Whatever Cause We Have

Whatever Cause We Have

*Memoir of a Marine Forward Observer
in the Vietnam War*

Dan Moore

McFarland & Company, Inc., Publishers
Jefferson, North Carolina

ISBN (print) 978-1-4766-9168-8
ISBN (ebook) 978-1-4766-5061-6

LIBRARY OF CONGRESS AND BRITISH LIBRARY
CATALOGUING DATA ARE AVAILABLE

Library of Congress Control Number 2023054484

© 2024 Dan Moore. All rights reserved

No part of this book may be reproduced or transmitted in any form or by any means, electronic or mechanical, including photocopying or recording, or by any information storage and retrieval system, without permission in writing from the publisher.

Front cover image: "Don't Shoot I'm Short,"
pen and ink drawing by Sergeant E.C. Sullivan (author collection)

Printed in the United States of America

McFarland & Company, Inc., Publishers
Box 611, Jefferson, North Carolina 28640
www.mcfarlandpub.com

For Pat, who has lifted me up in the darkest days,
and
For my father, whose silence during my tour spoke volumes,
and
For those who didn't come home

Table of Contents

Preface and Acknowledgments — 1

1. Generational Wars — 7
2. Keep on Truckin' — 16
3. Welcome Aboard — 42
4. Storm Clouds — 76
5. No Holiday Cheer — 108
6. Calm Before the Storm — 127
7. Hue — 149
8. Decompression and Reflection — 180
9. Echo Battery in Action — 193
10. Dead Man Walking — 210
11. Coming Home — 222

Epilogue: Aftermath and Return — 230
Glossary — 243
Recommended Reading — 247
Index — 249

Preface and Acknowledgments

This memoir has been a long time coming. It took over fifty years to examine my tour in Vietnam with any perspective and introspection. It could not have been written until I raised my family, retired from my career, and completed the cradle-to-grave biography of a fellow Marine. It is the story of one Marine, one experience among those of many other U.S. servicemen who served in the war. All our stories have similarities, yet each is profoundly different from the others; each combatant's experience unique. We all confronted moral and ethical issues to varying degrees. These problems have continued to haunt Vietnam veterans long after the war. Those who served have long had to deal with that unpopular war and its legacy—the futility, fear, frustrations, disappointments, anger, guilt, and for me the worst of it—the loss of friends and comrades.

Most of the stand-alone vignettes in this book are chronological, based on letters written home to family, a detailed daily journal kept a month before the 1968 Tet Offensive, and my recollection of events. When needed and possible, I have tried to corroborate my memories with those of Marines who served with me. The sketches are interspersed with passages that deal with topics that fit into the rhythm of the narrative but are not necessarily related to fragments before and after it. This is the way I remember Vietnam, the events that foreshadowed it, and what came after. My accounts, recorded soon after the events occurred, provide the detail and immediacy that recall could not re-create, without turning a nonfictional memoir into historical fiction. Where appropriate, I have filled in details to reflect my italicized thoughts at the time along with meditations that have emerged over the years. When possible, I have attempted to make clear the observational time period.

My letters home reveal a gradual skepticism toward the war and how it was fought. Questions emerged weeks after arrival in-country when I noted that Marines seemed to spend a great deal of time talking about the number of days and months remaining on their tour. In the ensuing weeks and months, as casualties mounted, I began to lose confidence the war would end well. I became aware of the chasm between junior and senior officers, between reserve officers and regular officers.

Unless otherwise noted, italicized quotes in this memoir largely have been taken from my letters to my family. Most of these letters from Vietnam—38 of 50—were written during the first half of my 13-month tour, when I supported Second Battalion, Fifth Marines, as a forward observer and artillery liaison officer. I wrote fewer letters as the months passed. The press of keeping an artillery battery running and general disillusionment about the war, particularly after the Tet Offensive of February 1968, drained my energy and dampened my motivation to write.

We all knew that in order to receive letters, we had to write them. Incoming was great. News from "The World," that is. Mail call—letters from home—kept us afloat. We lived for them. They helped buoy morale. Sometimes they brought bad news, but most of the time mail connected us to the everyday life of those we knew and loved. At the start of my tour, my letters to family consisted of descriptive accounts of first impressions. It was all new and different, even exciting. I had trained for a year to serve in Nam. I was now in the thick of it and wanted to contribute to the effort. But training for combat cannot prepare a person fully for what he may see and experience once the bullets begin to fly. As time passed, letter writing became something more than keeping connected with friends and family. It became a means of maintaining emotional balance and sanity in an environment where rationality sometimes seemed absent. Writing about observed events, internalizing and interpreting them, helped me deal with what I observed. Letters also became, without conscious intent, a personal record of my tour. They preserved an unvarnished, real-time account that made my memoir possible. They contained thoughts and feelings long gone from memory. Most memories detailed in the book remain vivid and I hope are accurate. They remain like an old book in some library, collecting dust, with torn and bent pages, sometimes barely readable.

I often wrote to vent. Regrettably, and perhaps selfishly, I gave little thought to how the content might affect my family. Unconcerned I might offend my father, who had his own strong views supporting the war, I wrote about what I saw, heard, and thought. He never once questioned or disagreed with what I wrote. Nor did he ask for clarification or challenge what he read. He rarely commented at all and never rebuked me. In retrospect, given the rocky relationship we had as I grew up, this was a gift I can now appreciate even more than when I was a 22-year-old artillery officer in Vietnam.

I wrote in a vacuum, not expecting any acknowledgment from my parents—especially, my father—the primary recipient of my letters. In part, they had their hands full dealing with my rebellious younger sister who had mental health issues. A survivor of World War II in the Pacific and having seen more than enough combat himself, my father seemed to understand and respect my take on a different war. His restraint, I like to think, demonstrated an unspoken but deep expression of love and understanding for which I have always been grateful.

I never expected my letters to have been preserved by my parents. In the 1980s, on a visit back home, my mother handed me a shoebox containing them, carefully organized in chronological order. A few envelopes included her doodling, done perhaps as she talked on the phone—scribbled telephone numbers, addresses, recipe fragments, reminders—all captured before she filed my letters away. It's been a trip seeing her hasty notes over 50 years later. I'm glad they served a useful purpose for her.

In-country, I sought to fit in and become an accepted, respected member of the team I worked with. That motive drove almost all my actions. I rarely confided private thoughts or views to others. Revealing any psychological or emotional trauma to others risked being singled out as a weirdo or troublemaker, but personal thoughts, concerns, and doubts could be put on paper in a letter home.

I understood search and destroy operations translated into a war of attrition. Often an encounter on the battlefield began with an ambush of a smaller U.S. unit, a platoon or company, by an enemy of superior force that quickly killed U.S. servicemen. Battles continued until our supporting arms gained the advantage, whereupon the enemy broke contact and vanished.

The Tet Offensive in February 1968 marked a turning point in the war for me and many others. Victory no longer appeared imminent or even an achievable goal in the near term, if at all. Whatever hope of "winning" the war I had on arrival in Nam faded. The shock of the Tet Offensive and the combat deaths of the two Marines who were like brothers almost crippled me emotionally and left me running on empty as my tour progressed. I knew I had to somehow keep going and not allow their deaths to affect my duties.

Vietnam vets have been comforted over the years by the friendships made and the pride of serving our country. There were good times along with the bad. There was levity, esprit de corps, camaraderie, laughing, and joking. But violence and sudden death lurked all around us, particularly for those who served in, or with, ground elements doing the fighting. The friends who smiled and joked with me one day, could be carried home the next. Suddenly-absent friends vexed us. We mourned alone and employed coping mechanisms for dealing with the stress and tedium to get through our tour alive, with dignity and self-respect. Our shared sense of professionalism, commitment, dedication to mission and duty were paramount and helped to sustain us. We did our best to serve America and represent its ideals. Most importantly, as the conflict ground on, many fought first and foremost for the buddies alongside them.

Coping strategies for many of us in Vietnam, survival mechanisms, included total immersion in the mission, counting the days with a short-timer calendar; graphic, sometimes humorous phrases written on helmets and flak vests, referring to time remaining in-country, and morbid humor. A tour in Vietnam was in some ways, to use a rough metaphor, like being involved in a game of high-stakes poker. That is, everyone began their tour with a set number of "chips"—an individual mix of coping skills, mental toughness, resiliency. To stay in the game as my tour wore on, I had to play those chips. As the days passed and casualties among friends and other warriors mounted, I strained to reach the end of the game, rotating back home, with some chips remaining—my dignity and self-respect intact, my efforts acknowledged.

The cumulative weight of the war led me to question whether I could complete my tour without revealing the depths of despair that filled my last months. I have regretted some actions I took in Vietnam out of impulse, boredom, or poor judgment. These missteps have haunted me. I look back now on my tour with some acceptance that I did my best. There was little I, the Marines I served with, or our country could do to alter the trajectory of events in Vietnam. But I will never forget the sacrifices and the courage of those around me.

I am indebted to family members, friends, colleagues, and fellow Marines for their valuable input. All were instrumental in the formation, molding, and completion of this memoir. I owe them all my deepest gratitude. Those who contributed their time and talent to the early, formative drafts of the manuscript include Michael Archer, Jim Gifford, Richard Kitchen, Richard Shepard, and Edwina Pendarvis.

Each brought a different optic on the war. Archer is a Khe Sanh siege survivor. Shepard is a Marine Vietnam vet and an artillery forward observer (FO) who served in the same area, in the same artillery battalion, as I did more than a year later. Air Force Vietnam veteran and long-time colleague Richard Kitchen pointed out holes and inconsistencies in early drafts. Pendarvis approached the manuscript as a civilian who knew little about the Vietnam War or the military. Others who read portions of early drafts include Bob Muir and Warren Robeson. Allison Kaukola and Michael Archer collaborated with me and provided the custom maps. Former Golf Company squad leader Barney Barnes, who served with me in

Golf Company, offered unlimited assistance with early versions of maps, photos of Marines he served with and his valuable memories. His accounts of the early days of the Tet Offensive in Hue constitute an important segment in a key chapter of this book. Al Claiborne provided advice and input at various stages of the project. My wife Pat reviewed the entire manuscript, suggested edits, and helped format it.

Others who provided key input and insights include:

On my assignment as forward observer with Golf Company, Second Battalion, Fifth Marines: platoon commanders Tracy Alton, Vern Arndt, Stewart Brown, Steve Hancock, Bill Harvey, Michael McNiel, Bill Rogers, and company commander Edgar "Buck" Dyer, Barney Barnes, Martin Dunbar, Bill Tant and Mark Oakes.

On my assignment with Echo Battery, Second Battalion, Eleventh Marines: John Augustine and Martin Dunbar.

On Chaplain Richard Demers: Christopher Demers.

My cousin, Gibbs Ferguson, provided my letters to him from Vietnam.

1

Generational Wars

Anchors Aweigh

Sons sometimes struggle to emerge from the shadow of their fathers and I'm no exception. By the time I reached my golden years, I understood just how much my decision to join the Marine Corps had been shaped by my father's career in the Navy and his strained relationship with me.

Dad came from an impoverished, broken family in rural Arkansas. He suffered emotional and physical abuse when young. He kept a family secret hidden for decades. Late in his life, he revealed that my grandfather had not died from a mule kick to the head as I had always been told. He had in fact died of a head injury in a fight with my grandmother's paramour. She later married an abusive husband. In their teens, Dad and his older brother came home from school to find their house empty except for their clothes. Their parents had abandoned them. A family who lived nearby took them in. Dad dropped out of high school for a year to work before returning to finish high school.

He soon found his groove, enlisting in the U.S. Navy in 1936 at age 19. He never looked back. Out of boot camp, he received his first assignment, the USS *Indianapolis*, later sunk by a Japanese submarine after delivering the first atomic bomb to U.S. forces in the South Pacific. He enjoyed three years on that legendary heavy cruiser, sailing the seas and visiting exotic, pre-war Hawaii. As he developed new-found confidence and independence, he began to write periodic letters and postcards to his mother with whom he had been estranged.

On 7 December 1941 he heard the call to man battle stations aboard the USS *Maryland* when the Japanese attacked Pearl Harbor. The following day he signed and mailed to his mother a pre-printed U.S. Navy–issued postcard, marking the appropriate text: "I am well … Letter follows at first opportunity."

The damaged battleship departed days later for Bremerton, Washington.

He wrote many years later: "In late January 1942 I was aboard the USS *Maryland*, then in Bremerton Naval Shipyard for repairs to damage sustained at Pearl Harbor when I volunteered for a new construction draft. I reported to the *Laffey* and was assigned to the engine room."

Since he would be assigned in Bremerton for several months while the *Maryland* was under repair, he sent a marriage proposal to his high school sweetheart, Polly Ferguson. She accepted his proposal and traveled by train from rural Arkansas to Bremerton. They were married by a justice of the peace on 17 January 1942.

After shakedown trials off the West Coast, the *Laffey* sailed into history. In a column of eight destroyers and five cruisers commanded by Admiral Daniel J. Callaghan, in the early morning darkness of 13 November *Laffey* encountered the Japanese Imperial Navy. The naval battle of Guadalcanal had begun. *Laffey* fought the Japanese ships with three main battery guns in a no-quarter duel at point-blank range. She was hit by a 14-inch shell, then a torpedo in her fantail put *Laffey* out of action. As the commanding officer reluctantly ordered to abandon ship, an explosion ripped the destroyer apart. The *Laffey* sank within minutes. The battle earned the ship a Presidential Unit Citation. Looking back, while attending a *Laffey* reunion in 1982, Dad told a *San Francisco Examiner* reporter, "We were below deck and didn't see fire, but we sure felt it. When the torpedo hit, that was it. We went top side and got into the boats. We barely made it when the ship blew up." Of the 247 crew members aboard, 59 were killed outright—including the commanding officer. My father received multiple fragmentation wounds in his legs from the exploding destroyer.

Although he rarely spoke of the war, one night at the dinner table about forty years later Dad recalled, choking back tears, jumping off the *Laffey* moments before the ship exploded and sank. He and a buddy from the engine room behind him climbed the ladders in the rush to abandon ship. Felled by metal beams of the crumbling superstructure, Dad's friend did not make it off the destroyer. Swimming to a raft, barely able to move his legs, Dad and his surviving shipmates spent a month on Guadalcanal with the Marines—at times manning the perimeter of Marine positions—before being repatriated to the Navy. After sustained prompting from *Laffey* survivors, retired Commander Moore applied for the Purple Heart Medal and received it 46 years after the battle.

What Do I Do Now?

That question must have been on my mind as I contemplated my first step. I stood upright, wobbly, doubtless concerned I might fall if I moved forward. I was nine months old. "Come on, you can do it," the encouraging words likely uttered by my mother as she framed the photo in early September 1945. She snapped the image for my father, who soon would be coming home. He had not yet met me. America had celebrated victory over Japan just weeks before.

My beloved 12-year-old uncle, Joe Pat, mother's youngest brother, kneeled behind me. He had just released me, ready to ensure I didn't fall. He taught me how to walk. He would stand by me, figuratively, all his life, positive, accepting, providing emotional support, encouragement, and unconditional love to me and to all his many nephews and nieces. He was one of the finest men I have known. There were times in my life that I wished he had been my father.

The author with 12-year-old Uncle Joe Pat Ferguson, September 1945, at the Ferguson homestead, Watson, Arkansas.

Sometimes-Difficult Father

I saw Dad for the first time about four months later. To his acute disappointment, for days I wanted nothing to do with him. I've always wondered if that reception somehow affected our early relationship.

I now attribute Dad's periodic flashes of anger, as I grew up, to post-traumatic stress disorder caused by childhood abuse as well as trauma from the war. I realized early on that pleasing Dad, winning his acceptance, would be hard, if not impossible. After one paternal tempest, I took refuge with my mother, but learned she could not be a safe harbor. She cautioned there was little she could do. I understood then: I had to navigate on my own and learn how to minimize and manage his occasional outbursts.

One day I realized Dad began to take a keen interest in my athletic ability: a pathway to connect had opened. Although wiry and slight in stature, I was a natural athlete. When he realized I had good hand-eye coordination and I began to follow college and professional sports, our relationship seemed to improve. He took me to a Bill Russell–led University of San Francisco basketball team at the Cow Palace the year the team won the national championship, and later to a Navy–Stanford football game. Sports became a safe, mutual interest for us, a common subject of daily conversation, especially baseball. We began to play catch and I grew aware that I now had a way of smoothing out our earlier, rocky relationship. Through Little League, Pony League, Colt League, then high school baseball, Dad kept nudging me along the baseball path. He was in fact more enthusiastic about my participation in the sport than I was, driven to give me the experience he never had as a kid. I wasn't that accomplished in baseball, and knew it, but Dad thought I was.

Marine Mentor Appears

Young men usually do not enlist in the Marine Corps without good reason. As Marines, they often credit an active-duty or former Marine for having inspired them to make the decision to enlist—perhaps someone who spoke highly of the Corps, or maybe someone they looked to as a role model. I had a friend who played a formidable part in my decision to enlist, a mentor assigned to the Marine barracks who befriended me and my best friend. Corporal Cliff Yoshida, a Japanese-American from Hawaii, must have understood I could benefit from having an older friend. He took us to a few San Francisco Seal baseball games and we sometimes hung out around him when he was on guard duty. His laid back, nonjudgmental, older-brother manner had a profound effect on how I viewed the Marine Corps. He reminded me of my uncle. I am sure his acceptance and friendship factored into my eventual decision to one day become a Marine. My best friend also joined the Corps and made it a career, inspired by Cliff.

Distant Conflict

In 1957 most Americans had not heard about the communist insurgency in South Vietnam. That distant conflict first came to my attention one Sunday aboard the USS *Los Angeles,* where my father was the chief engineer. The captain had invited the ship's officers to dine aboard with their families. The occasion offered a rare opportunity to view a sliver of the culture and wardroom protocols of the old Navy. We sat waiting until a Filipino steward marched around the room playing the chimes, the cue for officers to proceed to the table. I had, minutes earlier, picked up a magazine that featured a story of the communist insurgency in South Vietnam, with graphic photos. As I read the article, the events seemed faraway in a mysterious land, but disturbingly close as well. The U.S. had advisors and trainers there. The Cold War had been brought to life. I thought little more about the festering conflict for the next eight years.

Welcome Home, Dad. Greeting Lieutenant Commander J.D. Moore home from a sea cruise—mother Polly, holding sister Nancy, the author, and sister Paula. Long Beach, California, 1956.

Life-Changing Decision

I left home for college as soon as I could do so, anxious to make my way alone. Until my senior year in college, military service had not appeared on my radar. I held negative views of the Navy and military life in general. As a dependent I disliked the frequent moving, new schools, different people, the stifling prohibitions on military bases, the silly rules and regulations, the impersonal military medical care. While all that probably contributed to my long-term openness to change, as a youth I wanted a discharge from all of it. I wanted to go in a different direction. As a history major in college, I had a vague notion of perhaps teaching in higher education, but I had not formulated a conscious path. I considered law school, that too, only a vague option. In short, I was adrift.

By 1965 the Vietnam War had emerged from the shadows and the American public began to focus on it. The Marines landed near Da Nang in March 1965 and the Army arrived in-country two months later. The war drew closer one day when I viewed the April issue of *Life* magazine, which featured the war. There it was: we were deep into a Cold War and engaged in a world struggle with communism. Maybe I could help, it would take me in a new direction. My experience as a dependent of a career Navy officer enabled me to view possible military service in Vietnam as an honor, perhaps even a patriotic duty. My country could use me, maybe it needed me. More importantly, at that point I needed the Marine Corps.

The rapid build-up of U.S. troops in 1965–66 coincided with sharp social, cultural, and political changes in America. The segregated, private College of Charleston had not yet become the vibrant public institution it is today, attracting over 10,000 students from across the U.S. With the student population then hovering around 450, the College teetered on the brink of extinction. Most students at the College in 1966 were stuck in the button-down, traditional attire and lifestyle—loafers, madras shorts, short haircuts, the general Ivy League look. Politically conservative students far outnumbered liberals. As a senior, I began to hear—with some contempt mixed with curiosity—of wild, long-haired "hippies," some of whom lived in communes. I heard of drug use and alternative lifestyles, but for the most part the burgeoning counterculture still seemed far away, largely confined to major college campuses up north and on the West and East coasts. Yet, I knew the culture had begun to change everywhere, even in the south. Popular music played in dorm rooms—The Beatles, Bob Dylan, Joan Baez, Judy Collins, Donovan, and others seemed to me to grow darker, more experimental, more anti-establishment as the months passed.

While classmates around me began to fixate on avoiding the draft, I went in the other direction. I felt the pressing call of military service, the Marine Corps in particular. I was drawn to the challenge of Marine Corps Officer Candidates School (OCS); military service represented something noble. I needed to prove myself a man, maybe even a warrior. Was it all a fantasy? Did I have it in me, did I have what it took? As a risk-taker, I thought I did. I knew I fell well short of the stereotypical poster Marine: slight of stature, more cerebral than street fighter; and I was wary of the no-holds-barred, tough as nails, gung-ho enthusiasm I thought might be prevalent among Marine officers. But that made it even more tempting as I pondered the transition from college to what lay beyond. I wanted to keep my worldview simple. I distanced myself from the disturbing cultural currents I heard and read about in the last few months of college. I headed for military service, like my father and his generation, to protect the American way of life—another time, another war. I'm sure I wanted to show Dad that I could serve honorably like him, I could go to war in an elite, time-honored service. In part, my actions were self-centered. I had things to prove, particularly to myself, but also to my father. I knew little to nothing about the origins of the war in Vietnam or the cultural and political milieu of that faraway land. All that mattered to me was, our political leaders supported it. I had grudging respect for authority even while often questioning it.

Measuring Up

Could I meet the high standards and become a Marine? I wouldn't know unless I tried. Could I even begin to attain what my father had achieved in his career? No, but I wanted to write my own script, discover my own limits, become my own person. I wanted to accomplish something I could be proud of for the rest of my life. Service in the Marines offered that. Yes, the Marine Corps, I thought, would impress him, but if he disapproved, it didn't matter. Going a different route from the Navy would not constitute a rejection of him by any means. I knew he had the highest regard for the Corps, but I was committed to my path regardless of how he took it. When I told him I planned to enter the OCS pipeline, he understood. He said little and left the decision to me. His wartime experience with the Marines on Guadalcanal must have factored into his approval.

Yes, my motivations for service were just as much personal as altruistic or patriotic. The Cold War argument for fighting in Vietnam—the Domino Theory—fearing the spread of communism to other countries, saving the Republic of Vietnam, seemed a little vague, not entirely persuasive. But it had some currency and provided cover for my decision. What else resonated and pushed me forward? The call to do something for my country and stand up for the values we espoused as Americans, service to the country. These notions had been instilled in me almost through osmosis as a military dependent. Military service, in the abstract, was something I could relate to and believe in. Without my father's career in the Navy, I might not have been so motivated. I began talking to friends at college about my intent. Most expressed shock or surprise. A few told me joining the Marines could be hazardous to my health. But the near-total positive feedback from friends I respected further encouraged me to contact the Marine Corps recruiters in Charleston. A gunnery sergeant connected me with Marine Officer Selection Officer Captain Carl E. Mundy, who would become a future commandant.

In early 1966 the Marine Corps was ramping up fast for Vietnam. Clearly, officer candidates were needed, lots of them. Captain Mundy welcomed my inquiries about the program. We met for my interview in Charleston and I signed the paperwork for the Reserve Officer commissioning program. I had justified the decision in part on Mundy's assurance the government would pay for post-service academic education—the GI Bill. That was all I needed, I was all-in. The Marine Corps approved my application for OCS after I jumped through a series of medical hoops. A physician—a distant cousin in Arkansas—at my request stated sight unseen that I was physically fit to serve. After my government physical exam, I obtained a series of medical waivers for my poor eyesight, flat feet, and heart murmur. I looked forward to the next chapter of my life. Two roads had diverged and, as Robert Frost wrote in "The Road Not Taken," I took the one less traveled by. That has made all the difference.

Summer 1966

When my senior class of 80 men and women graduated in May, I was the only student planning to join the armed services right away. A few others followed the next year. The college athletic director had earlier asked if I would oversee a youth summer sports school program while he attended graduate school courses. A Korean War–era Marine, Tony Meyer entrusted me with managing the school and the care of the Depression-era gym and pristine clay tennis courts. It was Tony's way of looking after a Marine-bound graduate. My association with the Marine Corps had already begun to pay personal dividends. I hired two college students to help run the summer sports school. The four clay courts required frequent sweeping and watering each day. I spent hours on the tennis court myself, keeping in physical shape. I came close twice to defeating top players on the college tennis team. When Tony returned to Charleston for a couple of days half-way through his summer school, he dropped by the gym. I had not yet completed sweeping the basketball court that morning, a cardinal sin to Tony. I received my first, thorough Marine-style ass chewing. It was a suitable introduction to what I would soon experience at Quantico.

2

Keep on Truckin'

Anticipating OCS

I made final preparations before leaving for Quantico. Relaxed and confident, I read and re-read the booklet describing what to expect and how to prepare for OCS. Clearly written, it pulled no punches, emphasizing that OCS would test my mental and physical fitness. It would be no picnic. I knew that already. Acculturated to military life from an early age and through the example of my father, I understood the discipline and commitment required. I had no real concerns that I might not succeed, but I harbored a resentful acceptance, and some distrust, of authority. I welcomed what I knew would be a huge adventure and a milestone in my life. I had no concerns regarding my conditioning and ability to keep up with the physical demands of training. The harassment and pressure I anticipated at Quantico, I knew, came with the turf. The course would be a psychological game of sorts. Play by the rules, go with the flow, keep a low profile—it all came natural to me.

Still, expectation of what I might encounter in OCS did not come close to actually living through it. As it turned out, the daily harassment and accompanying physical exhaustion—while constant and intense—paled in comparison to the self-imposed mental and psychological burden of living with possible failure. I would become my own worst enemy, full of self-doubt, sometimes second-guessing my actions and thoughts, too often concerned with how I might appear to fellow candidates and the instructional staff.

OCS Approaches

I spent a relaxed two weeks with my family in New Jersey before reporting to Quantico. My father refrained from offering any advice.

2. Keep on Truckin'

Perhaps ignorance was bliss, but I recall no anxiety, only expectation, no remorse, only the prospect of entering a new phase in life filled with purpose. I thought my immediate goals achievable. I felt assured that, because of my earlier experience growing up, I could fit into the Marines as my own person. The day before beginning what would become my long association with the Marine Corps, I prepared a small bag of personal belongings, as recommended by the OCS candidate handbook. A few toiletries, not much else. I took no stationery, thinking I would have little time or inclination to write during the ten-week course. I was later amazed at the volume of letters other candidates managed to write and receive. The morning of departure my mother—anxious about how to navigate downtown Philadelphia—drove me straight to the bus station in center city. I said little during the drive, lost in thought about the day ahead. When we reached our destination with minutes to spare, she got out of the car with me. I knew she was nervous and hoped she would not get emotional. She did not. After a hug and a quick goodbye, I boarded the bus and presented the military payment voucher to the driver.

About ten other young men had already boarded and sat quietly at first, but began to talk excitedly as we got underway. Most appeared to be clean-cut college graduates, some with longer hair than I expected. All of us were headed for Quantico. En route, we stopped several times to take on new travelers. Throughout the morning I sat listening to conversations of others, amused at their comments. One passenger in particular caught my attention. He sat near the rear of the bus and had a loud voice. At times he would belt out unsolicited advice to no one in particular, voicing concerns about the training ahead. He apparently assumed we shared his views. The outspoken passenger, Paul, would wind up in my OCS platoon, where he would wash out early and serve as an enlisted Marine for the next few years. He eventually would be assigned as an office clerk in the rifle company I would support in the field for five months in Vietnam.

We disembarked at Quantico in early afternoon 22 August 1966. The staff divided us into groups to draw the uniforms and gear we would have for the remainder of the course. The screws soon would begin to tighten.

Training Begins

Quantico Marine Base has been the flagship of Marine Corps officer training since 1917, when it trained qualified officers to serve in the American Expeditionary Force in Europe. Following the war, the commanding general of Quantico, Major General John A. Lejeune, established the Marine Officer Training School on base. The Basic School (TBS) was later established in a more remote area to train lieutenants in small unit leadership. Today, Quantico's 100 square miles sit astride I-95, twenty miles south of Washington, D.C.

My home for the next ten weeks would be a two-story World War II–era wooden barracks situated almost within spitting distance of the heavily travelled main rail line on the East Coast. The barracks shook when the train came barreling through, horn blasting, at 0500 hours every morning, announcing imminent reveille. By that time, many of us had already dressed, made our racks, and performed morning ablutions, ready for another beautiful day at Quantico. Echo Company, First Platoon, inhabited the structure with three other platoons, two on one side of the building and two on the other. My platoon was located on the bottom deck, near the railroad. Passageways, offices, and the heads—containing showers and commodes but no stalls—filled the space between the two wings of the building. Each squad bay held about 25 double bunks—50 Marines—on each side. I occupied the less desirable top rack of a bunk near the passageway that connected one side of the building with the other. Green, wooden footlockers fit under our bunks and contained what personal belongings and other small gear we had.

Like each of the 16 platoons in Officer Candidates Course 41, mine included men from all over the country, from all walks of life and experiences. More than 80 percent of the candidates in the course had a degree, be it from a tiny Midwestern college or an Ivy League university. Eleven percent were selected from the enlisted ranks. Of the roughly 50 candidates in my platoon who began the course, 35 would graduate. Collectively, we were a true socio-economic representation of America, with one stark exception. We had only one Black candidate in our class of 800. My platoon contained an unusually large number of candidates bound for flight training once they received their commission.

I later learned candidate motivations for enlisting were complex and varied widely. In general, we were self-selected, motivated, and patriotic men. In late 1966 to early 1967 most of us believed the Vietnam conflict was a just war worth fighting. We believed our nation needed us. We wanted to serve—and to prove ourselves. Our political leaders framed the Cold War as a conflict between good and evil, a necessary means to halt the spread of communism in Southeast Asia. Better fight the communists in Vietnam than at home seemed a fitting cry to arms. And we answered the call. Wrapping ourselves in the flag also provided camouflage to some, like me, who also acted on personal, self-serving, or selfish motives.

My senior staff platoon sergeant, Staff Sergeant Murray, a rugged World War II survivor of the island campaigns in the South Pacific, was a no-nonsense Marine who played no favorites and held everyone to the same high standard. I don't recall ever seeing him smile or laugh. We candidates looked up to him, even after we discovered one evening when we had to clean the staff offices that his field pack, along with those of the other platoon staff, contained weightless Styrofoam blocks. In contrast, candidates carried heavy field gear in our packs during forced marches and runs. We kept the revelation to ourselves, but surely the staff knew we would uncover the ruse. It remained a quiet joke among all of us, and possibly among the staff as well. The lesson learned, if there was one: don't try to fool the troops.

Our sergeant-instructor, Sergeant Booker T. Taylor, a short, stocky African American, projected a stern exterior, but often made witty comments that relaxed and amused us. Inspections of one kind or another filled every day. At one rifle inspection Taylor found nothing wrong with my M-14 rifle except an unacceptable loose sling. He handed it back with a frown, asking if it was my rifle or a bow for shooting arrows. Taylor inspected our individual racks and footlocker contents each morning while we ate chow and did physical training. He doled out reams of dreaded chits for deficiencies and imperfections. Morning inspections created a mental pressure point on candidates. My chief concern? I feared an excess of chits might draw the unwanted attention of our platoon sergeant, Staff Sergeant Murray, and platoon commander Captain Owens for possible unsuitability. Taylor knew that most of the candidates under his care would one day soon become officers. Sure enough, when commissioning day came, he made a point of standing in the squad bay to receive the traditional dollar bill from lieutenants, given to the first enlisted man to salute them. Murray was nowhere to be found.

For me, the most challenging, but in the end, least important part of OCS? Perfecting the details of military housekeeping in the squad bay—"squaring away" equipment, maintaining the rifle, cutting off the ubiquitous threads ("Irish Pennants") from our uniforms, polishing brass, shining boots, blocking our utility covers (hats), neatly organizing and aligning the various items in the footlocker, well-made bunks. Yes, the daily chores of a well-ordered military mind, prized "attention to detail." A tidy footlocker reflected a disciplined mind. We all sought to be "Candidate A.J. Squared Away."

Within the first few days at OCS, the three shortest candidates, which included me, were directed to mow the steep, hilly grass lawn in front of our barracks. The thermometer exceeded ninety degrees, with high humidity. I've wondered if we were being tested for our attitude and work ethic and whether the staff watched to see how we performed the tasks. Maybe not, but I prefer to think they monitored us. During the course, I witnessed no discrimination directed at us runt candidates, but marching columns were organized with taller candidates at the front, shorter ones in the rear. Perhaps it was tradition, the practice pleasing to the eye, but I soon learned it placed shorter candidates at a distinct disadvantage during forced marches and conditioning runs.

Captain Owens

A tall, mean-looking officer with a perpetual scowl and a flat-top haircut, Platoon Commander Captain Owens seemed to be on one mission, which he relished—identifying a man's weakness and exploiting it. Candidates despised him. He relentlessly pushed them to voluntarily leave the program—to drop on request, or DOR. He threatened many with expulsion, some more than once. It appeared to me that Owens made life especially tough for the African American in our platoon. Owens attempted to "board" the candidate and have him expelled, but Theodore "Ted" Williams made it through the course, and, as a lieutenant, later graduated from the Basic School. A few of us thought Owens appeared racially biased against Williams.

Walk, Don't Run

No, I'm not referring to The Ventures' 1960 megahit, recorded during the golden age of small-band, rock-n-roll instrumentals featuring several electric guitars. I had little doubt I could deal with endurance tests when I began training. Well-conditioned and in top-notch physical shape, I thought I could run all day, if I needed to. As the course progressed, however, doubts emerged. At times I worried whether I could power through endless runs and forced marches in full battle gear. Any candidate who lagged behind or dropped out of a run earned the unwanted attention of the staff and risked being washed out.

The primary objective of runs and forced marches? To expose the "weak sisters," who lacked the stamina or will power to maintain the pace set by Captain Owens. Falling behind a fast-moving column of Marine officer candidates—straggling—could be the kiss of death for a marginal or out-of-shape candidate. As any run or forced march developed, the column would stretch out and contract, stretch out and so on. We in the rear, focused on the backs of those immediately in front of us, often could not determine if a candidate just ahead of us had fallen behind the moving column of candidates. I often ran slightly to the side of the column to gauge my position—was I running and keeping up with the main body,

2. Keep on Truckin'

or not? Sometimes we runts found ourselves falling behind one or more stragglers. When we realized the danger, we had to accelerate and pass the stragglers to join the main column.

I anticipated the forced march that morning would be challenging but, I thought, more than manageable. We were vaguely familiar with the route—the Powerline Trail, up and down gently rolling hills, several miles to the western edge of Quantico Base bordering I-95 and back. No problem, I thought. This looked like business as usual. I wrestled with my loaded field pack. Perfect weather greeted us—sunny, comfortably cool—ideal, I thought, for a forced march. As usual, the captain would set the pace, with Murray monitoring and hectoring from mid-column and pulling out stragglers. Taylor, a tad overweight and I suspected often strained to keep pace—would bring up the rear, corralling, harassing, humiliating those who fell behind.

Before we began, I was a little suspicious of the captain's matter-of-fact cautionary announcement. There would be absolutely no running. Candidates could only walk at the pace set by the captain while keeping in formation. It sounded like a piece of cake, I thought, unless the captain was misleading us. It ended up a trap. For the first mile or so, Owens stretched it out at a comfortable pace, especially for taller candidates, I thought, but more challenging for us smaller guys. At the mile marker, I maintained the steady, quick, long strides with relative ease, even as a few candidates began to falter, then lag behind the column. When we hit the two- and three-mile marks, Owens kicked it into another gear, still walking. Murray harangued those who struggled. I could not see Sergeant Taylor but heard him bellowing behind me. Was it fair, I again asked myself, that candidates with longer legs might have an easier time keeping up with Owens? No, I answered my own query, it was never a question of fairness.

As the minutes passed, seeming like hours, I began to feel my shins strain. I worried that they might fracture or that my tendons might tear from the stress of the walk. If only I could run, I'd be fine. Onward we pressed as moans and cursing grew louder from candidates around me. Now more men fell back. How could anyone devise such exquisite torture, I thought. I feared my own pain and exhaustion might be nearing a breaking point. Was I only minutes away from collapse or a physical breakdown? I was near panic. My legs wanted to run. Only sheer determination kept me going. Stop and you're a failure, I told myself, keep going and you will attain your goal. It became a pure mind over body struggle. I held on for what seemed like another hour, but I had in fact lost all track of time. I wanted to scream out in pain and frustration, but if I did, I'd be a dead man, out of the program.

Then Owens stopped for a short break. Had he reached his own breaking point? Is that why he stopped, couldn't take it anymore? Over the collective wheezing and gasping of candidates around me, I could hear the distant thrum of trucks and cars speeding down I-95 as I collapsed on the ground along with everyone else. It was psychological torture of sorts. People outside the base were enjoying the freedom of their daily lives while we candidates were caught in a vortex of pain and exhaustion. Had I been hallucinating? The civilian world, freedom from OCS and the all-encompassing stress beckoned, enticingly close, just beyond the high metal fence separating Quantico Base from the interstate. Life on the outside seemed agonizingly within reach, but still a world away.

Now, walking down the column of candidates reclined on the ground and gasping for air, Owens taunted us. "Failures, pussies," he spat out, "you'll never graduate." His sarcasm led me to doubt for a moment that I could stay with the column on the return to OCS if we had to walk at the same pace. Then, like a gift from heaven, on the return the captain ran at a comfortable pace. Weakened by the trip out, some candidates straggled until we arrived back at our starting point. I exulted inwardly as we concluded the run, realizing I could push myself beyond what I thought was the limit of my endurance.

During those ten weeks at OCS, I would feel pressured time and again, but, somehow, I broke through the barrier of fear and anxiety and kept on truckin'. Failure would never be an option. I would do whatever it took to run the gauntlet. Whenever doubts arose during the endurance runs and marches, I vowed to stick with it. If I made it through the course, I reasoned, it would be a lifetime accomplishment, an enduring source of pride no one could ever take away.

Unexpected Encouragement

Despite his malicious reputation and reprehensible treatment of some members of my platoon, Captain Owens uttered not one negative word or made a threatening gesture to me during the entire 10-week course. I'm not sure why. One day, about halfway through the course, Sergeant Taylor approached and told me to report to the captain's office. A thought flashed to the fore. Was it bad news? I centered myself in the doorway and knocked three times, announcing as forcefully as I could, "Sir, Candidate Moore reporting as ordered, Sir." Owens sat behind a desk as I stood at attention. I stared past him, out the window. The sparsely furnished office contained a government-issue heavy, gray, metal desk with a chair, and a few tall metal lockers. It could have passed for a stage set, nothing on the walls, not a single piece of paper on the desk, an exemplar of military austerity.

Owens ordered me to enter. "At ease," he snarled. Then his demeanor changed in an instant. He relaxed, lowered his voice, and began asking questions in a normal, conversational tone. He inquired about my background and family in almost a getting-to-know-you tone. Looking straight ahead, I responded to his questions. The meeting seemed to last no more than five-to-ten minutes. At the end of our conversation, he frowned, and said, "You may be smaller than most candidates here, but don't let anyone ever tell you that you can't make it through this program and become a fine Marine officer." That seemed to be the whole reason for the meeting, to send that message. I tried to suppress an enormous sense of relief, responding with a robust, "Yes, Sir!" I knew then I would make it through OCS. I have since wondered if Owens might have been what Fred Rogers, of Mr. Rogers fame, once called "a helper." I was not a child, not the kind of person Mr. Rogers had in mind, but I might have been on the receiving end of someone who wanted to help. That meeting with Owens served as a life lesson for me. A small word of encouragement at the right time can mean all the difference to someone in need of it.

The captain intervened twice more in my training, neither incident showing any particular favoritism toward me. On a forced march on the infamous, muddy and treacherous Hill Trail one morning, my mess kit shifted in my pack, rubbing an abrasion on my back. We changed into PT gear that afternoon for a running of the obstacle course. Owens stood by, arms crossed, observing the platoon. After I completed my running, he called me over, scowled and said blood had seeped through my red and gold USMC athletic shirt. He asked me to turn around. He lifted the shirt and examined the area. He sent me to sick bay to have it attended to. During the final week of training, I developed painful Achilles tendonitis from my heavy, thick black leather boots. Observing my slight limp while marching during drill, the captain sent me again to sick bay for evaluation. Upon my return to the platoon, he told me I could complete the final week of the course, including Field Day competition between platoons in the company, in tennis shoes. I considered myself fortunate he did not consider a recycle in training. Physical injuries could sometimes result in a candidate's repeating the course. More severe injuries could result in a discharge from the service altogether. I later learned that at least two candidates who broke a leg during the last week of training were eventually medically discharged. Recycling in training and medical discharges happened with some frequency in each course running.

Candidate Dynamics

OCS opened a window to the wider world. Classmates came from every walk of life, from every state of the union, from the farmlands, from the suburbs, from the cities. Some had even served in the Peace Corps. That seemed a little strange to me: was there a commonality at all? Whatever our previous experience before the Marine Corps, we were all in the same boat. It remained a self-contained universe, a cocoon that locked out distractions beyond the confines of Quantico Base. There were no dummies among us; everyone met the same intelligence requirements. In fact, I knew several men who scored in the high-IQ spectrum. The one unmistakable goal we all shared? Getting through training and serving in Vietnam. A few in my platoon had served as enlisted Marines before selection to the program. Without doubt they benefited from previous active-duty experience. Of the 16 platoon honor men in our four companies, 10 had prior enlisted, active-duty experience. To their credit, these candidates often served to teach and inspire their classmates and helped ease our transition from civilian life.

I maintained a low profile, viewing student billet assignments as a thankless, potential threat to successful completion of the course. I tried to avoid the attention of the platoon staff to the extent possible. Survival depended in part on blending in, avoiding becoming a lightning rod for the OCS staff's punishment. Some candidates on the cusp of washing out would receive critical assignments such as platoon or company commander to determine how they performed under pressure. It appeared that the staff applied maximum pressure on candidates deemed marginal. On the other hand, exceptional candidates at times were rewarded with a billet assignment as an illustration to us run-of-the-mill candidates of what a leader should look like and how he should comport himself. I thought it strange there seemed little effort by the staff to forge my platoon into a cohesive unit until the final week of training. Apparently, time was too short and building esprit de corps not a primary objective.

Peer reviews and rankings were a fixture at OCS. I judged the rankings as popularity contests of sorts. Candidates could be ruthless in their assessments and treatment of other candidates whom they thought fell short in one facet of the training or another. Still, knowing I would be judged by my peers, I made an effort to create a favorable impression without losing my sense of self-respect. I tried to project a positive attitude and to be helpful when possible. Unfortunately, struggling candidates and those marked for almost certain failure often found themselves isolated, shunned, and viewed as on the way out. In some respects, OCS became a Darwinian jungle where, as Jerry Butler pointed out in 1969, in a different context, "Only the strong survive."

We lived in a competitive world—"every man for himself" and "better the other guy gets screwed than me"—yet I recall countless instances of candidates helping others in some way. Yes, we operated in an intense environment, but aiding one's fellow candidates often stood out as a generous gesture of common humanity. It appeared widespread and sincere. Candidates might have been training to be hardcore Marines, but many extended a helping hand to others. A candidate's character and integrity came under scrutiny by others in the platoon, and I am sure the staff observed that. Lasting friendships were made in OCS, and later in TBS. Bonds of brotherhood that would last a lifetime had begun to form as a result of our shared experiences in a training environment.

The platoon usually received liberty on Saturday afternoons. Some bachelor candidates would pile into a car and rent individual rooms wherever they landed. Some partied the night away in Georgetown bars and crashed wherever they could find a bed and perhaps a willing partner to share it with. Others sought more quiet companionship in Fredericksburg, home of Mary Washington College, then the all-women counterpart of the University of Virginia. By late 1966, Mary Washington students were deeply divided on the Vietnam War, split about 50–50 between those who deigned to date Marines and those who would not. When Marines visited the campus on reconnaissance, they were immediately identified by their high and tight haircuts. The ladies sorted themselves out. Those who opposed the war or disliked Marines made themselves scarce when we arrived on campus, while the others welcomed us. I met girlfriend Cheryl there. We dated during TBS and for two years following my return from Nam. She sent care packages throughout my tour, writing almost every week, a faithful supporter and morale booster. Cheryl had marriage designs, but matrimony was far from my mind at the time.

The War

The 800-pound gorilla thrived at OCS—the Vietnam War—the chief reason most of us joined the Corps and our destination once we completed training. Service in a combat zone motivated most of us. Clueless as to what war was actually like, I plunged ahead, doubtless thinking I would soon be walking in the heroic footsteps of John Wayne's Sergeant Stryker in *The Sands of Iwo Jima*, with a beautiful damsel waiting back home. Classroom instruction took place in aging tin-roofed buildings. These stifling metal structures dated from the Korean War-era or earlier. The instruction often referenced Vietnam, but the war did not dominate the syllabus, as it would later, at the Basic School. Classes after meals in a building with little to no air conditioning put candidates to sleep. Exhausted, we tried to keep awake and alert. We were warned to stand against the wall of the room to avoid falling to sleep, but I recall only seeing a handful of candidates daring to do so. I learned it's possible to sleep without appearing to be sleeping.

During a rare instance of downtime one afternoon in the squad bay, after listening to Question Mark and the Mysterians' "96 Tears," on AM radio, a number of candidates gathered round to discuss the training week ahead. The song had caught my attention with its raw, repetitive beat and wailing, rhythmic organ. Paul, the talkative one who rode the bus with me, and who ended up washing out of OCS, commented cheerfully that the pressing demand for junior officers in Nam augured well for our collective prospects of making it through the course. Paul laughed amid silence. A cynical, contemptuous candidate looked at him and said, "Don't count on it." Poor Paul was clearly on his way out at that point. The reply seemed cruelly humorous at the time and we all chuckled nervously at the response to Paul's observation. But, I thought, possibly along with others present, would my head soon be on the chopping block as well? It appeared to me that certain candidates were targeted early on by the staff for unsuitability and urged or told to DOR. One weekend after graduation from OCS, another lieutenant and I had dinner at the officer's club. We were waited on by a former candidate in my platoon who had dropped out. It was awkward. I was embarrassed at the situation, how a once-fellow candidate was now serving me at the club. I felt deeply sorry for him but I could not think of anything to say that might have made him feel any better.

We knew the Corps was, in fact, in dire need of junior officers to fill the gaps of those rotating from Vietnam and those who became casualties. Rumors of recent battles in Vietnam trickled in. Anecdotes spread of notable experiences in-country. One report involved the death of a candidate's relative. When the news reached us, it brought us all a little closer to the fighting we would experience ourselves in less than a year. The war, for me, was still out there, somewhere. I did not focus on it simply because it was not on the immediate road ahead. I could only concentrate on one obstacle at a time. That hurdle was getting through training.

We candidates were insulated from the outside civilian world most of the week, existing in a bubble where we breathed Marine Corps air, ate Marine food, and swore like Marines. We sometimes listened to the Top 40 on transistor radios while cleaning the squad bay, working on our uniforms, or "shooting the shit." There might have been a two-minute news segment at the top of the hour, but I cannot recall having any discussion with another candidate concerning current events. The world outside Quantico did not exist for me except when Saturday rolled around. The pressure of uncertainty and possible failure forced me to live in the moment. Our actual training curriculum at times also seemed detached from the war, but for us candidates and, later, young lieutenants, it was all, as author Michael Herr ended his book *Dispatches* in despair, "Vietnam Vietnam Vietnam."

Graduation at the end of October could not come soon enough. We shined our shoes, clipped the Irish Pennants, random threads which always seemed to sprout while preparing our uniforms. My parents drove down from New Jersey. I was grateful they were there for me. Dad wore his Navy officer's uniform, which still fit him like a glove more than three years after his retirement. I was proud of him. I noticed after the graduation ceremony that numerous lieutenants had no family or friends in attendance. They asked other graduates—some unknown to them, but who happened to be standing nearby—to pin on their bars. Classmate Wes Lamoureux many years later recalled,

> At the end of the graduation ceremony, we were milling around and looking for our families and friends. Richard Wiseman came over to me and said he had no family there. He then blessed me with a great honor, one that I have

The author with parents after commissioning ceremony, Quantico, Virginia, 28 October 1966.

come to appreciate far more than on that day. He asked if I would pin his new brown bars on his collar. We never crossed paths again.

Lamoureux learned of Wiseman's death sometime after the latter's first day in-country. Graduation was a poignant moment for all of us. We had survived a trial by fire of sorts. Other challenges beckoned.

At a reception in the officer's club after graduation, Captain Owens seemed transformed. He was relaxed and smiling. I introduced my father to him. Dad and the captain exchanged pleasantries and Owens said good words about me as I stood by uncomfortably. The newly-made lieutenants from my platoon avoided him. While I do not recall the incident, a classmate told me years later at a reunion that Owens announced midway through the course that he hoped he would never serve with any of us.

When I returned to the barracks after graduation to retrieve my belongings, Sergeant Taylor stood with a grin in the center of the squad bay and saluted me smartly. I smiled, returned his salute, shook his hand, and thanked him for what he had done for us. I handed him the traditional dollar bill. In retrospect, I owed him, Staff Sergeant Murray, and Captain Owens much more than that. With new-found self-confidence and pure pride, my goal secured, plenty of other challenges and disappointments awaited me, but I had cleared the first hurdle.

The Basic School (TBS)

Located about eight miles from main side Quantico, TBS emphasized teaching second lieutenants the basics of small unit leadership and military skills. The heart of the campus included the enormous, now-demolished O'Bannon Hall, built in the 1950s. It housed the bachelor lieutenants, a large mess hall, and a reception area containing the Hawkins Room ("The Hawk") bar. Lieutenant William D. Hawkins received a posthumous Medal of Honor for his actions at the Battle of Tarawa in 1943. Early in the war Hawkins received a battlefield commission without attending Basic School, so the bar at TBS bearing his name—still in existence in a new building—was intended as a special honor in his memory.

The main headquarters building and attached classrooms were a five-minute march from O'Bannon Hall. We undertook water survival training at a large indoor pool located on the other side of a rarely used grass parade ground. We sometimes used a nearby blacktop parade deck for drills and a track field. Other training areas, including the mock-up of a "Vietnam Village" and the rifle and pistol range, were located within a ten-minute marching distance of the main campus. We were trucked in attached trailers called "cattle cars" for other weapons and tactical training exercises scattered away from Camp Barrett.

More than 500 new lieutenants in TBS 3-67 reported for duty on 28 October 1966. We received an extended weekend liberty, then began training the first week of November 1966. The 21-week course would span, unfortunately, the entire winter season. I remember those months as the coldest of my life, largely because so much of it was spent outdoors in the wet snow of Quantico. The harsh weather remained a constant enemy, sapping our spirit at every turn. But the morning of graduation from OCS, I was on a high when I left main side Quantico.

The war began to come into much sharper focus as the training centered on the hard and soft skills required to be a small unit combat leader. Most, if not all, of us expected orders for Vietnam. Despite the frigid weather, we knew we had to absorb as much instruction as possible if we were to lead Marines and improve our collective chances for survival. Unfortunately, 47 of our brothers in The Basic School 3-67 would not return to live their lives as the rest of us would. That misfortune has long plagued me.

The Reserve Lieutenant

Few of us new lieutenants likely considered making the Corps a career. I took pride as a commissioned officer, even though I was a reserve one. I had three years of obligated active duty before returning to the civilian world, followed by three years as a reservist on standby reserve. Officers who held a regular commission—and there were very few who emerged from the TBS 3-67 course—usually became careerists. I would later call them "lifers." The difference between a reservist and a lifer would become more evident and pointed in Vietnam and beyond. In training, I couldn't have cared less about the difference. At TBS, we were all rowing in the same boat.

A TBS student is a commissioned officer to be sure, but in an environment led by more senior career-oriented regular officers, he was low-man on the totem pole, sucking hind tit, as the saying went. I recalled this frustration in a letter from Vietnam a year later, written to my cousin, who was going through TBS.

> By now you have probably experienced what I call Basic School disenchantment. The entire temper of the Basic School is unnatural and always a little contrived. It is the infantry that's pushed at Basic School. I have seen the bitter disillusionment of so many grunt

> [infantry] officers. I did not care for the Basic School, to be truthful. You do have the opportunity to learn a lot there. I don't agree with some of the doctrine taught. Also, I disagree with the way lieutenants are treated. Try not to get discouraged. Enjoy your weekends and relax, enjoy the things that make you happy.

I seemed to have had no problem dispensing gratuitous advice. Now in my late 70s, the negative memories of the Basic School in 1966–67 have mellowed. I now look back with some affection on my stay at TBS, wishing I could relive those times, perhaps changing the trajectory of some events in Vietnam.

The TBS Platoon

Just as enlisted recruits were trained to be riflemen, The Basic School taught lieutenants the basics of how to lead a rifle platoon. The course left little idle time for getting better acquainted with classmates, something I have long regretted. We were placed in platoons of about forty officers, in three squads. Most of us had not known one another in OCS. There were two bachelor officers per room in the sprawling O'Bannon Hall, with a married officer assigned to operate out of the room during the training day. The spare room contained a sink, a metal desk, and a metal bunk bed, to which we secured our M-14 rifles. Two residential rooms shared a small bathroom with a toilet and shower.

My staff platoon commander, Captain Brian Fagan, was a far cry from Captain Owens. He was a different animal altogether, recently returned from a tour in Vietnam. Reserved by nature, Fagan represented the epitome of what I imagined a Marine officer should be. He was an Irish Catholic from Ohio. Not a large man, lean, he had the chiseled features of a poster Marine officer, an ideal choice to lead a TBS platoon. He treated lieutenants with firm dignity and respect and exhibited a keen sense of subtle humor, as if he did not buy-in completely to the culture there. He seldom chewed-out one of us in front of other lieutenants, but when he did, he accompanied the criticism with wit and compassion. Lieutenants responded to the student environment of TBS with cynicism and humor. When we thought we were being harassed, shouts of "attitude check," and "Motor T [Motor Transport officer], out in three," would echo down O'Bannon Hall corridors. We loudly complained of unexpected uniform changes during the winter requiring us to change into, or out of, our clumsy cold weather, rubber-insulated "Mickey Mouse Boots." Fagan surely heard the shouts, but said nothing to discourage it.

We considered the Captain to be on our side, nearly one of us. He was only a couple of years older than most. Had we been in Nam, I am sure we

Captain Brian Fagan, Vietnam, 1968 (courtesy Brian Fagan).

would have laid down our lives for him if needed. He would return to Nam a second time as a company commander and survive a grievous gunshot wound to his neck. He eventually retired a decorated colonel and remains deeply respected by our TBS platoon.

The Basic School Classmates

As TBS began, I thought I had little in common with some fellow lieutenants. A few, frankly, were not men I chose to spend my limited free time with at the time. None of us were adept practitioners of small talk. We were often blunt, if not brutal, in our comments to one another. I recognized my social limitations, preferring to observe and allow others to take the lead and the risk. I discounted the "Follow me" stereotype of a combat Marine officer. That was not me, I didn't even try. I winced at the loud, gung-ho demeanor of some lieutenants. Was it their real personality on display or feigned enthusiasm intended to impress their classmates? Their dramatized enthusiasm sometimes struck me as phony. Looking back on that time, I now believe I was far too quick to judge others, sometimes too critical. To provide one notable example, going through the course I developed an early negative view of an officer I considered boisterous. Built like a tank, Lieutenant Carl (Bud) Myllymaki had played college football and made it clear to everyone in the platoon that he wanted to be a gung-ho infantry officer, a macho recon Marine. Near the end of the course, I had an opportunity to spend some time talking alone with Bud and found him almost the opposite of that public persona. He struck me as a man who shared the same self-doubts and concerns about the future in Vietnam that I had. In Nam, Bud excelled as a leader and was beloved by his men, never asking them to do something he would not or could not do himself, never placing them a needless risk. He was killed in action just days away from the end of his tour as a Recon company commander when he insisted on leading a patrol to break in a newly-arrived officer.

Like OCS, TBS had a peer evaluation system. Officers graded one another on billets they held and rank-ordered their platoon peers at the end of the course. In my view, peer grading encouraged unhealthy competition, prompting some officers to be hyper-critical and demeaning toward others. I thought it also unnecessarily divided officers rather than bringing them together. I have since learned that peer evaluations were not factored in to the official rankings, but served as a "truth-teller." The staff platoon commander looked at the student rankings as just another element in a lieutenant's performance. Peer rankings were not included in the official assessments or end-of-course class standing.

In late 1966 and early 1967, the standard training schedule had been compressed. It conditioned us to deal with physical exhaustion, something we would experience our entire tour in Vietnam. The nonstop schedule included instruction during the long winter in overheated classrooms. During training films, with lights dimmed, lieutenants would often doze off and sometimes fall out of their chairs, to the laughter of those who managed to stay awake. Weekend breaks, when we had them at all, started mid-day Saturday. Married officers and their wives seemed to establish social relationships with other married couples. Their wives formed supportive bonds with other student wives. Bachelors were on their own to make mischief in D.C and Fredericksburg or hang around the BOQ, sleep, and watch football games on one of the few TVs.

Demanding Integrity

On one of our early, timed conditioning runs we had to run a mile and a half down a paved road to a checkpoint and return to the start point near O'Bannon Hall. On the way to the halfway point, several Marines running together decided to turn around early. Thinking they would not be noticed among the throng of lieutenants running on the road, they made their way back to the start with impressive times. Hours later we learned that they had cheated and were reported on by other lieutenants who observed them. After an investigation they were discharged from the Marine Corps. It was an object lesson for all of us new lieutenants. Those who cheated or violated ethical standards would not be tolerated.

Focusing on Artillery

I knew early on I would not be a fit for the infantry, even though platoon leaders seemed to be in greatest demand in Vietnam. My introspective personality, I thought, would probably not fit what the Corps sought in an infantry platoon commander. I gravitated to the artillery, the king of the battlefield. If infantry was a non-starter, I wanted a job that would put me in the field with the infantry, or "grunts," a term of the greatest respect. I wanted to serve at the "pointy end of the spear," on the front lines. The risk of being an artillery Forward Observer with the grunts didn't faze me. I began to realize that "arty" was the best fit for my skill set. Captain Fagan doubtless knew it as well. I recall at the end of the course when I had my last interview, he acknowledged my limitations and supported my choice of artillery rather than infantry.

Lasting Bonds of Brotherhood

Over the years, I have regretted not having known my OCS and TBS brothers better when we undertook training. The chief obstacle, besides my own reserve, was the lack of opportunity to know each other in a more relaxed environment. Nam lay just ahead and that was more than most of us could deal with. As the 1969 Guess Who hit noted, there was "no time, no time, no time left for" … others. Married officers had their wives and clusters of other married couples off base. The unattached lieutenants scattered to the winds on weekends, some swooping to Georgetown nearly every weekend and sometimes during the week. They would scramble to return to Quantico, change into their uniforms, and make morning formation. Only decades later did I feel the lost opportunity of knowing other officers better. My TBS class reunions started in 2011.

Unfortunately, politically partisan divisions began to surface around the 2016 general election, reflecting trends in the U.S. population at large. These differences have buffeted, but not destroyed, our brotherhood. I hope in due time we will all come to bask in the warm glow of our shared experiences during a critical time in our nation's history and to remember our lost brothers.

Farewell Feast

Following graduation from TBS in late March 1967, I began driving to Fort Sill, Oklahoma, stopping to see friends and relatives along the way. Charleston was my first stop. While there, I had a fresh seafood dinner at what was then the preeminent restaurant in the Holy City, the esteemed Henry's. The food was always fresher than fresh. A professor who frequented Henry's in the 1960s once told me that when he once squeezed lemon on a plate of raw oysters, the bivalves reacted, standing up out of the shell. While in college, friends and I would occasionally have a beer there, but dinner was out of reach. The Maître d' and other waiters were African American, in white jackets. All of them were long-time employees. The superb head chef was also African American. The restaurant had two rooms, one with a bar containing booths for dining, and another with starched, white tablecloths for families and polite society. That room had its own entrance so the ladies would not have to walk through the bar. Marguerite Gruber, the restaurant manager and sister of the owner, and bartender George Groover were both tough as nails, but each had a heart of gold. Neither countenanced untoward behavior from the customers and ran a tight ship. George had a degree in journalism from the University of Georgia.

That evening I sat in the bar and talked with George as I ate. I told him I would be leaving for Vietnam in several months. Shortly afterwards, Marguerite walked up and said, "I hear you're headed for Vietnam. If you can come here tomorrow, I'd like you to have dinner with me." I was surprised, but accepted immediately. Marguerite knew me from my visits to Henry's when I was a student, but we had never talked much. I arrived as scheduled and Marguerite escorted me to her apartment above the restaurant. I sat on a stool and watched in awe as she cooked and assembled a meal worthy of Julia Child: roast squab with a delicious sauce and all the trimmings. It was an incredible meal. I am sure Marguerite was paying her respects not so much to me personally. I was more a symbol, a young man heading off to war. It was a kind and generous gesture on her part, one I have never forgotten.

Fort Sill

The need to get lieutenants through the training pipeline to replace growing casualties became more acute throughout 1967. I sensed the urgency at the Field Artillery Officers Basic Course. Fort Sill was built in 1869 and named by Civil War General Philip Sheridan in honor of friend and West Point classmate Brigadier General Joshua Sill, who was killed in the war. The expansive base of 94,000 acres has been home for U.S. Army and Marine artillerymen since the early 20th century. The base's varied, rolling terrain is especially ideal for the training of Forward Observers (FOs), in addition to teaching all aspects of employing field artillery.

Listening to AM radio most of the day during the days-long trip, I sensed pop culture—reflected in the music—was changing, gaining momentum in new directions. Over the next few months, four unusual songs sat atop the Top 40 charts. Scott McKenzie's "San Francisco (Be Sure to Wear Flowers in Your Hair)," memorialized the city that became the symbolic ground zero for the Summer of Love, while Procol Harum's haunting "Whiter Shade of Pale," pushed the envelope of pop music into the classical realm. Both songs endure as signal recordings of the era. And soon after arrival at Fort Sill, while checking in and preparing for the course, I heard two other songs of the times that, again, signaled currents of change in the air. Aretha Franklin's defiant version of "Respect," penned and recorded first by Otis Redding, and Bobby Darin's plaintive "If I Were a Carpenter," written by folk artist Tim Harden.

The new, six-story BOQ at Fort Sill appeared luxurious compared to the older, austere BOQ at Quantico I left behind. The day after arrival, I wrote:

> I have an outstanding room, all to myself, with carpeting, large desk, bed, chest of drawers, walk-in closet, night stand, book case, record player and easy chair—palatial compared to a room at TBS. This morning I met a Marine artillery captain by the name of Harvey Barnum. You might've read how he took over a rifle company after its commander was killed and by doing so, received a Medal of Honor. He was an FO at the time.

Friends

I stayed in touch with friends, some of whom were dealing with the uncertainty of the times. The war eventually touched the lives of nearly everyone I knew. Friends made sometimes hard decisions that would affect their lives for years to come. I heard from Colleen, a girl who worked on the college newspaper with me. We were close, but not yet romantically involved. Following graduation, she took a job as a reporter at the Charleston *News and Courier*, but complained that she didn't want to "dry-up" there. The following year after I arrived in Vietnam, she got married, I thought at the time, for the "stability." Another friend a year ahead of me at the College of Charleston planned to leave graduate school in chemistry. Perhaps reacting to an imminent induction notice, he would begin Naval flight training that summer. Following active duty, he noted, he wanted to return to grad school in English. I had always told him he was on the wrong frequency. Others I knew embarked on academic or law careers to avoid military service.

The Forward Observer (FO)

During the Vietnam War era, a Forward Observer deployed with infantry units, usually a company, to provide artillery support. He usually traveled with the company commander. He requested fire missions by contacting the battery Fire Direction Center (FDC), which computed the target firing data (range, trajectory, shell, and fuse type). The FDC then passed the firing data to the gunline. Once the rounds left the battery, the FO would observe the effect and adjust the rounds on target.

At Sill, 30 Marine lieutenants from TBS 3-67 joined newly commissioned Army lieutenants in my Field Artillery Officer Basic Class. Another group of TBS artillery lieutenants followed weeks behind. We would be tutored in the critical, complicated battlefield art of FOs and running an artillery battery. I soon realized that FOs were as much in demand as platoon commanders, and they became war casualties at the same rate. Senior Marine instructors at the base expected Marine lieutenants to excel and to outshine our Army counterparts. It was all about pride, typical of the interservice competition the Marine Corps embraced. The ten-week, intensive course sped by as the reality of an impending deployment to Vietnam started to come into focus. As I recall, field exercises outpaced classroom instruction. I maintained a 90 percent average until a Cannon Mechanics and Theory test pulled it down. But consistently high field scores on FO Shoots, calling in artillery and adjusting fire on assigned targets, such as those on the undulating hills of "The Washboard," boosted my confidence. Given my success on that shoot and others I was convinced I had found my calling. Artillery was where the rubber met the road. I noted in a letter that I wore ear plugs during a four-hour team-exercise firing the World War II–era 105mm-howitzer, but admitted, "it was hard on the ol' eardrums."

Unfortunately, cannon-cockers in Nam would not wear them for various reasons, machismo a prominent factor.

In one memorable exercise, we became air observers and called in a fire mission. I became completely disoriented as the pilot of my small aircraft made sharp turns, "pulling Gs," nearly making me sick to my stomach. Sensing my struggle, and perhaps the cause of it, the pilot assisted with the fire mission required to bring rounds on target. During another exercise that had direct application to what I would experience in Vietnam, we called in artillery close to our bunker. I would experience incoming again in Nam as a target of enemy artillery.

Gunnery instructors were selected for their aptitude and ability to teach. My homeroom gunnery instructor was a brilliant, sarcastic army captain with a wicked sense of humor. I attempted without success to determine his view of the war in Vietnam. I suspected he might have been critical of it. I never learned whether he had served in Nam. He taught us the detailed intricacies of getting an artillery round on target, to include the various jobs of running an artillery battery—the complex logistics, how to organize a Fire Direction Center, how to repair a howitzer, among other skills. We students all respected and looked up to him. I did not meet a more knowledgeable, intelligent artillery officer on active duty.

I directed most letters home primarily with my father in mind. After craving positive feedback from him when I was younger, and receiving little in return, I still worked to secure an emotional connection. In a Memorial Day note, I mentioned planned home leave before deployment to Vietnam: "I'm looking forward to July. You and I will have to go out and slurp a couple of brews one night. I'd really like that."

Instead, he took me deep-sea fishing for the first time, at my request. I was fortunate I had not chosen the Navy. Within ten minutes of leaving port, I became seasick and spent the rest of the day leaning over the rail of the boat or reclining on a bench, pure torture.

Bad News Arrives

I wrote on D-Day 1967: "Everything bad seems always to come in flurries." Near the end of the course at Fort Sill, disheartening news arrived from my family. My oldest sister had run away again without notice, this time to San Francisco and Haight-Ashbury. She would stay there for months living the life of a hippie. She had suffered from a mood and personality disorder since childhood. Her behavior produced continual disruptions in the family that preoccupied my parents during my tour in Nam and afterwards. At the time, I didn't know about the damage and self-destruction mental illness could cause. My parents had no idea how to deal with it.

Then, days later, my parents informed me of the death in Vietnam of Ensign John McCormick, a naval gunfire liaison officer assigned to Third Marines. John and I were friends as youths at Hunter's Point Naval Shipyard, on San Francisco Bay. The excitable Johnny I knew bore little resemblance in my mind's eye to the courageous Ensign John McCormick I later read about who received a posthumous Silver Star for valor. As a naval gunfire officer, his Marine assault force was ambushed by North Vietnamese Army (NVA) regular forces near the Demilitarized Zone (DMZ) that separated North from South Vietnam. It was a strain to get my head around the news. John's father, a retired World War II–era Navy captain, and his mother, friends of my parents, built a memorial in their backyard and became vocal anti-war advocates, scandalizing some of their retired Navy friends. When news of John's loss reached me at Sill a week or so before graduation, I responded to my parents:

> His death hit me very hard. I can't explain why, exactly. But he and I were close. You know how it is; you're always attached in some way to another person you once knew very well. Johnny always hated pain and never took it easily. I hope—well, you know.

I received further disturbing news about the same time:

> I have heard today of several of my Basic School comrades, infantry types, being killed or wounded already. One Army lieutenant here at Ft. Sill left after learning of his brother's death in Vietnam, a lieutenant a year older than he was.

I knew that grunt lieutenants, especially those assigned to the 3rd Marine Division near the DMZ, were at high risk, but the reports still shook me to the core. The converging reports triggered a brief, unexpected dark period. I became convinced I might not return from Vietnam. The cloud didn't last more than a couple weeks, but I asked two friends if they would consider visiting me in Oklahoma. They responded without hesitation. One drove from South Carolina, the other from Indiana, to spend separate weekends at Fort Sill. I did not anticipate they would respond with a "yes," but they did. We were all aware it might be our last meeting. Weeks later, however, the thought of possible death in Nam dissolved completely. It coincided with an uptick in my test scores. I am sure talking with reassuring friends helped. Maybe just putting one foot in front of the other aided in vanquishing the gloom. Once I arrived in-country, I never again dwelled on the possibility I might not return home alive. Still, I had my share of close calls and always understood life could end in an instant.

2. Keep on Truckin'

As the field artillery course wound down at Fort Sill, the band played on at the officer's club as it did in military bars across the country in those trying days. Students at Fort Sill and the wives of absent husbands serving in Vietnam sometimes partied the night away at the club:

> Saturday at the Officer's Club I talked with a young German officer, also going through the course, about WWII. He danced with some 18-year-old girl he met there. She was separated, not divorced, from her husband. I enjoyed the band, a group that played the old-time band music of the 1940s. People sure were having a great time.

Of the Marine officers who attended field artillery school at Sill with me, I knew well three of the six who would die as FOs applying the skills we learned—Texan Hank Norman, Harvard graduate Charlie Ryberg, and Ted Edwards. Hank was one of the few married officers in our Marine group, a low-key, soft-spoken officer with a perpetual smile. He was universally liked and respected, felled by an enemy mortar round at Khe Sanh during the siege in spring 1968. Charlie Ryberg won a scholarship to a prestigious New England prep school before studying English at Harvard. One of the 22 graduates memorialized on a plaque at the university, he died from enemy incoming artillery near Con Thien. Ted Edwards, a tall, genial, low-key officer, received a posthumous Silver Star in the early days of the Tet Offensive. When his company near the DMZ was attacked by a battalion-sized enemy force, Edwards acted instantly, calling in pre-planned defensive fires. Disregarding his own safety, he moved to various vantage points along the defensive perimeter skillfully adjusting fire from three batteries, halting the enemy advance within meters of his company's position and blocking their retreat. Shouting encouragement to his men, he steadfastly remained on the front lines until he fell mortally wounded.

I did not know Dennie Peterson, who received a posthumous Navy Cross, an award for valor second only to the Medal of Honor. The only child of a former World War II combat, and later commercial airline, pilot, Dennie was killed in action in September 1967, weeks after his arrival in Nam. In a battle against a large enemy force, fearing for the life of his radio operator, he took the radio and carried it during the hours-long battle across fire-swept terrain. To observe and adjust artillery fire on the enemy, he left the company perimeter and in contested ground drew fire from five enemy automatic weapons. Although painfully wounded, he remained in place for two hours adjusting artillery. When darkness fell and the enemy repulsed, he crawled to assist another wounded Marine into the perimeter. After being medically treated, he organized groups of Marines and led them through enemy lines on three occasions recovering and carrying casualties to protected areas. His citation read,

By his calm courage, intrepid fighting spirit and dynamic leadership, Second Lieutenant Peterson served to inspire all who observed him and contributed materially to the accomplishment of his unit's mission. His great personal valor reflected the highest credit upon himself and enhanced the finest traditions of the Marine Corps and the United States Naval Service. He gallantly gave his life for his country.

Home Leave

Graduating from Fort Sill in June 1967, we lieutenants scattered to the winds, taking home leave and spending several weeks with family and friends before departure for Vietnam. I packed my father's underpowered 1961 Chevy Monza and, following a couple close calls on the road trying to pass cars on two lane roads, reached my home of record in Long Beach, California. For many of us Marines headed for Nam, home leave was filled with nonstop wish-fulfilling activities—seeing people we might not see again, doing things we might not do again. For me, it was not a melancholy or foreboding time at all, rather happy weeks filled with fun, good food, and plenty of rest and downtime. I wanted to enjoy my time to the fullest, but Nam was never far away in my thoughts. Counting down the time I would depart for Nam, I wanted to live every hour to the fullest. I spent hours in the pool with my younger siblings—11 years separated me from my brother and sister twins. Long-time family friends from Dad's career in the Navy dropped by. Some invited my parents and me to dinner. These were times of unspoken, quiet goodbyes—"just in case we don't see one another again" meetings. They were not at all sad times, but upbeat, see-you-later affairs.

I was surprised and moved when I spoke with my father the day before I left to deploy to Vietnam. Standing in the dining room, I began reviewing my life insurance policy and designated beneficiaries in the event of my death. He held his hand up indicating I had said enough. Although he almost never displayed much emotion, he teared up, patted me on the shoulder, nodded, and said he understood. The day of my departure for Nam in mid–August, my parents drove to Camp Pendleton from Long Beach to say goodbye. They watched from a distance as I boarded a bus for El Toro Marine air base. My mother told me years later it was hard for her to believe I was going to war.

Okie

The chartered Boeing 707–stretch Continental Airways flight stopped to refuel on Wake Island before landing in Okinawa, where the final battle against Imperial Japan was waged in 1945. Following the war, the U.S. installed numerous bases on Okinawa. The island became the chief launching point for Marines destined for Vietnam, a couple hours away by air. At Okinawa, Marines would complete final administrative check-outs and check-ins, waiting for flights and stowing their seabags filled with civilian and stateside uniforms and other personal items. The pause sometimes included a trip to the post exchange to purchase more personal items for in-country, plenty of eating and drinking, and perhaps time for activities off the base with Okinawan ladies.

3

Welcome Aboard

Arrival

Someone must have been eager to get me in-country. I spent just eight hours in Okinawa, leaving at 0230 on 14 August. I landed in Da Nang with a Valpak—a government-issued, olive-green military suitcase—and two small hand bags. One of them contained my mini-library of about twenty paperback books I planned to read when time allowed. I would receive an education in Vietnam, but it would not be a literary one.

Da Nang was the primary entry point for Marines arriving in Nam. We landed about 0430 in the morning. I was struck with the overpowering heat and high humidity, like a blast from a furnace. After checking in with a Welcome-to-Nam desk at the Terminal, I boarded a bus and rode through a fortified, military sector of the city containing one headquarters compound after another, each enclosed with barbed wire, bunkers interspersed on the perimeter. I saw few people on the road, only a smattering of military vehicles. I wrote a day later:

> Da Nang is more of a primitive base than I expected. Planes of all sorts were flying around. I was really surprised how the weather saps your strength when you are not used to it. The humidity was violent and of course the sun doesn't help much. I'm in a hut waiting to see the 1st Marine Division commanding general. All officers who report in talk to him. Afterwards I will be assigned to a unit. I hope it will be with the artillery.

Yes, it was the ultimate test, I thought, and the objective of a year of rigorous training and preparation. I had a lot to prove to myself and others. I wanted to do what I could to help win the war. I had no doubt that we would defeat the communist forces; it was only a question of when. America did not lose wars. The idea of not prevailing over what we imagined to be an inferior enemy in every respect never crossed my mind before arriving in Vietnam. I looked forward to the experience of eventual combat

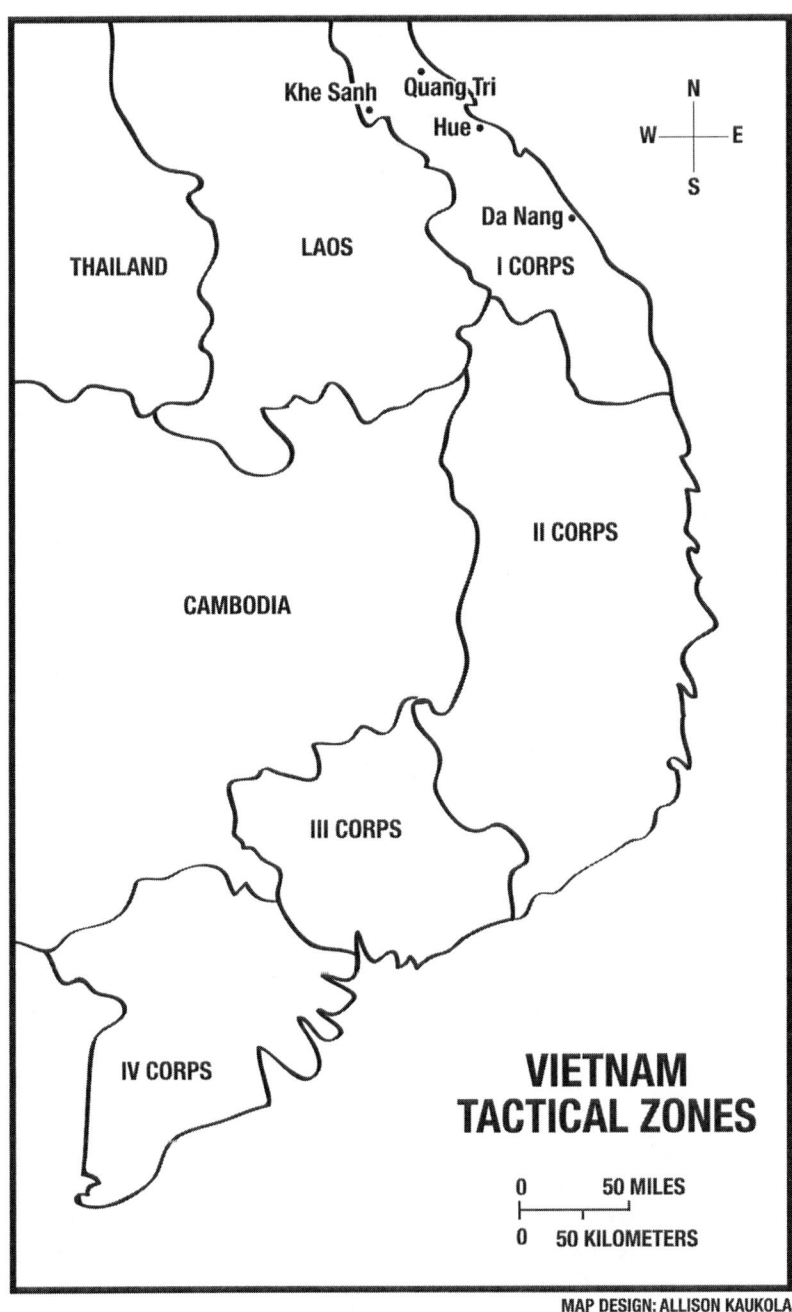

Vietnam Tactical Zones. Graphic by Allison Kaukola.

with excitement and curiosity. I recall no fear, no concerns, only positive anticipation. Subsequently assigned to the 11th Marines artillery regiment, I billeted at the transient officer quarters for several days in a spartan plywood hooch, sleeping on a cot. "The outdoor toilets are bad news." I would soon grow accustomed to the urinal tubes and multi-holed outhouses.

The following day, along with about ten other officers, the assistant division commander in attendance, the commanding general—in an impeccable, pressed utility uniform—provided a traditional 15-minute overview of the tactical map of I Corps (pronounced "Eye Core"), where all Marine units were located. His monologue left me, and likely everyone else, none the wiser. The general's briefing made little sense to me. I had no context, no familiarity of the order of battle. There were no questions when the general completed his briefing, but he didn't ask for them either. Highly decorated World War II veteran Major General Donn Robertson struck me, nonetheless, as a competent and approachable officer.

There was no intimidating "look to your left and right; one of the officers sitting next to you won't leave Vietnam alive." A regimental executive officer (XO) in the 3rd Marine Division reportedly had said just that to a group of just-arrived TBS classmates about the same time. It might have been an accurate statement, but this was not a college sociology class. In this instance, it was callous. I boarded a bus back to the regiment, anticipating another Welcome Aboard at Eleventh Marines artillery compound. I stayed in the transient officer's BOQ a couple days, but never met the CO or received a welcome aboard. The contrast between the division commander's professional reception and the artillery regimental CO's no-show made an impression. It proved consistent with the questionable leadership I would experience with more senior artillery officers in Nam over the next 13 months.

One afternoon at regiment, I wandered into the small, empty, plywood officer's club and sat down, enjoying the calm and gentle breeze created by a slowly-turning fan overhead. It must have been siesta time. I could hear booms, explosions somewhere out in the boonies, perhaps in no man's land. The sound of aircraft and trucks passing by could be heard, but no voices. The neat, clean room contained about a dozen tables and a small bar. After some time, a beautiful, poised, and dignified-looking young Vietnamese woman wearing a traditional, silk ao-dai entered and glided silently across the room. I greeted her with a smile and a nod. I thought she might be a waitress, but no, she was the manager-bartender. She smiled politely in return and went about her business without speaking.

At least my first encounter with a Vietnamese was positive. I wondered, however, is she a friendly, or perhaps a secret Viet Cong (VC) supporter? Obviously, a year of insurgency training and indoctrination had an effect. I couldn't trust the locals entirely over the course of my tour. I would remain ambivalent about the Vietnamese I encountered, oscillating between admiration of these proud and resourceful people in general, fear of and respect for the VC and North Vietnamese Army (NVA) in the field, and general contempt for the U.S.-allied Army of the Republic of Vietnam (ARVN), Popular Force (PF), and Regional Force militia.

After a while I wandered outside and watched a twin-rotor helicopter land on the regimental headquarters landing pad. The aircraft—officially grounded for mechanical problems at the time—brought back inspectors from some battery in the field. I guess the ban on flying the aircraft did not apply to the inspectors' travel. In the far distance, to the west, through the haze I could see small hills in the foreground, giving way to more imposing features that appeared to be high hills or mountains. The flatlands in front of those distant features would become my primary area of operations for the next five months.

Personnel assignments for arrivals in-country were largely based on which units had the most immediate need for replacements. At 11th Marines Regimental headquarters, the adjutant, the chief personnel officer, said I would be assigned to a well-regarded arty (artillery) battalion—Second Battalion, Eleventh Marines (2/11, pronounced "Two Eleven")—and taken to the field. It sounded good to me, what I had been trained for attained. I wanted to get on with it. As the lone passenger, I finally hopped a helicopter for the 20-mile trip south to Hill 63 (later called LZ Baldy), not far from the national, north-south, Highway 1. The two-lane, rutted hardtop road near the South China Sea would remain the chief ground transportation artery for U.S. forces in I Corps—the primary Marine tactical area of operations during the war.

The two machine gunners informed me, when I asked as I boarded, that small-arms fire could bring down the aircraft if it struck the engine in a vulnerable location. Loud pops of rounds passing through the thin skin would be unmistakable, they noted. I scanned the interior and identified at least a dozen bullet holes that had been patched. His head tilted back, the chopper's door gunner fell into a deep sleep within moments of lift-off and slept the entire, noisy, bumpy, 30-minute ride, proof positive that Marines can sleep anywhere, anytime. The window gunner on the other side of the chopper remained awake and vigilant in case we received ground fire.

As we landed at Hill 63, the rotors kicked up enough dust to envelop the aircraft. After the chopper left, I found the adjutant's tent and checked-in. The base looked like a temporary installation. I learned the battalion had been on the hill for five weeks, a bleak, dry place with large 32'×10' GP (general purpose) tents, smaller, 10'×5' tents, and a few scattered hardback hooches. Marines in the co-located artillery battery and 2/11 headquarters had been working 16-to-20-hour days filling sandbags, hardening their positions against any possible enemy attack.

The formal, obligatory "Welcome Aboards" kept accumulating. I

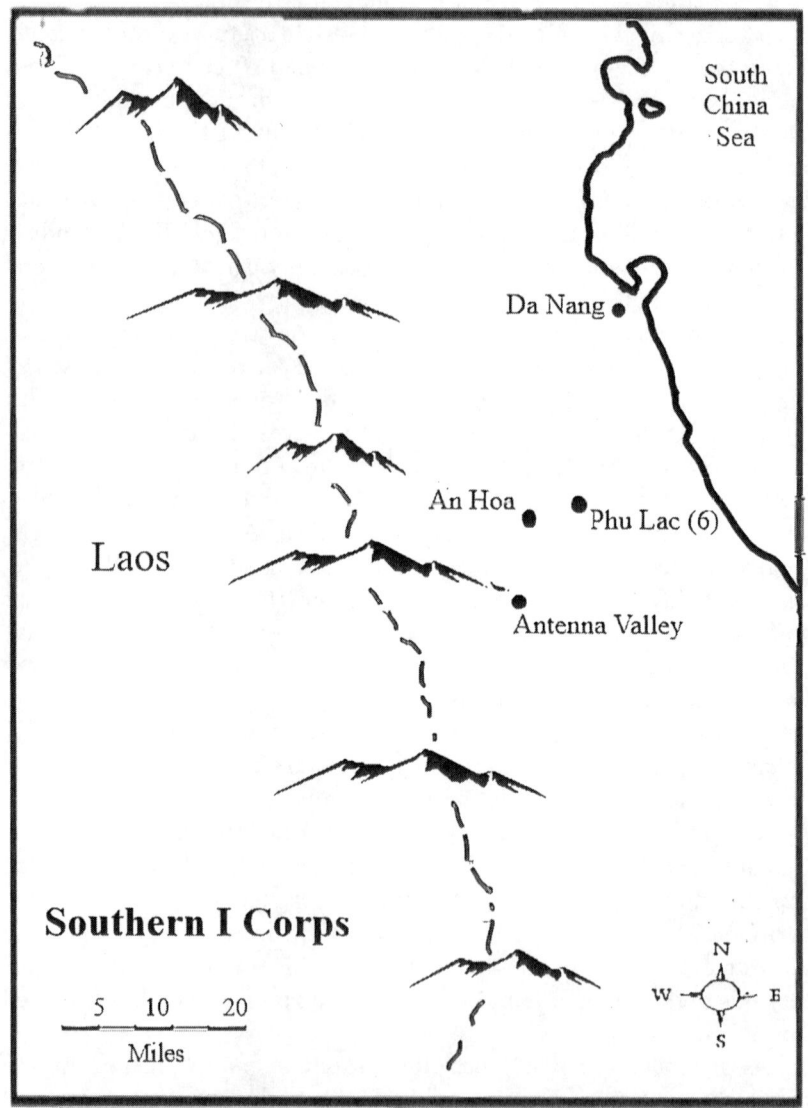

Map of Southern I Corps. Graphic by Michael Archer.

received them from the artillery battalion executive officer and the operations officer. The XO informed me I would be assigned to E Battery (pronounced "Echo Battery"), "the best in the battalion," he emphasized, one eyebrow raised, checking whether I was impressed. A sharp outfit, he added, supporting the infantry Second Battalion, Fifth Marines (2/5). The CO was in the field on an operation, he noted. As I waited his imminent return, I drew plain olive jungle utilities, a .45 pistol, and a Ka-Bar combat knife. I also had Dad's World War II knife. The operations officer informed me no rifles were available to issue at the time. The entire armory had been taken to the field for an operation and would not return until after I left for An Hoa combat base, home base of Echo Battery. I thought it unfortunate, particularly after he mentioned that they expected to be hit by the enemy anytime. Don't worry, he said, there will be plenty of artillery illumination rounds available. Did he intend those to be comforting words?

An Hoa

After waiting two more days for the no-show artillery battalion commander, I received the green light to proceed by helicopter to my artillery battery at An Hoa. Designed for an infantry battalion with its supporting artillery battery, An Hoa lay in a remote area of Quang Nam province, the southern-most of the five northern provinces of the RVN composing I Corps. By mid–1967 Marines manned most of the major I Corps bases. Marines had taken the isolated base over from ARVN troops the year before when ground combat units began to arrive in Vietnam and expand Marine presence beyond the immediate Da Nang tactical area. The base appeared large. Its 1,000-meter-long runway could accommodate the large C-130 transport plane. Numerous 30 by 10 foot tin-roofed plywood hooches dotted the base, providing billeting and office spaces. Wooden pallet walkways were scattered around. Red dirt dominated everywhere I looked. Once the monsoon settled in, the ground would turn into a sea of red mud. Not more than 6,000 meters west of An Hoa base rose imposing hills covered with impenetrable canopy.

Scanning the area around the base, I could see more high hills to the south, partly obscured by low clouds. I would soon learn that NVA regular forces streamed around An Hoa, traversing the outlying rice paddies, headed to the coastal regions to the east. The enemy used the nearby mountains and valleys as safe harbors. Marines viewed the local villagers in the area as mostly unfriendly-to-hostile, active in laying antipersonnel mines and setting booby traps in areas patrolled by Marines. No more than 2,000 meters from the southwest perimeter, I learned, a German Red

An Hoa Base, choppers approaching the airfield, late 1967.

Cross compound overlooked the base. The handful of German doctors and stunningly beautiful blonde nurses were allowed to eat in our battalion mess hall, but kept to themselves and provided no information on the enemy. The German medical team provided care to villagers in the area and, we were convinced, also tended to occasional wounded enemy. I heard years later, sometime after I left the country, that the NVA kidnapped German medical personnel there.

Echo Battery

Echo Battery lay in the southeast corner of the base. I confirmed, from talking with Marines in the battery, that it enjoyed a respected reputation supporting 2/5.

> It's the best [battery] in the battalion, supposedly, and I believe it. It's real "tight," meaning the morale is high, and the battery is operating at a high state of proficiency. I talked to the battery commander, who seems real fair and hardworking.

Captain Cates, a stocky, serious, gruff career officer, was of medium height and wore a crew cut. A Texan, he positioned his pistol low on his right hip, ready to draw if needed. Had he worn Western attire, he would have been at home in a John Ford movie. He informed me I would be assigned as the FO for G Company (Golf Company). I would soon observe and experience his stern micromanagement of junior officers and his cultivation of staff noncommissioned officers and gun crews.

Over the next few days, I would form impressions of battery officers and senior staff NCOs who held key positions. They seemed rather cool and distant. Sure, I was a "friggin' new guy," who knew nothing. In ground units like the infantry and artillery, having a buddy or big-brother figure with time in-country to show you the ropes and break you in was critical. The infantry, grunts, seemed to develop an effective buddy system from the start. Not so the artillery officers, in my view.

> *The officers in the battery are not too friendly. Everyone has to prove himself in the field before one is "accepted." They are not unfriendly either, just disinterested.*

Perhaps most surprisingly, within days I was struck by how many Marines of all ranks were openly counting the number of days left in their tour. They flouted it with more recent arrivals, or "boots."

> *Everyone talks of how "short" they are, meaning when they will be going back to the States. Short timers always look down on the boots.*

Did they want to leave Nam that badly? I had no idea of this dynamic while in training. To me, the attitude marked an early indicator of overall morale. I filed it away for future reference. It bore watching. I spent a week in the battery preparing for the field, drawing a rifle and other equipment.

Echo Battery Gun Pit, October 1967.

The battery's officer FO tent of heavy canvas often stood empty. The battalion's four rifle companies—where the FOs were assigned—spent a good portion of the time in the field. The tent interior was hot, allowed little circulation, and smelled of mildew.

> I fired the M16 and have the dope on my weapon. I will carry it when we leave An Hoa for Phu Lac (6), a base surrounded by a hostile area about 6,000 meters from An Hoa, probably 1 September. I will also carry my .45 and Dad's knife. We'll be getting a new Golf Company CO next week.

In the battery admin office, I enrolled in a 10 percent payroll deduction savings plan for my $300 monthly salary and $60 monthly combat pay. Those savings, along with a $200 savings account left behind in the states, would become a source of cash I would use a year later to buy a white 1968 Mercury Cougar, four-on-the floor, low-mileage demo when I returned home.

Before joining my grunt rifle company, I stood duty several nights with experienced battery officers. An early, unexpected attack of homesickness surfaced one evening while I was on watch in the Fire Direction Center (FDC), just a week after arrival:

> Tonight, our battery has been taking some sniper fire, a common occurrence. Our 81mm mortars took care of that. I don't think of home except when I have to, when there isn't anything else to think about. I love you all and think of you a lot, but when I have to, I think only of my job in the field.

A Rat Race

I was impressed with the sanitation measures taken at An Hoa:

> The doctors are always around and inspecting. There is a Vietnamese village about a thousand meters to our front. They don't pay attention to us when squatting on a nearby hill to do their business. Unfortunately, they are not as clean and sanitary-minded as they should be.

A urinal tube was situated a convenient 40 feet away from the FO tent, and the three-hole outhouse a relatively safe 100 meters or so away. The smell of human waste burning in drums of kerosene always filled the air. The latrine sat at the far end of the battery's ten howitzers. There was rarely more than one person at a time occupying it. Understandably, no one wanted to linger. I soon learned of an occasional rat race that took place near it. Marines built wooden rat traps in the scrub behind the outhouse.

Trudging toward the outhouse at Echo Battery, An Hoa, October 1967.

When two or more creatures were trapped, they were doused with kerosene and set aflame and the doors were opened to see which unfortunate rat could run the farthest. That was certainly one form of rodent control. I was never present when a race was run.

Battery Vibes

Battery gun crews considered artillery FO teams as outsiders, associating them more with the infantry companies they supported than as the integral members of the firing battery they were. A physical, social, and cultural chasm separated us. The barriers prevented establishment of valuable professional and personal relationships. Lieutenants led most of the battery FO teams when I arrived. The FOs would typically spend up to six months with their infantry company before rotating back to the artillery battery. Few arty officers, however, spent six months in the field. They either became casualties or were recalled to the battery to fill critical billets that kept the battery functional—assistant executive officer, assistant fire direction officer, fire direction officer, and executive officer—before rotating back home.

Soon after I checked in, a senior battery officer informed me that I had replaced Lieutenant Bill Wilk, who had been killed instantly two weeks earlier by a falling metal cannister from a large-caliber U.S. illumination mortar round. Perhaps in a macabre effort to scare or to impress me, the officer pointed out the deceased officer's helmet. It had a six-inch indentation on the crown from the impact. I thought at the time that showing me the helmet seemed pointless and disrespectful to Lieutenant Wilk's memory. Down the road, I would revisit the incident in my mind each time we used friendly illumination in the field. Tragically, Wilk left a wife and a newborn son he never saw.

I looked forward to the opportunity of leading my own team, inherited from Lieutenant Wilk. My assistant FO—Lance Corporal Ken Stetson—would become my trusted right-hand man. Two other team members and a radioman would rotate off the team within the first two months. Stetson joined the Marine Corps not long after high school graduation. He had married Jan, his high school sweetheart. Quiet and earnest, even-tempered and laid back, he spoke with a slow, western drawl and had a dry sense of humor. I had the fullest confidence in him from the outset. I wrote with enthusiasm, "I am going to really shape [the FO team] into a topnotch unit." Eager to apply what I had learned at The Basic School and Fort Sill, everything seemed possible at that point. I believed without a doubt that I could make a positive contribution to the war effort.

Grunt–Arty Dynamics

In Marine Corps culture, "grunt," is a term of endearment and respect for the Marine infantryman. Grunts valued having a good Forward Observer with them. Marine artillery and air support were critical to retaining battlefield superiority in an environment where encounters with the enemy often began with an ambush resulting in the death of U.S. combatants. Rarely did the enemy stand and fight once artillery and air support had been brought to bear on the battlefield. The enemy had much to lose and little to gain locked in combat with a Marine unit, unless they had a decisive numerical superiority in troops and favorable weather or terrain.

During training I understood little about the nuances of how FO teams interfaced with the infantry units they supported. That was something that had to be worked out in the field. It depended on personal relationships to a large degree. The FO teams were administratively attached to infantry companies, not fully integrated to them. Before I deployed with Golf Company, the battery executive officer (XO) provided guidance on how to deal with the infantry in the field. He cautioned against allowing my team's participation in Golf Company night watches, clean-up details, and other infantry duties. He stressed I should make it clear, if necessary, that my team's obligations with the grunts would be restricted to providing fire support in the field and advising and instructing on all-things artillery. The FO teams had their own radios and each man on the team stood radio watch 24×7 monitoring the arty radio frequency.

At the time, the guidance sounded counterproductive to me, and in the end only served to drive a wedge between our FO team and the grunts. It created a negative optic: that FO teams were not team players. I understood my administrative chain of command would be through the artillery, but my team had to support and live with the grunts in the field. Strictly adhering to the battery policy placed us in an untenable position. It provided a source of friction going forward, at times making for awkward moments. In retrospect, it was not a good policy. My FO team and I violated it on occasion. At the same time, I tried to protect the team from being exploited. In the end, I had to find some accommodation that made us more integrated into the company.

Joining Golf Company

Following battery orientation, I reported to Golf, the rifle company I would call home for the next five months. Repeating the guidance I received from the battery XO, I reviewed with the acting CO of Golf the ground rules of how my FO team would operate. As instructed, I explained that my FO team could not participate in working parties or be assigned to nighttime watch duty. My guidance from the battery was clear, I explained: arty was there to provide support, but my FO team could not serve as grunts in the rifle company. I noted my team would be giving classes to the company's Marines and providing arty support in the field. We had to man our own radios all day. Anticipating my comments, he shrugged glumly and walked away, giving a reluctant nod of acceptance. He had heard it before. With his rotation only days away, he appeared more than ready to put Nam behind him.

The tense partnership in the field made for an orphan-like status for the FOs. We worked with the infantry, but were not recognized or accepted as full-fledged grunts. These boundaries did not diminish the profound respect my FO team members and I had for our infantry brothers. The longer an FO remained in the field, the closer he identified with them. When I finally left Golf months later, I felt an acute loss of camaraderie I thought I could never duplicate in the battery.

It quickly became clear to me that the infantry likewise stood in awe of arty, but had an inherent fear of it—wary for good reason of the potential Friendly Fire that could kill them. And Friendly Fire accidents happened with some frequency. It was the FO's duty to win grunt confidence, teach them how to use artillery, and demonstrate how safe and effective it could be. Deploying on patrols and field operations provided opportunities to build trust in supporting arms and develop the personal relationships important in a combat environment.

Crackerjack Platoon Commanders

The awkward relationship with the grunts did not prevent me from forging close ties with the superlative platoon commanders I worked with. I enjoyed their company in and out of the field, and I remain friends with them to this day. All were good leaders, with integrity, respected by their troops. Right away they impressed me with their energy and

The author (left) with Lieutenant Bill Harvey at the Golf Company officers' hooch, fall 1967.

professionalism. I hung around them every chance I got during down time, learning from them. They all understood the importance of artillery support and appreciated it. Bill Harvey, the senior lieutenant, would spend a career in the Marine Corps. A man of few words, he was laser-focused and all business. Bill was one of the best field officers I met. From Vermont, he was married with a young son he had yet to see.

Vern Arndt was a Basic School classmate, a tall, talented field Marine from Pennsylvania, a former enlisted Marine recommended for the officer program. He was a super-competent field Marine with a sense of where he was on the map and an inspiration to his men.

Tracy Alton, the junior platoon commander, arrived in-country a month earlier than I. Tracy had the misfortune of losing a squad of Marines in an NVA ambush on the treacherous An Hoa–Phu Lac road soon after his arrival. He had been in Da Nang drawing funds for company payday. Tracy suffered the long-lasting shock of losing them. He had to identify each at the morgue in Da Nang.

For months the ambush would weigh heavily on the company. The

Lieutenant Vern Arndt, Nong Son coal mine in background. October 1967 (courtesy Vern Arndt).

surprise attack by a larger enemy force overwhelmed the squad in minutes, well before a quick reaction force led by Lieutenant Harvey could arrive on the scene from An Hoa. He said the NVA had time enough to line up the dead Marines neatly, side by side, and escape without a trace into the nearby hills. The event took a psychological toll. The incident would continue to spook Golf Company Marines long after it happened.

The Strategic Tableau

By the summer of 1967, with the battlefield in Vietnam in relative stalemate, each side maneuvered for advantage. While the Johnson Administration proclaimed success on the battlefield and urged patience, Hanoi prepared for an offensive. In July the Communist Party in North Vietnam approved the impending General Offensive and General Uprising that became the future Tet Offensive, a strategic plan intended to break the military standoff. The strategy called for simultaneous attacks on South Vietnam cities and military bases to rally supporters to overthrow the Republic of Vietnam. Viet Cong military commanders would take the

Lieutenant Tracy Alton (left) and Lieutenant Ken Lee, An Hoa, September 1967.

lead; they met in Cambodia to begin planning. In August U.S. military intelligence seized a high-level VC internal document describing a new situation on the battlefield and a mission that would lead to a climax in the war: "The time is right for violent military moves."

The same month, in a news conference that stepped up a public relations effort, President Lyndon Johnson asserted that the Vietnam War effort remained on track, but more troops were needed. Secretary of State Dean Rusk also saw signs of progress, stating the enemy was hurting badly, but still a tough foe. He said a long task lay ahead, one that would require continued U.S. troop commitments. With the troop ceiling raised to 525,000, Johnson's civilian adviser Clark Clifford and retired General Maxwell Taylor visited Asian allies and reported back a broad level of support for U.S. effort on the battlefield. Army chief of staff General Harold K. Johnson announced he detected the "smell of success" in the war. Subsequently, the Marine Amphibious Force (III MAF) headquarters in Da Nang collected intelligence suggesting that NVA forces had begun to mass forces in I Corps, according to the official Marine Corps History's *U.S. Marines in Vietnam, The Defining Year, 1968*. Moreover, the NVA appeared to be planning large-scale offensives in the region.

In August 1967 Marines were fighting two different wars. In northern I Corps, near the DMZ, 3rd Marine Division units were engaged in near-conventional ground war against large NVA regular forces. In southern I Corps, the 1st Marine Division usually fought a small-unit war—principal threats included mines and booby traps in addition to a growing NVA presence. Almost imperceptibly, however, Marines in An Hoa had come into more frequent contact with the NVA, calling them VC all the time. Although it did not appear clear to us in the field, what we were experiencing was a slow, quiet build-up of regular forces from North Vietnam.

To the Field

Liberty Road connected An Hoa to Phu Lac (6) and on to Da Nang. In early September 1967 Golf Company and my FO team walked to Phu Lac, my first time in the field. Marines feared the narrow, twisting, pot-holed dirt road, one of the most dangerous in I Corps. Marine engineers swept it for mines and booby traps after daylight each morning from An Hoa to Phu Lac, accompanied by a squad of Marines providing security. Mines and booby traps seemed to sprout overnight on the road and in surrounding paddies, where flank security would walk. At times the enemy planted larger landmines that could take out trucks. In some places, low hills along the route were sometimes used by the enemy to ambush small Marine units.

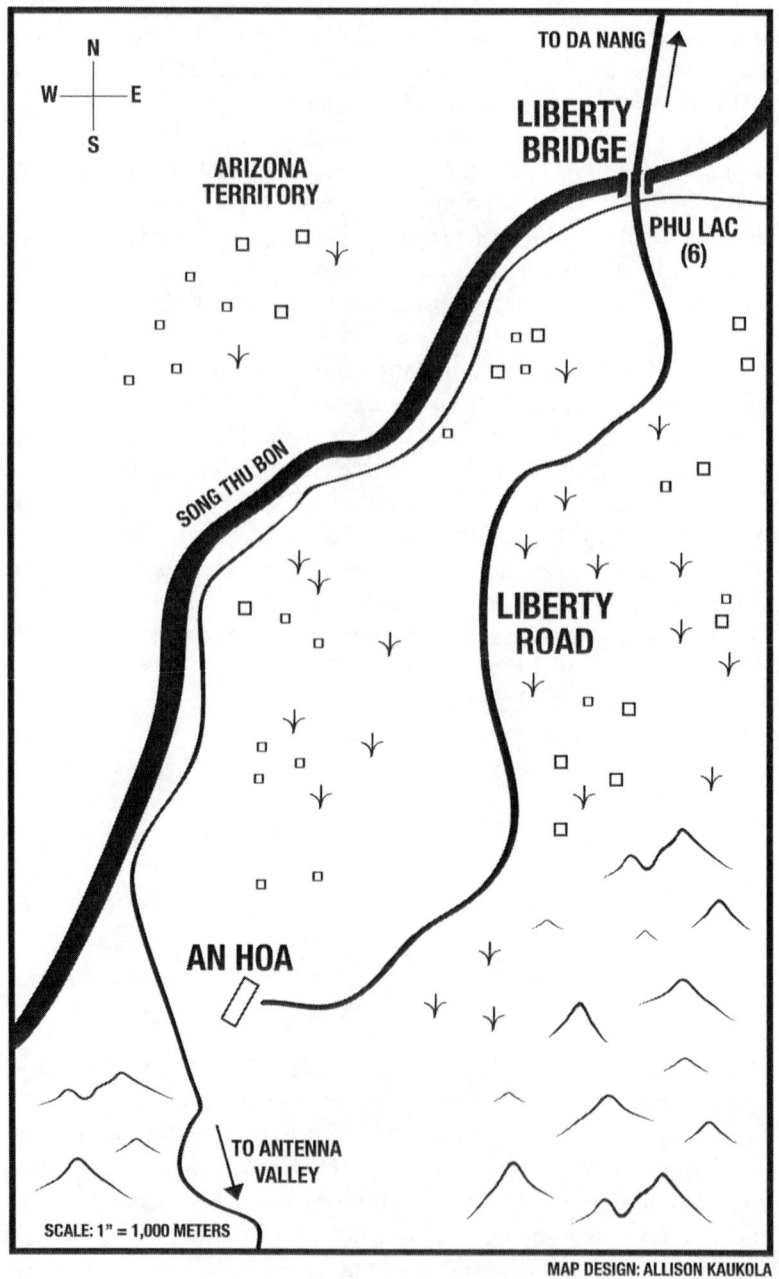

Map of An Hoa–Phu Lac 6, showing Liberty Road. Graphic by Allison Kaukola, with input from Barney Barnes.

Phu Lac base provided security to Seabees building the strategic, wooden Liberty Bridge spanning the Song Thu Bon River:

> Earlier the bridge was blown in one part by a VC who swam up the river and placed a satchel charge under one of the I beams. I take a bath in the river nearly every day. It's not too dirty. Local Vietnamese wash our dirty clothes.

Phu Lac overlooked the river and contained deep, underground bunkers. Marines occupied two low hills during daytime. On the main knoll, a 30-foot tower afforded excellent 360-degree lines of sight, but it also exposed any Marine who used the tower to potential enemy sniper fire. At night most of the company withdrew to the perimeter of the primary hill and to bunkers dug several feet deep into red clay, leaving a Listening Post of four or five Marines on the other hill. My FO team had its own bunker, and we settled in upon arrival. Just weeks into my tour, I began to develop an early aversion to C-rations. The high energy, high calorie, canned entrees were boxed with fruit and condiments. Within weeks after arrival, I had begun to tire of them. I also absorbed the stories and the unsavory, sometimes frightening, usually embellished, lore of recent operations told by members of Golf company old-timers:

> We eat C-rats—nothing else—I plan on eating 2 per day, about 11 and again at 5 or so.
> After C-rats any semblance of real food makes me hungry. I don't like to hear of the things that are done by and to Marines. I will probably understand why they [the grunts] do the things they do when I get out to the bush.

Mail soon began to arrive in a trickle, then almost a torrent as friends of my parents, several old girlfriends, and friends from college began to write. Receiving letters became a source of great comfort to all of us in Nam. With notable exceptions—Dear John letters and the like—mail boosted morale for all U.S. combatants. I wrote as if I had been in-country for months, not weeks, complaining about the rear echelon personnel who supported the war from the relative safety of large bases:

> That is one of my pet peeves—there are more people in secure headquarters and bases than there are in the field and they can't appreciate how the troopers feel.

New Grunt CO

Soon, a fresh Golf company commander arrived, a senior captain named "Buck" Dyer. A career officer from Tennessee, he was a gruff, rugged, tobacco-chewing former farm boy sporting a large moustache and deep Southern drawl. Dyer would prove a highly skilled field tactician, a naturally born "field Marine," an excellent map reader who had some doubts about what artillery could do for him. A week after meeting him I wrote home:

> After a week's impression, he is a good man. He often offers to take radio watch at night when we're short of men. I will be glad to take up the slack also since I don't have to go out on night ambushes. Not yet anyway. Things could definitely get worse. The captain asked me if I would like to help him make out schedules and do other time-saving chores. I told him I'd like to very much and pitched in. He's easy going and understanding, yet demanding.

You Got to Walk That Lonesome Valley

For me, earning the respect and trust of others became a priority goal. By late 1967, nearly all Marines arrived in Vietnam alone, as replacements for someone who rotated, was wounded, or killed in action. Each of us was a lone soul yearning for acceptance. Establishing myself as a reliable, valuable member of the team became paramount. Those who had more time in-country tended to regard "Newbies" with some contempt until the Marine demonstrated a certain level of competence. Trust, as always, had to be earned. Every new guy had to prove himself to those with whom he served. Could he be trusted in a firefight? Was he dependable, or too self-focused? Did he have a sense of humor? Was he cautious enough? Did he have what it took to look after his brothers and to share the good times and bad with them? For those who met the expected standards, enduring bonds were forged day by day over time, especially among the grunts, who bore the brunt of the pain.

I strived to gain the confidence and respect of the grunts I supported. Traditional artillery battery doctrine stated that a lieutenant Forward Observer should accompany the company commander to the field, but my arty battalion protocol allowed a lieutenant FO discretion to go with a rifle platoon:

> When the company commander goes out, I also go. I also accompany any grunts whenever I feel like going out, even when Capt. Dyer is not present.

During my first two weeks at Phu Lac, our activity was limited, consisting of squad-size patrols of 12 to 14 men that covered an area not more than 3,000 meters—usually less—from the perimeter. Initially, I assigned each of my FOs to support a specific platoon, but as team members dwindled in the ensuing weeks, that practice ended. I joined a platoon on a routine patrol days after we arrived at Phu Lac. Nothing came of it. I was surprised to see some Marines sleep without setting up proper security. Disappointed, but now aware of the deep fatigue grunts always dealt with, I did not report the incident.

Counterinsurgency

Long before I began my tour in Vietnam, "winning hearts and minds" had become a well-worn adage for combatting the insurgency in Vietnam. "Ambassadors in Green," military-civic action efforts, played a key, early role in combat operations. Counterinsurgency warfare doctrine had in part evolved from the Banana Wars of the 1920s where the Marine Corps exercised police force actions in the Caribbean and Latin America, and later studying the pro-communist, nationalist insurgency in Malaya in the 1950s.

Following insertion of U.S. forces into South Vietnam in 1965, counterinsurgency principles and rural pacification had an important champion in Lieutenant General Lewis W. Walt, the commanding general of the Third Marine Amphibious Force (III MAF), headquartered in Da Nang. He and the commanding general of the Fleet Marine Force Pacific, Lieutenant General Victor H. Krulak, conceived of Combined Action Platoons (CAPs), comprised of squads of Marines, Navy corpsmen, and a platoon of Vietnamese paramilitary Popular Forces. The CAPs would be established in rural villages to prevent VC access to the local population, provide protection to friendly villages, and identify and destroy communist infrastructure. While the CAPs remained effective in certain areas held by the Marines, the commander of U.S. forces in Vietnam, General Westmoreland, had little regard for the concept. Instead, he chose to accelerate a war of attrition, gambling that U.S. forces could kill more of the enemy than the North Vietnamese Army could replace. Although Search and Destroy operations yielded often-inflated enemy body counts, the principal measure of battlefield success, high U.S. casualties sapped the morale of Marines who did the fighting.

New Life Village

Three weeks after my arrival in Vietnam, I ignored battery guidance out of curiosity and accompanied a squad of 16 Marines, the battalion civic affairs officer Lieutenant Ken Lee, and two Kit Carsons on a visit to a New Life Vil. The Kit Carson Scouts (also known as Tiger Scouts), were former VC or NVA defectors used as intelligence scouts, translators, and interpreters for infantry units:

> Each battalion has two Kit Carsons—they have a death sentence on their heads if caught by the VC. They are excellent. A New Life Vil supposedly is where all the comforts and advantages of clean, Western-type living are introduced. In turn, the vil is expected to be friendly and keep us informed of VC movement (you don't get something for nothing).

On the way to the vil, my mind wandered, as it often would in the field. Some thoughts were not at all rational. Typically, they filled the time as I absorbed the scenery during our silent movements from one objective to another. What beauty, the green landscape appeared calm and peaceful. If a VC took a shot at me, I thought, maybe I could hear the report of the rifle and dodge the bullet. I realized that was a fantasy, but the mere thought offered some relief from the boredom. If I could not evade the bullet with my name on it, I thought, I would rather die from an enemy who took the effort to single me out before pulling the trigger, not get blown apart by a hidden booby trap. Dying that way seemed more personal, something I preferred, if I was going to "buy my lunch," a popular expression at the time. While I judged the likelihood of my death in Nam varied between slim to none, if I did perish, I wanted it to be because some enemy combatant intended to kill me.

When we arrived in the New Life Village that morning there was no CAP presence and no local or South Vietnamese government official to show us around. I wondered at the time if the New Life Village concept itself was just a mirage. As I moved about and observed the few actual Vietnamese standing in front of the huts, I felt there was something artificial, misleading, and unreal about the set-up—stage-managed perhaps. I saw mostly old women, a few old men, some children. Like other villages I would see over the next few months, this one was quiet, almost devoid of any real life. The women shrank from us, holding infants or carrying young children, their eyes fearful. A few resourceful Vietnamese who could speak a word or two of English approached us selling items. What happened here at night, I thought? Did the occupants turn away NVA regulars passing through, or did they feed and give them shelter? Did the young men return after dark, perhaps carrying weapons? I bought a pair of one-dollar Ho Chi Minhs—rubber sandals made from tires—paying in piasters, the military scrip. In addition, I purchased a candle and some dry rice cakes. I did not visit a New Life Village again during my tour, but I did have an illuminating meeting with a CAP Marine in a "friendly" village two months later.

Under Fire

On 10 September I joined the Golf Company command group and a rifle platoon on a Search and Destroy mission—an exercise looking for the enemy and, I soon concluded, a tactic that offered up the lives of Marines to engage with the enemy. Before the morning departure, I coordinated with the chief of the 81mm mortar section, discussing our planned route. I had confidence in the competence of the mortar team, a highly-motivated and well-trained resource. Mortars could get rounds on target much quicker than my artillery battery in An Hoa, which had to go through a more time-consuming clearance process requiring approvals from higher headquarters.

The planned route that morning would not exceed the mortar's maximum effective range of about 5,000 meters. We left the An Hoa–Phu Lac dirt road and crossed a series of dry, empty rice paddies south of the base without incident. As we neared the maximum effective range of the mortars, we began taking sporadic small arms fire on our right flank from a tree line about 200 meters away. We fell to the ground, receiving automatic rifle fire now from the right rear. Two rifle grenades impacted about 30 meters away from our command group, not dangerously close, but of some concern. I called in my first fire mission and peppered the tree line, walking the mortar rounds down a line of about 200 meters. At the end of the mission, we ran into a cluster of huts in an adjacent tree line to our left. Marines set fire to the huts there. I later wrote,

> *It was a little exciting. I didn't love it because I could hear the rounds zinging over our heads and around us. On the way back to the base we found a machine gun position and numerous 5" wooden punji stakes. After blowing a homemade grenade booby trap, we sat down to a quick lunch of C's. When we rose to leave, we saw another booby-trapped grenade 10 feet away.*

I later mulled over my first moral conundrum. While I began to understand the enemy threat grunts faced every day, I also began to understand the limited choices and the poverty of rural Vietnamese. It was a no-win situation for everyone:

> *The Vietnamese own so very little, just eating utensils and perhaps a bamboo couch bed and a couple of jars. Maybe they will have a couple of empty Pepsi cans to drink from. They are ingenious in that they*

> construct what they have from unlikely materials—mirrors out of beer cans, etc. The poverty is depressing. The people are caught in a pincer, between the U.S. troops and the VC, both of whom demand assistance and will go to almost any extent to attain it.

I thought it wrong, an overreaction, to burn the homes of local villagers. Yet we were directed to destroy them in retaliation for being fired on. Three weeks into my assignment with Golf Company, and my first trip out meeting hostile fire, I witnessed the complexities of fighting an insurgency:

> After we were ambushed, we burned hooches. That was protocol set by higher headquarters: burn any hooches in the vicinity from which you are fired upon. It sounds inhumane and I do regret the policy, but like some other things done here, you must accept it.

There would be no remedy to the problem. Inconsistent, vengeful Marine behavior in the field only added to our frustration and futility while confusing and angering Vietnamese who might otherwise have been inclined to support us.

Reflecting on my first exposure to hostile fire that afternoon, I realized I should have conducted an artillery Recon by Fire, calling in fire missions on the tree lines on three sides of us—the structure of a horseshoe-shaped ambush the enemy often used—to flush out or suppress any VC or NVA planning an ambush. We were fortunate to take hostile fire from what appeared to be only a couple of VC, rather than a large enemy force.

At Sea in the Countryside

We often did not, could not, understand the insurgency environment in Vietnam. The Basic School's compressed curriculum left little time to educate young lieutenants in the history and culture of Vietnam. Despite a year of military training, I soon realized I was woefully ill-prepared for what I saw. I did not understand the language and knew little of the political forces at work in Vietnam. I understood from their facial expressions and body language that Vietnamese locals feared and resented us. Mothers held children close and often cried. Fear filled the eyes of peasants anytime we entered their village. In rural I Corps, the local villagers often assisted the VC and NVA troops and planted mines and booby traps that took the lives of our Marines. Escalating retaliation only worsened our relationship with the locals.

Nor was I mentally prepared to deal with the inevitable mounting combat losses of fellow Marines. The Basic School trained lieutenants to lead in combat, but even an hour of instruction or advice—perhaps from a chaplain or psychologist, or both—on how to manage the aftermath of battles that produced combat casualties would have been useful. It could have perhaps had an impact on limiting the trauma of losing fellow Marines. The unrelenting violence and the death of friends angered and frustrated us, heightening our fear and frustration and making Vietnamese civilians an easy target for retaliation.

Boredom

I tried to keep busy, engaged, and productive during long stretches of time inside the wire at Phu Lac. One day I had my FO team make a drawing of our hill. We shot in mortar night defensive fires and drew in the targets on our map, along with existing artillery targets. I gave classes to squad leaders. On 11 September, about a month after my arrival in-country, two of my FOs in the base observation tower called to me and asked if they could conduct a fire mission on a group of Vietnamese. I assumed the target included individuals with weapons or suspected weapons. Foolishly, I told them to proceed and rushed to the tower to observe and supervise. In retrospect, I should have climbed the tower to assess the situation before providing the go-ahead with the fire mission, but I wanted to show the FOs I had confidence in them. As I reached the tower platform, before the fire mission had begun, Captain Cates contacted us on the radio and asked if the Vietnamese had weapons. One of the FOs holding the radio handset replied no, they had no packs or weapons and were dressed in white. That meant they were likely a group attending a funeral. End of mission:

> *Mistakes like this are embarrassing. I am going to explain to the captain that it will not happen again. It needs closer supervision. I'm learning all the time. I find it a challenge and interesting job. It requires much attention to detail. I am doing alright, I think, and will do better.*

While no one was killed or wounded, my blunder did not sit well with me or the CO, as I would learn days later.

Night Raid

I was a bit troubled when I heard the plan: two platoons, along with the company command group, would execute a rare and tricky night maneuver. I later wrote:

> Today at 0300 we began a two-platoon sweep. We headed for a hamlet where [our intelligence reported] 15 confirmed hardcore enemy resided.

The planned movement over unfamiliar terrain, in total darkness, sounded risky to me. As we moved out, without ambient moonlight, I feared losing contact with the Marine in front of me. I trusted he could see the Marine in front of him.

The noise made as the company command group inched towards the objective must have been audible for miles around. I could hear water sloshing in canteens. In tense conditions such as those, the imagination plays tricks, the unseen looms large, threatening, the unknown scary. The approximate two-kilometer-plus move took three nerve-wracking hours. We stopped about a hundred meters from a cluster of huts just before daylight. How the Marines in the company vanguard managed to locate the objective seemed to me a minor miracle. They were natural map readers. There must have been a detailed planning and orientation exercise at the base I did not attend, I thought. I always marveled at how grunts seemed to find the objective in the worst of conditions:

> We snooped and pooped and stumbled into the hamlet and surrounded it by 0600. They were completely taken by surprise. In the twilight, ghostly figures appeared to dash out of huts but I could not determine conclusively that they were people running or imaginary figures springing from fear.

Two Marines near me opened fire with their M16s, followed by an ear-splitting cacophony of small arms fire from others. I lifted my rifle to fire on what I thought was a fleeing figure in a nearby paddy—or was it a specter? Moments later, a Marine who had been kneeling and firing five feet in front of me sprang up, firing his rife. He jumped into my line of fire. I had squeezed off a round a split second before, but managed to lift my finger from the trigger and raised my rifle in just the nick of time. I have pondered that close call for many years. It could have ended tragically for both of us.

> The VC hatted out [got away] quickly. The Gunny shot and killed a VC suspect, a woman, when she ran from him and did not stop when warned three times. I heard him shout, "dừng lại, dừng lại, dừng lại" (stop, stop, stop) before he shot her. We entered the vil and found two dead Vietnamese, a young girl of 17-18 years—pretty—and a 70-year-old man. No one believes he is VC. Perhaps he was not an actual combatant, but a supporter of the enemy. The girl was carrying $60 (6,000 piasters) and some suspect she was a VC prostitute.

That was debatable. Our rules of engagement allowed us to shoot at anyone running away from us, but was she a legitimate target?

> She had a small mirror trinket one might find in 5-cent candy machines. I had to walk over the dead woman. It was not at all pleasant. She had been shot in the small of the back and lay crumpled all over the trail leading into the vil. Her visible intestines were piled on the ground beneath her.

The intelligence report pointing to the village as an NVA or VC refuge seemed to have been accurate. But were we justified firing on all or any Vietnamese running away from us? That was the battalion's Rule of Engagement. As a second lieutenant, two months into my tour, I thought it not my place to question it.

> We recovered packs and other equipment. I picked up a VC bush hat— or I thought it VC—until on closer examination I found it to be a North Vietnamese item, a red star inked in three places around the brim with other writing on it. A souvenir. We are positive the NVA used the vil to rest in. A pot of hot tea was still on the fire. We caught them with their pants down. They'll be watching closer next time. We did win a psychological victory—a surprise, pamphlets, three kills and a hard-hitting night movement.

The nights often belonged to the enemy, but not this time.

An Ass-Chewing

A month after my arrival in-country, I found myself the recipient of a ferocious, humiliating take-down by the battery CO. Perhaps I had it coming. It was the only such confrontation I had in Nam. On 22 September, we had returned to An Hoa for two days before the division commander directed the company to return to Phu Lac, tear down some of the bunkers on the hill down and rebuild them. While in An Hoa, I ran afoul of Captain Cates. The FOs would typically stand watch in the battery Fire Direction Center and Exec Pit whenever they came in from the field for a few days with their rifle companies. It provided good experience for the FOs and gave the battery officers some relief. About midnight, on watch in the Exec Pit with my communicator, we received a routine illumination fire mission following an aborted friendly ambush. Cates must have heard the activity on the gun line. His tent sat less than a stone's throw from one of the gun pits.

Cates soon appeared in the small, ten-foot-square bunker built to hold two. I tried to ignore him and focus on the mission. He stepped in closer to watch, hands on hips. He leaned in and listened to the radio transmission and my landline exchange with the crew chiefs who would shoot the mission. Cates began to interrupt, raising his voice and questioning my actions as the mission proceeded, each time commenting on or criticizing what I passed to the gun crews. I grew distracted. I completed the mission despite his effort to interfere and take it over. He humiliated me in front of the radio operator—who kept his head down during mission—and the gun line, which could overhear his rant on their headsets. What must they have thought? I almost walked out of the bunker. I came close to telling him to run the mission himself, but did not. I really wanted to say, "Up yours, asshole." I felt I was seconds away from exploding and saying something I would regret as soon as I said it. His actions were disheartening, poor leadership on full display. The mission ended after inordinate delays on the field side of the transmissions. Cates then left the Exec Pit without further comment. I wrote afterwards,

> I'd rather be in the field than in the battery. The battery CO hovers over me when I'm in the Exec Pit running fire missions. I learn, but I get nervous, too.

What explained Cates's objective—simple harassment, an attempt to break, or break-in, a lieutenant? A test of some kind? Had he been drinking? Was it a planned intimidating power play? Had the earlier botched fire mission on the unarmed Vietnamese funeral party been a factor in his actions? Perhaps he was well-intentioned. At minimum, he had anger

Exec Pit, Echo Battery, An Hoa, 1967 (courtesy Martin Dunbar).

issues. Cates also had career ambitions that years afterwards propelled him to general officer rank. I soon shook the incident off and recovered. I had too much to prove to paralyze myself over the episode. Cates and I had no more tense exchanges while he remained CO. He later offered faint praise, telling me that Captain Dyer had said good things to him about my work with the grunt squad leaders. Cates and I would work together again several months later when, as the arty battalion operations officer, he came to Echo battery to investigate a friendly fire incident. Only many years later, when I began to revisit and reconstruct old Nam memories, did the illumination mission work its way to the fore of memory.

Doubts Emerge

Unexpected thoughts began to take hold in quiet moments a little over a month after I arrived in-country. I wondered whether there was something wrong with me. I had limited experience to date, I still considered myself a new guy, an "FNG," but I began to question why we were in Vietnam other than to assure the survival of the South Vietnam regime. What was the end game? What did we hope to accomplish through fighting? How would we know we had won? After a possible "victory" sometime in the future, then what? Granted, the answers to those cosmic questions rested far above my paygrade. It was a disquiet I expressed only through letters home, mainly for an audience of one—myself.

My letters usually contained a reaction to family news and concerns along with a section on recent Nam experiences. I assumed my parents were involved with their own lives and raising four other children, making my observations of life in-country more of a venting exercise mixed with self-dialogue, an echo chamber. Still, doubts emerged and began to weigh on me. I had too much time left in country to dwell on leaving Vietnam, but I too started to track the days left in Nam. It seemed as if what I had signed up for—victory over the communists—might not be near at all. Guess I had begun to think like other Marines around me.

> *Time passes quickly in the field. I've been here 40 days and have 355 to go. I know I shouldn't be anxious to get back home. I look on this tour with a "why not make the best of it?" attitude. I want to feel as though I have contributed in some form or another to whatever "cause" we have here. If you can speak of it as a cause.*
>
> *I rather doubt it. It's more of a personal war than anything else. You play the game, try not to be scared, and do your best. Everyone wants to go home, and I can't blame them. It's the type of war we're fighting that makes them feel that way.*

I would leave Vietnam exactly 12 months and 20 days from the time I arrived, which would put my departure date at 2 September 1968.

> The months will pass, won't they? There's no way they can stop time from passing, can they? I will have R&R in January or February.

In the meantime, I wanted to document my experience in Nam on film. I arrived in-country with a miniature 16mm Minolta camera that shot black and white film. I wanted a 35mm single lens reflex for color slides and that's what I soon purchased. My letters and my photos would be my personal record of the war.

Short of Field Gear

In September 1967 the Marine Corps supply and logistics system seemed broken, the warehouses empty of serviceable and useful gear. Years of pinching pennies and doing more with less, a time-honored Marine budgetary tradition, had come home to roost. Frontline Marine rifle battalions received M16s months after the Army had fielded them. We needed jungle utilities, jungle boots, and other field equipment. The uniform shortage in 2/5 grew worse when combat operations intensified in late 1967, with Marines wearing serviceable uniform items and boots taken from the wounded and the medevaced. The available gear sometimes dated to the Korean War or earlier. Military-issued olive drab tee shirts had just begun to come on-line and stocks were scarce. I arrived in Nam with white tee shirts dyed neon green by my mother. They quickly faded to a sick, faded green. Standard issue olive-colored tee shirts did not appear until late 1967.

There were more critical items than jungle utilities unavailable in the battery supply system. Within weeks of arrival, I asked my father to purchase a simple compass—the few in the battery supply room were unreliable, clumsy, difficult to operate, and dated from World War II or Korea. I also asked him on separate occasions to send acetate plastic contact paper to waterproof my maps—a critical need in the damp climate—and a slipover or zip hooded rubber rain jacket. Again, none of the items were available when I checked in. Dutifully, my father responded to each request by going to retail military surplus stores and sending whatever I asked for as soon as he could find it.

All You Need Is Love

Popular songs heard in Nam on Armed Forces Radio still run through my mind on occasion, carrying me back to a particular place and moment each time I hear them. One hot afternoon at Phu Lac I listened closely to The Beatles' "All You Need Is Love." I had stepped out of the FO bunker under a blinding noonday sun, no one else in sight, when I heard the song emerge from a bunker farther down the hill. I walked along, listening to the haunting, puzzling lyrics, pausing until the song ended, lost in my own thoughts. The irony was overwhelming. I dug the song, the music and harmonies, the message I thought it sent—but it seemed out of sync, out of place, out of time, for those of us in Nam.

The sentiments juxtaposed with a battle zone stood out, an impossible ideal, not the grim reality we faced each day in the field. The popular music of the emerging counterculture back home seemed increasingly out of step with the conditions we were facing and unrelatable to those of us doing the fighting in Vietnam. I listened to the songs and the lyrics, sometimes yearning for sentiments they expressed, but mostly just puzzled by the messages they conveyed. The music did not fit in a combat zone, but we listened to it anyway and tried to understand it. What hope did we have? Only that we might serve honorably, to the best of our abilities, while surviving our tours. As time passed, popular culture seemed to be leaving us in-country further behind. Not that we loved the war—we hated it, but expressions of support for troops in Nam had begun to disappear. It affected morale and opened a fissure in American society that has only widened over the years.

More Moral Failures

I began to experience situations I could not have foreseen while in training at Quantico. Life at Phu Lac combat base could be deadly slow. Time often dragged. I worked to find ways to stay busy and productive. Giving classes to squad leaders on procedures for calling in fire missions was always useful and helpful to the grunts who struggled with their fears and doubts regarding arty support. Fifty-five years later a former squad leader still recalls having benefited from our arty classes.

But offering tutorials to grunts could only fill up part of any day. Out of boredom one afternoon, I stood near the base perimeter watching for any movement in an area known to contain booby traps. I saw a man walking on a trail about 600 meters away, well over the maximum effective range of my M16. I began to track him through the sights on my rifle until he came into full view for a moment, walking away from me. He had no visible weapon and, after peering through my binoculars, I could not determine with certainty whether he carried anything suspicious. His progress was partially obscured by brush. Without any expectation I could hit him, perhaps out of frustration, I raised my weapon again and with little hesitation squeezed off a shot. I thought of it as a means of harassment and lost sight of him. Like some other actions in Nam at the time, I have come to regret this.

A few days later, in a similar incident, I scanned the distant rice fields from the observation tower, looking for some activity or group of Vietnamese I thought might be the enemy. I saw a cluster of young men on water buffaloes grazing in a dry paddy an estimated 7,000 meters away. I wanted to disperse them. Why? I don't know, other than—again—being bored, angry, and frustrated with the invisible enemy that caused us harm. I asked the team leader of the 106mm recoilless rifle section whether the direct fire weapon had an indirect fire capability. The M40 recoilless rifle was a deadly direct fire weapon, but, he confirmed, it also could be fired with the tube slightly elevated. The 106-crew seemed eager to try it. First examining the map, the crew chief took a couple minutes with his team to compute the gun data. When ready, we cleared the area behind the weapon. We fired a round, the back blast throwing up a huge dust cloud. The group in the distance scattered as the projectile landed about 200 meters from them. I ended the mission with no known casualties, almost immediately regretful that I had initiated the mission. What if I had killed or wounded innocent kids?

Sudden Death

Death sometimes visited without warning, at unexpected times and places, and for various reasons. An estimated 11,000 of the over 58,000 deaths of U.S. servicemen in Vietnam resulted from non-combat causes. Sometimes it came as a surprise, amidst calm and quiet times. One hot afternoon at Phu Lac a Marine, clowning around to pass the time—and showing off to clapping bystanders—jumped on the front of a moving tank and dangled his legs over the side. After a few seconds, without uttering a word, he was dragged under the tank when he caught his trousers in the treads. Before anyone could react, he was lost.

On another quiet morning at Phu Lac, I heard a pistol discharge near the corpsmen's aid station nearby. I ran over to see what happened. A Marine had shot himself in the thigh. I stood by as a corpsman tended to him and asked him if it had been an accident. No, the Marine replied with a smile, he shot himself to get out of the field. He might have shattered his femur and lost normal use of the leg. As we glared at him, the now-relaxed Marine smiled at us through the pain, satisfied he had done the needful. He would now be going home. Within an hour he would be medevaced, another casualty whose story would end without any known resolution. It was not a rational act at all, but the incident illustrated the high level of fear and anxiety some Marines had of the field and their desperation to escape the danger it held. Others would follow.

An Enigma

I planned to go on a platoon-sized night ambush in late September. In preparation, I worked with my radio operator, PFC Raub, and got to know him better. Thirty-years-old, called "the old man," he had asked to leave the battery to become a radioman for an FO team. He had to learn on the fly how to operate the radio from grunt radio operators. Raub already had eight months in-country when I arrived and he extended an additional eight months on his tour. Did he have a life at all back home, I wondered?

> He is a worker in the field, very quiet. He wanted to be a grunt, but now seems happy being with the FO team humping the radio. He is afraid of the radio now, but practice and familiarity will correct that. He has endurance, got to give that to him.

Private First Class Raub, Operation Essex, Antenna Valley, 8 November 1967.

Yes, Raub was quiet, very quiet, but easy to get along with. He never complained, seldom initiated any conversation. He appeared to have trouble getting words out, problematic for a radioman, but he would respond with a few words if asked a question. Several Marines prodded him about his past, with limited success. I learned he was from Oregon and had been in the Corps eight years previously, was discharged, then returned to active duty as the Vietnam War revved up. In the context of the war, Raub's past wasn't important. Although he would remain a mystery to me to the end, I viewed him as a dedicated, brother Marine in a combat zone. He wanted to serve. That's all I needed to know.

At the time, I wondered if Raub had joined the FO team to prove something to himself. Didn't all of us have some of that in common? Perhaps, or had he experienced some past emotional or psychological shock that rendered him the way we saw him? He might have had a disability of some kind. I respected Raub and gave him plenty of space. I avoided intruding—he fit in with the team and became close with my main man on the FO team, Stetson. Raub also had the stamina of a horse and the heart of a lion. I never had to worry about him.

Wouldn't You Rather Be a Marine?

In late September I caught up with letter writing in An Hoa. My cousin, Gibbs, in law school at the University of Arkansas, had tired of fighting off the draft board and had decided to enlist in the Marine officer program. He had no remaining deferments and solicited my views. I was quick to reply, suggesting that while the Vietnam War might be problematic, becoming a Marine was an admirable goal. I doubtless came across as more gung-ho than I felt myself at the time. I did not reveal my own emerging skepticism about the war, perhaps I should have. If I had begun to question the mission and how we conducted it, it did not include criticism of the Marine Corps. I managed to keep the two separate. Whatever my motivation was at the time, answering his letter allowed me to pose as the wise and experienced Marine I was not.

> Your invitation to tell you about the Marines is a chance for me to give you the true hot scoop. No, there is not much difference, if any, between being in Army guerrilla warfare or the plain old Marine Corps. Fighting a guerrilla war is the Marine way of life now. If you went into the Army and graduated from OCS, then headed for guerrilla war training, you would probably emerge as an interpreter or advisor. Army OCS lasts six months, Marine Corps OCS is 10 weeks, during which you must prove to the Corps' satisfaction that you can take the physical and mental strain. Then you are sent to Basic School, Quantico, where you are groomed into the mold of a Marine officer. You get intensified guerrilla war instruction. You learn basic conventional Marine doctrine and discipline [and history].
>
> At OCS, candidates are not encouraged at all—in fact they are harassed and asked many times to quit and become enlisted Marines. The philosophy is that if you are determined enough to become an

officer, you will put up with all the shit they deal out, and come out a better man as a result. Wouldn't you rather be a Marine? Think of the tradition, the future that the Marine Corps has. It is unique to be a Marine. Who raises their eyebrow when they discover someone is in the Army? I am prejudiced, but if you have a sense of adventure and desire to do well, the Marines is the place for you.

4

Storm Clouds

Antenna Valley

Remote, nearly unpopulated, "Antenna Valley," as Marines called it during the war, had few if any cultivated fields. Former rice paddies had fallen into disuse and ruin. By 1967 most of it had become a "free-fire zone," a place that U.S. forces could fire in without having to obtain prior clearances. The assumption? No friendlies lived there.

Marines first operated there in 1966, when we took over An Hoa from the ARVN, and again earlier in 1967, removing approximately 3,000 refugees from the Valley, according to the 2/5 battalion command chronology. Only 200–400 farmers remained, most clustered for protection near the Nong Son coal complex. Former farmer-inhabited hamlets bordered by overgrown bamboo and thick hedgerows dotted the valley, surrounded by large expanses of empty paddy. Stunning, lush vegetation and triple-canopy covered the surrounding hills. We did not know that most hamlets had been turned into deadly, interlocking, fortified enemy strongpoints with underground tunnels.

We knew now the enemy probably inhabited Antenna Valley in force—at least two battalions, our intelligence had reported weeks earlier. It served as a transit area and safe haven for NVA troops coming down the Ho Chi Minh Trail.

> Tomorrow three companies go into Antenna Valley looking for contact. My company will head straight up the valley, while two companies will be on the ridgelines to our east watching our flanks. There were two battalions of NVA there a few days ago.

Our mission, according to the warning order received at the company, was to protect the farmers while they harvested the rice before the big monsoon approached. Protect farmers? I didn't buy it. The rationale seemed like something senior officers in safe bases might conjure up. A strange,

4. Storm Clouds

obtuse rationale, out of touch. We all heard Antenna Valley had long been populated by known VC and NVA sympathizers, and we knew it contained the headquarters of hidden enemy ground forces. Rice had not been cultivated in most of the valley for years. Farmers were confined to the nearby river area protected by friendlies.

Our intelligence suggested—accurately—that the valley served as a way station for NVA regulars. Without question, the probe into Antenna Valley sought to locate and flush out the enemy. I could accept that—I just disliked the more evasive rationale of higher headquarters for going there. The temperature had cooled, intermittent monsoon rains had begun to appear, but not yet settle in. I ticked off the items I planned to carry for the anticipated five-day operation:

> gas mask, entrenching tool, hard hat, flak vest [never zipped or buttoned], cartridge belt with three full magazines of 5.56mm ammo, two canteens of water, compass, poncho, first aid packet with halazone tablets for purifying water, insect repellent, three meals of C-rations, heat tabs, foot powder, rifle cleaning gear, two pairs of extra socks, VC bush hat, M16, 45mm pistol, and a book or magazine. The places where we will be going are all under water so I doubt I'll be dry long.

My mistake involved the canteens. I did not carry sufficient water. I had room for a couple snacks—smoked oysters and some cheese from home. Before leaving, I asked someone to take my photo. I stood on a berm in full combat regalia, my arms crossed, a cinematic stogie in my mouth. "All the world's a stage," Shakespeare informed us. So far, the role I sometimes felt I was playing seemed to fit.

A Marine combat photographer joined the company before we left the perimeter. Did that portend anything, I wondered, perhaps expected imminent engagement with the enemy? Did he have access to information that I did not? I was conscious of his presence during the next few days. I felt a little like John Wayne. Would I be captured on film doing something memorable? I sometimes posed, thinking he might be "shooting" me.

Caught in a Typhoon

It could have been emblematic of a tour in Vietnam, and the scene of a battlefield drama—entrapped in the valley, our lives threatened by a deadly flood. The typhoon struck almost without warning. I summarized what happened after returning to An Hoa, safe and sound, if water-logged.

> After a quick hot breakfast, the battalion moved into the valley. We left An Hoa at 0400 on 8 October and walked the entire 5-6 miles to

> the valley in a steady downpour. I had struggled [earlier that morning] to get up at 0245—it was pouring down and my cot seemed a warm, secure place to be.

We reached our first objective at 1400 without stopping as the heavy rain continued. Captain Dyer expressed concern and spoke with battalion on the radio. We were aborting the next objective. By now alarmed by the gradually rising water in the floor of the valley, we headed at a rapid pace for a small hill near the western end of the valley. We reached it before nightfall. That evening, a typhoon blew in from the sea, 15 miles to the east.

> There have been nights when I have been more miserable than I was there, but not many. Radioman Raub and I could not build shelter with the wind blowing. We tried putting down a poncho and throwing another over us and keeping close for warmth. It failed miserably. The wind blew the rain horizontally, there was no respite, no escape from the water and cold. We ended up each using his own poncho and trying to keep himself as warm as possible.
>
> Surprisingly, it cleared up the next morning and I enjoyed drying out the entire day. I shot in some night defensive fires. With clothes drying, sitting on the high ground, we saw the whole of Antenna Valley flooded, seven feet of water on the valley floor. Stetson helped Raub and me build a good hooch with ponchos to help face another possible typhoon on the way, lurking sixty-five miles SE of us.

We stared at the fearsome flooding below us with awe and gratitude that we now occupied a small hill well above the waterline. Had there not been adequate high ground, we could have drowned. I also briefly thought about snakes that might have had the inclination to join us. We waited for the water to recede.

> The second night I slept on my inflated air mattress as the second typhoon missed us and water began to drain from the valley. I was the only Marine in the company who brought a "rubber lady." We pulled up stakes the following morning, and after tracking through neck-deep rice paddies, boarded amtracs to go back to An Hoa. We returned after light enemy contact and no casualties. You can always rely on amtracs—that is, rely on them to break down.

Leeches and Fish

Fortunately, the amphibious tractors made it back without incident, but before we could board them, we encountered other obstacles. After wading through a 20-foot-wide, five-foot-deep stream, we were advised to check for leeches. Dropping my utility trousers, I discovered several two-inch-long, blood-engorged leeches on my lower legs. I removed them easily, no pain. They left marks that lasted a couple of days. The experience took me back to my college dormitory several years earlier, where a senior class dorm proctor kept a pet leech in a fish tank in his room. He would feed it by sticking his hand in the water every so often as we underclassmen gawked in disgust.

After surviving the attack of the leeches, I ran out of drinking water. In the bush I usually carried only two canteens on the expectation that water replenishment would not be an issue. While I wanted to reduce the weight I carried, I learned the hard way that scrimping on water was a bad idea. In desperation, just a few thousand meters from base, I partially filled a canteen with paddy water and put in two halazone tablets. I shook the canteen well to dissolve the tablets and took a drink. Before I swallowed, I felt something in my mouth. I opened wide and carefully extracted a small dead fish. As bad as it was, I was relieved it was not something more distasteful.

Once safely back at An Hoa base, we heard we would return to Antenna Valley in two days. The prospect of enemy contact seemed to encourage higher headquarters to push farther into the known NVA stronghold. I noted with some contempt that the battalion commander appeared determined to stir things up with the enemy. While search and destroy seemed the chief reason we operated in the field, I resented his readiness to place our lives on the line—likely, I surmised, for his career. After all, I had begun to think, that's how senior officers got their next promotion. I checked the Red Sox–Cardinals World Series scores. I had been pulling for the Sox and Jim Lonborg, but the favored Cards prevailed in seven games. I normally pulled for underdog teams, unless my beloved Philadelphia Phillies or Arkansas Razorbacks were involved.

Talk with the Skipper

Days later we returned to the west end of Antenna Valley, to a large hill overlooking South Vietnam's only coal mine. As the battalion reserve in the event that the other maneuver companies in the battalion ran into trouble, we would remain there nearly a month guarding the coal mine and the Vietnamese officials who ran it. I wrote on 13 October:

> A big hello from Nong Son, an enormous hill that our company is now manning, Nong Son has four levels. A company of VC overran the top-level on the 4th of July. The Marine platoon up there had 13 killed, the rest wounded, 100% casualties.

> I'm with our company commander on the CP [command post], second level. Our bunker is good—lights at night, provided by the large coal complex. That's why we are here, to protect the government supervisors and coal mining activity. These first few days, I've shot in a few night-defensive fires and looked the hill over. And also have plotted some H and I [Harassment and Interdiction] rounds shot at random times] targets in the area.

I didn't describe a frank, sometimes tense, conversation with Captain Dyer, soon after arrival on the hill, whether to shoot-in the already-plotted and verified Night Defensive Fires (NDF). The four targets, designed to defend against an enemy night attack on the hill, had been registered months earlier by other FOs. I tried repeatedly, without success, to persuade Dyer that shooting in the targets, even with white phosphorous (WP) marking rounds, carried a risk of accidentally and unnecessarily wounding or killing Marines, even if they were sheltered in bunkers. The CO wouldn't listen. He insisted the plotted targets be fired in again on all levels of the hill while the company occupied it. I realized then he sometimes would ignore my advice—not good. My artillery expertise would not be automatically accepted by the CO. Frustrated and concerned about the safety of the Marines, I reluctantly complied with his direction.

Nong Son from the air, showing the summit and coal mine, undated image taken by Sam Kelly, The Basic School Class 3-67 and 41st OCC Reunion and Memorial Book, 2016.

Before shooting the NDFs in, I consulted with the battery executive officer in the fire direction center at An Hoa, who also questioned the wisdom of proceeding with the mission. Cates, the battery CO, to my knowledge, did not weigh in. I recommended that all hands on the hill take cover in bunkers before the fire missions began. For about fifteen minutes, everyone hunkered down. To my great relief, four WP rounds landed where had been plotted earlier, with no issues or harm done. I am sure Dyer felt vindicated in insisting I shoot them in; I was just glad no one was hurt. Going forward, I knew earning the CO's confidence in artillery—and in me—could be an issue. I could advise, but whether he would act on it remained problematic. I tried to shrug it off. The captain could be hard to figure out, at times moody and inconsistent. He veered between humorous casual exchanges with his subordinates on one hand, and leaving us out of lone-wolf decisions he made on the other. For the most part, however, his actions as a field tactician remained unquestioned.

Downtime

The extended downtime and relaxed moments we enjoyed those weeks at Nong Son would soon be only a memory, overshadowed by savage combat with the enemy. In the meantime, I reveled in the calm. The company CP was large, comfortable by bunker standards: about 12 feet by 30 feet, large enough to house the CO, XO, and me, plus radios and a couple communicators. At various times as I scanned the valley for possible enemy activity, I recall listening to Armed Forces Radio play "Never My Love," by The Association, masters of the "sunshine pop" or "easy listening" genre, and hearing Lulu's distinctive voice in "To Sir with Love," from the movie. The laid-back tunes seemed to fit well with the relative quiet days we had on the hill. To kill time, I quick-read books I had bought in college and hauled to Vietnam, finishing François Mauriac's *Vipers' Tangle*, Barbara Tuchman's *The Zimmerman Telegram*, Albert Camus's *The Fall*, Virginia Woolf's *A Room of One's Own*, Carson McCullers's novel *Member of the Wedding*, Robert Bolt's play, *A Man for All Seasons*, Aldous Huxley's *Brave New World*, Thomas Mann's novella *Death in Venice*, and re-reading Shakespeare's *Julius Caesar*. Afterwards I gave some of the books to other Marines and discarded others. No one could afford to carry around heavy items, and books seemed a little inharmonious with the environment. I was fortunate to have held on to them that long and had the occasion to read them. I would not have an opportunity to repeat the experience.

> The captain made some hobo stew tonight from C-rats. We added generous amounts of hot sauce and chili sauce and hydrated onions along

> with rice from Stuttgart, Arkansas. We will be here at Nong Son until
> the second week of November, then go back to An Hoa to hot meals
> and other operations.

I could have lived on Nong Son for another ten months, no problem.

In mid–October Marines assigned to the local Combined Action Platoon informed us that an ARVN lieutenant had requested instruction on how to call in an artillery fire mission.

> Seems he doesn't know how to shoot a [compass] direction to the
> enemy, a critical bit of information.

Captain Dyer smiled and shook his head when he learned of the request, commenting that my efforts with the lieutenant would probably not succeed. I met and worked with the officer nevertheless and he seemed to understand my instruction in handling a compass and determining the direction to the target.

Clouds on the Horizon

The remainder of October was reasonably quiet on the hill, but time to read would soon vanish. November approached. Talk of a possible impending operation in force into Antenna Valley filled the air. I wrote my cousin:

> The war we are fighting here is, at times, frighteningly deceptive.
> Wait, wait, then, all of a sudden, I'm in the midst of it facing the possibility of death. But isn't that something everyone must face sooner or later? Better later, I know, but I can't help but feel I'm doing what is right and hopefully I'm doing my country some good.

We ran a few company patrols into the mouth of Antenna Valley, with directives not to exceed 2,000 meters from the hill. Concerns of encountering a larger enemy force kept us close to the hill. One day I accompanied a patrol that crossed the river and penetrated the valley no more than a thousand or so meters, a show-the-flag exercise, not an effort to provoke the enemy. I am sure a Marine recon team on the top of a mountain overlooking the area observed our route. We drew no fire and the so-called friendly villagers on the patrol route welcomed us, children smiling and waving. Domestic water buffalo, on the other hand, watched us warily, their ears twitching, nostrils flaring.

During a brief stop a smiling, young boy no more than six- or seven-years-old approached and said a few words in English. He wore a tee-shirt incorporating the yellow and green striped colors of the Republic of Vietnam flag. I could not help but talk with him for a minute, allowing him to hold my M16 as I took his photo. He stood at attention, proud, with a serious expression on his face. It would always be a good reminder for me: not all Vietnamese we met in the field were the enemy, or enemy sympathizers. I have often thought of that kid over the years, hoping that, somehow, he made it out of Vietnam and settled in America.

I wrote on 25 October:

> *I lost my chief FO Stetson today. He was medevaced, a virus, the corpsman thinks. He was sent to Da Nang with two others for diagnosis. He'll be gone for at least a week.*

Stetson would miss the major operation that would kick off in early November, but would later return. He had malaria. The FOs remaining on my team were marginal at best, including one who misled me at Phu Lac when they tried to direct a fire mission on unarmed mourners. One in particular had a toxic attitude problem that explained why he had probably been ejected from the battery before assignment to my FO team.

> *He is extremely lazy and has continually tried to get away with as little work and effort as is humanly possible. He is definitely bad for the team's morale, a chronic complainer, a bad egg.*

I joined the company officers at a dinner with several coal mine managers one afternoon in late October. It was my first face-to-face meeting with South Vietnamese officials. They were polite, educated men, but I later wrote,

> *How I would hate to live in Vietnam permanently, as they do.*

The battalion commander paid a brief visit in late October—a rare occurrence, I noted with sarcasm—to look at Nong Son. He flew in by helicopter and stayed no more than a few minutes, reportedly explaining to Dyer why he had chosen Golf Company to occupy the hill. According to the skipper, the colonel told him we were one of two companies in 2/5 that he could rely on to clean the hill up. We had built up Nong Son almost from scratch, installing better razor and concertina wire and hardening the bunkers. Dyer relayed the compliment to his lieutenants and directed them to spread the word to their Marines. I wondered—was the battalion commander blowing smoke with those compliments? Perhaps, if not likely. Why not stay longer with us, colonel, I thought, as he prepared to board the chopper and return to An Hoa. I wanted to tell him Nong Son at night was a special experience. The battalion commander also likely told Dyer of a planned multi-battalion operation into Antenna Valley just days away, but the skipper said nothing to us about it at the time, perhaps for security reasons.

I reminded my parents:

The Marine Corps Birthday is 10 November. Are you going out to celebrate? We might not have much for Christmas here, but we'll have some good stuff for the birthday—beer, maybe steak.

I suggested an idea I had heard from other Marines:

Mail a pint of brandy packed in popcorn or in a plastic container with a good lid and packaged well.

On the whole, I could not have asked for a better group of grunts to serve with. I felt like I belonged with them. Dyer proved himself to be a talented field Marine who could read a map better than almost anyone in the company, apart from one platoon commander and the XO. All the company's platoon commanders were more than adequate map readers, with an innate sense of where they were on a map. I wasn't bad with a map either, but not a natural like they were. I had to study my map and refer to it often in the field. Holding it on the move, with Raub carrying the radio behind me, I likely drew the attention of any enemy who tracked us. Within three months, however, none of the officers on Nong Son would still be with the company, including me. That's the way it was in Nam.

On 28 October, one year exactly since my commissioning, wearing my NVA bush hat, I accompanied the skipper to the top of the hill and carried his binoculars. Dyer stood alone for several minutes scrutinizing the lush valley, perhaps making mental notes of the terrain or simply admiring the stark beauty of it. I talked with Lieutenant Arndt and an arty lieutenant who had arrived in-country just a month before. The latter commanded two four-deuce (107mm) mortars there. I envied his command experience, with reservations. Time in-country mattered. I wrote, with some satisfaction:

He's more boot than I am.

Although my own morale had taken a hit or two since my arrival in-country, I remained generally positive two-and-a-half months into my tour. But, I mused,

The months will pass, won't they? There's no way they can stop from coming.

I had experienced no debilitating trauma. I had yet to see real, sustained combat. I had no regrets. There were no dark thoughts to ponder, no experiences to replay in my head. All systems were still "go." Yes, I had made mistakes in judgment, like any new officer. I acknowledged them. I did not dwell on them at the time. I could ill-afford the luxury of self-reflection, but memories buried for decades would later return.

The Enemy Stirs

At the end of October, our elusive adversary began to stir. Through most of October, small-sized patrols had carefully explored the western end of the narrow, six-mile-long valley. On the 25th my problem FO helped bail out a Golf platoon on what we anticipated would be just another routine patrol. The platoon took no casualties, but we were put on edge.

> I have been going on patrols with platoons. Nothing happened when I went out, but one of my FOs called in a mission a few days ago—102 rounds. This was the same FO with an attitude.

The experience should have motivated him and boosted his morale, but it did nothing to improve his disruptive behavior. The battery had placed him on my FO team before my arrival in-country—thanks guys, most considerate. Previously, he could not or would not fit in a gun crew, causing morale issues. What is a common choice for any organization that refuses to deal with a difficult personnel problem? Move that person on to another organization. I worked with him as best I could, unable to pinpoint the cause of his disgruntlement after several talks. With his hoodlum comportment, he would have landed in the brig if he were stateside. But in a

Antenna Valley, February 2008. The valley was off-limits to the public, according to our government-approved guide.

combat environment, he had to be isolated from the grunts the FO team supported. Back to the battery I sent him, never to be heard from again.

Something large and important seemed to be brewing in the valley, I thought, but what? The unknown beckoned—the promise of meeting the enemy in combat. I savored the possibility of a major operation for the first time, in the lion's den, the almost mythical Antenna Valley.

As a junior arty FO attached to Golf Company, I had no visibility into what must have been intelligence of growing concern collected days, perhaps weeks before, at higher levels than our infantry battalion. In conversations, the company platoon commanders and I assumed the enemy occupied the valley, but knew of no intelligence that pointed to a specific location. I had no insight into the enemy order of battle. I wasn't sure what lay hidden in the valley.

A Soccer Match, Then a Banquet

On 2 November Golf Company Marines played a friendly soccer match with the local Vietnamese coal mining team and lost 3–0. It marked the first time I had seen coal mine employees since we had arrived on the hill. Tight security and our inability to move off our defensive positions on the hill had prevented us from contact with the workers and villagers occupying the small settlement at the base of the mountain. "I played left forward and was rewarded with cut feet and sore joints."

My soccer experience had been negligible, as it had for most of the other Marines. I had no idea what I was doing out there. It was all in good fun, diplomacy on the soccer field. Locals watched, laughing hysterically at our clumsy ineptitude as the Vietnamese team ran circles around us. For a change, it seemed to me, figuratively, the boot was on the other foot: large, defenseless Marines versus diminutive, nimble, skilled Vietnamese. Playing in bare feet could have led to the painful plantar wart I developed weeks later on the ball of my right foot.

We enjoyed a sumptuous banquet later that afternoon with mine officials, held to celebrate the election of Republic of Vietnamese President Thieu. Since the Vietnamese present spoke only broken English, I tried to translate some of the conversation using my elementary French, with marginal results. The banquet included delicacies, mostly unidentified but tasty. One included fish from the nearby river. "It's delicious!" I managed to convey to the Vietnamese, "how did you get it?" "With grenades," one of officials replied, with laughter all around. I began to chew with greater care. One of our most experienced officers drank so much "Tiger Piss" beer he had to be medevaced with alcohol poisoning, an unfortunate loss. He returned some days later, but we missed this proven warrior on the first day of the operation to come. Our time at Nong Son coal mine was drawing to a close. Tensions seemed to mount. It was time to move on, but to where?

Operation Essex Looms

Then the Frag Order came in—we were alerted without warning. Operation Essex would kick off in Antenna Valley on the 6th. I welcomed it, my first major Search and Destroy operation. We had inhabited the hill for a month while the enemy roamed free to build an offensive infrastructure that would support the communist Tet Offensive. As always, it seemed, we had operated in a defensive, reactive mode. I wrote home on 3 November:

> *Four companies will participate, two from my 2nd battalion fifth Marines (2/5), one from 3/5, and one from 1/5. We want to locate and destroy a gigantic NVA field hospital, rice caches, and the headquarters of the 2nd NVA division. We will be out in the valley for 10 days. I won't get to write during that time, so you'll understand why you won't be hearing from me.*

I knew nothing about the enhanced medical support team that had been flown to the Battalion Aid Station (BAS) in An Hoa—according to the battalion command chronology written after Operation Essex—in anticipation of what would turn out to be close to 300 Marine battle casualties, not including the more than 30 Killed in Action. The wounded would be treated in an average of seven minutes after being wounded. A modified kitchen would be established at the BAS to ensure the wounded received prompt hot food and beverages.

I would miss Stetson, but I was pumped.

> *I will be slightly short-handed, my radio operator being my only artillery sidekick. I'll be with the company CP so don't expect I'll be stranded. I'm looking forward to the operation. Not only is it my first named operation, but here is a chance to call in artillery on some real NVA and VC and see the effect—I hope.*

In preparation for Essex,

> *The Gunnery Sergeant and I went down to the friendly Nong Son village [at the foot of the hill on the river] to exchange some piasters [RVN currency] for rice. I've taken some C-rats and traded them for some condensed milk to take on the op.*

Completing our transactions at the market, with some haggling, we received two cans of Black Label beer thrown in. I only realized years later

I was lactose intolerant. I had always wondered why Dad didn't touch dairy products. My reference to "friendly village" was not an entirely accurate description. I heard rumors the inhabitants were subject to enemy extortion and some of them doubtless supported the Viet Cong.

A squad of CAP Marines was embedded in the village. The CAPs were probably the best counterinsurgency tool U.S. forces had in Vietnam. Any Marine serving in a CAP unit had to be level-headed, self-reliant, and street-smart. By virtue of their skills and courage, they commanded respect from the locals. Most had served with distinction in infantry units before volunteering and competitively selected to serve in a CAP. Removed from main battle units, they operated independently and effectively with RVN Popular and Regional Forces and often had little immediate armed support from Marine ground units in the event of an enemy attack. Grunts also respected the CAPs—some of them hoped to someday be selected to serve in a CAP unit.

For the first time, I spoke for about ten minutes with a CAP Marine, a sergeant, during our visit. The clean-cut young Marine could speak some Vietnamese—impressive, I thought—and seemed to have a good relationship with the villagers—also admirable. From what he told me, I gathered the local villagers trusted and respected him. I wondered from our conversation if the Vietnamese admired him because he understood and appreciated their culture. To some degree, I thought, he had almost gone native. Knowingly or not, he must have had contact with VC sympathizers, I surmised, if not covert enemy operatives, given the nature of his duties.

Upon return to the Golf company command post, I learned of additional significant events just ahead:

> In December, the battalion will be moving from An Hoa, our [Echo] battery with it. All we know is that we should send all valuables home.

I would have to jettison what remained of my mini-library once I returned from the operation. The books had been a security blanket of sorts, a tangible reminder and link to the life of the mind and imagination, an avenue of escape from the reality of war. I wrote on 4 November,

> It's raining now. We're all in hopes Essex will be put off a day at least. The rivers have risen 6 ft. already.

I shivered, recalling the earlier flooded valley. We would have to cross the fast-flowing river at the base of Nong Son on amphibious vehicles. The rain stopped. Operation Essex proceeded as planned on the 6th.

4. Storm Clouds

Into Antenna Valley

I was not privy to the order of battle intelligence the battalion received on the eve of the operation. We were informed that aerial photos, signals intelligence, and other intelligence sources indicated the enemy had constructed fortifications throughout the valley—bunkers, trenches, and fighting positions. According to intelligence we received, "should a division or regimental headquarters be present, it is likely the enemy will defend the area vigorously and attempt to reinforce it from adjacent areas." An NVA battalion, a VC battalion, and an NVA company had been positively identified as operating in the valley the week before the operation began. Just where, we didn't know. Additional, unidentified enemy components waited there as well.

Hours before Operation Essex kicked off, Golf Company officers informed their platoons that significant Marine casualties were possible. That led one new arrival to ask his squad leader, "If we are expecting to suffer many casualties, why are we going in the first place?" The question was posed by a clear-eyed "Newbie" puzzled by the logic of it all. He failed to understand: we were fighting a war of attrition. His squad leader replied with a profanity-laced admonishment. But, indeed, why? Because if we were to rack up enemy casualties, we had to accept we would absorb casualties of our own. That was the nature, the terrible irony and tragedy, and the frequent outcome of Search and Destroy Operations. Win some—enemy KIAs. Lose some—Marine casualties. It was all part of the game, the deadly compact we shared with the enemy.

I was packed, my rifle locked and loaded, before daylight on 6 November. The adrenaline rush had kept me awake. Throughout the night, in the command post bunker, tactical radios crackled with updates, orders, and reminders. I had readied my heavy pack before night fell, hours before. In addition to the usual items, we carried extra ammo and water canteens, entrenching tool and gas mask. I included only two C-rat meals and a couple cans of condensed milk. I counted on receiving more meals delivered to the field. After a steady diet of Cs over the past month, however, I had little tolerance for them and chose not to be burdened with food I wouldn't eat.

I had some time to think of what might be out there awaiting us, but did not have the experience to draw a clear mental picture of just what we might encounter. I felt excitement, mixed with the unknown. I would carry my .45 pistol and M16 rifle, which I had cleaned and oiled the night before. I placed Dad's knife in my field pack. I was ready to go. Bring it on, I thought. Over the next 12 days, I would have little time to process or make much sense of what I would see and experience. Some details of the operation to this day remain hazy, but other memories remain clear now, more than 50 years later.

The Battle Begins

We left Nong Son hill before dawn. The rains soon stopped, the sky cleared, bright blue the morning of 6 November, even though the official monsoon season had begun. With the sun out, the temperature moderate, it was as good a day as any for a battle. As I recall, with no previous combat experience that generated deep fear, I had little anxiety over what might lie ahead in Antenna Valley. For several hours, we ticked off designated checkpoints along our route. It appeared at first to be shaping up as another walk in the sun, a routine search and destroy op with no contact. During a ten-minute pause to eat late that morning, I finished a can of sweet, thick condensed milk and reclined on the ground. It quieted the hunger pangs, but in due time my stomach began to gurgle.

Shortly before 1100 we observed the arrival of numerous helicopters carrying Hotel Company from An Hoa. At a distance we watched them

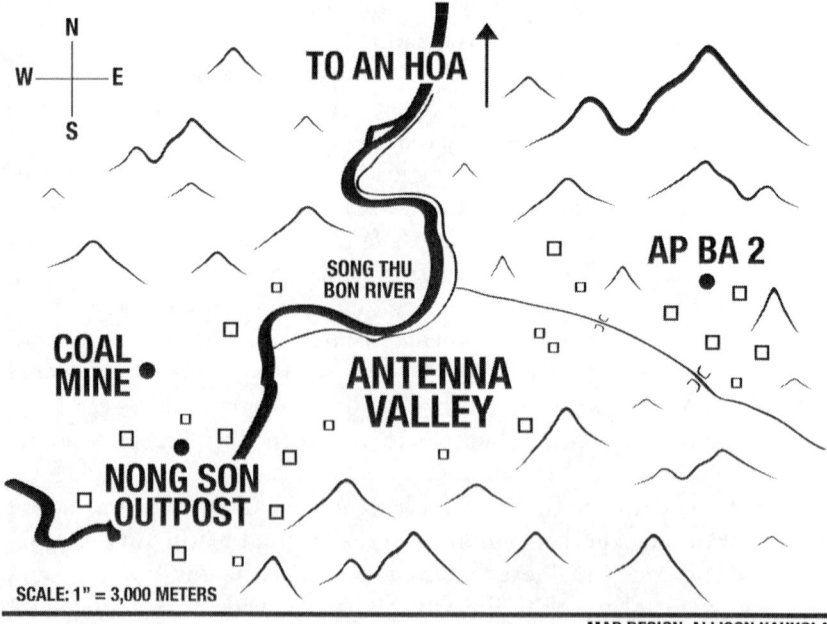

Operation Essex and Antenna Valley. Graphic by Allison Kaukola, with input from Barney Barnes.

land with rotors turning, then lift off, one after the other. From the outset Hotel received sporadic sniper fire, but moved ahead toward its first objective, a village called Ap Ba. About an hour later, we began to hear the deep, staccato thumping of heavy machine gun and mortar fire about 2,000 meters away. It didn't sound to me like a normal firefight. Hotel had engaged the enemy, which had been waiting for them. I have long questioned why Ap Ba had not been blown to smithereens by our aircraft and artillery before the grunts approached the village, crossing an expansive paddy field. Battalion after-action reports later stated that the village had been prepped with artillery and air, but I do not recall having heard or seeing it. Consistent with the doctrine of Search and Destroy, senior officers planned for the Marines to first draw fire, then engage. The enemy could then be destroyed by supporting arms—air strikes and artillery. I failed to grasp the basic logic. Exchange Marine lives for enemy lives—a war of attrition. The enemy had learned to play the deadly game: stand and fight on their terms alone, usually with an initial numerical advantage on the battlefield, following a surprise ambush. This time would be no exception.

Numerous radio reports followed over the next several minutes. Although Raub and I were still with the command element, I could not hear Dyer's urgent outgoing transmissions responding to battalion directives. I surmised that Hotel Company had taken heavy casualties from a fortified village. The battalion commander, on a nearby hill overlooking the operation, ordered Golf Company to advance posthaste to the battle to reinforce Hotel.

> At noon we were in the heart of Antenna Valley, on the move to reinforce Hotel Company. An entire platoon was wiped out as they tried to move into the village. NVA with at least three automatic weapons opened up from behind strands of camouflaged barbed wire when the Marines were 10 meters away in the kill zone.

Some of the dead and wounded Marines were retrieved that afternoon, but others could not be reached, littering the paddy where they fell. Two platoons had assaulted the village on-line from a tree line about 100 meters away. Marine dead and wounded began to fall as the assault element pushed ahead. As they neared the village perimeter, they discovered the NVA had strung four strands of camouflaged barbed wire anchored every six feet with eight-foot-tall stakes in the thick hedgerow, making it impossible to enter the village. The assault stalled and the surge retracted. In addition to the dead, numbers of wounded lay unable to move away from the line of fire. Some would not be retrieved until the following morning due to the heavy volume of fire coming from the village. Others were recovered late that afternoon and evening and brought back to Hotel's lines by volunteers who dared to brave the enemy fire.

Career Officers

The battalion commander and his staff stood observing the battle through binoculars from a safe distance on a hill overlooking the valley as they directed the Marine maneuver companies in contact with the enemy. Each tactical move ordered by the battalion commander had lethal consequences for his Marines. I understood the chain of command and accepted it. Each Marine had a critical job to do. I knew battalion commanders could not and should not be leading from the front on a battlefield. This was not the Roman Army or the American Civil War. On the other hand, it did not seem fair to me that day-in, day-out, senior career officers in command or in staff positions often avoided the dangers of subordinate Marines doing the fighting.

I was just a junior reserve officer. Approaching three months now into my tour, I had begun to feel and to observe what I thought was a distasteful chasm that separated the more senior, regular officers, with their military careers ahead of them, from the junior lieutenants, most of whom were reservists. Career officers needed their command time ticket punched. Most junior officers planned to serve three years of active duty and return to what we hoped would be a country that looked similar to what it did when we left to pursue whatever cause we had in Nam.

I felt then and, to some extent feel even now, that senior, regular officers at times made tactical decisions that caused the deaths of Marines, for unclear or unnecessary reasons. To be fair, I understood that they doubtless sought to accomplish the mission as they saw it. Surely, these career-minded officers did not want to lose their Marines. But resentment—the reserve-regular and the senior-junior officer dichotomies—would gnaw at me the rest of my tour. I began to harbor the impression that junior officers were considered expendable along with enlisted Marines.

Enemy Contact

The crescendo of gunfire rose to ear-splitting levels as Golf Company double-timed toward the fighting to reinforce Hotel Company. In the din and confusion, as we approached the NVA-held village on a run with our equipment banging, Raub and I became separated from Captain Dyer and the company command group. Within a minute or two I

4. Storm Clouds

found friend Lieutenant Alton and his platoon. Raub stayed with me as we rushed through the battle haze. To my left, I tried without success to catch a glimpse of the paddy where I had heard the Marine casualties lay. I struggled to get my head around what might have happened in the ambush, but could see nothing that made sense.

In the hubbub, a platoon began an assault on the far-right side of the village, took dead and wounded, and then fell back. Smoke and gunfire enveloped us. Mortar rounds landed all around. As the chaotic battle raged, I stayed near Alton, making sure I did not lose sight of him, trying to comprehend the tactical situation. I strained to overhear his radio transmissions with Dyer. I caught a word or two here and there, but could not grasp the plan. Close air support soon arrived, directed by the battalion staff. Aircraft began to strafe and bomb the village complex.

Time stood suspended and the noise of battle disappeared when I understood that the skipper had ordered Tracy's platoon to attempt an envelopment of the village from the far-right flank. Near a dry creek bed, under cover of a tree line, we began cautiously to work our way toward the enemy. Then, as Raub and I trailed Alton's command group, we thought we had identified the outline of the village perimeter. The attack would require descent down the bank, crossing the two-meter-deep, dry, rocky creek bed, then a scramble back up the other side before we could reach a dense hedgerow of bamboo and jungle brush that obscured our objective.

As the lead element of the platoon maneuvered for assault, we thought we detected what appeared to be a small entrance to the village, an almost invisible opening in the interlocking bamboo and thick brush. It would require us to channel an attack toward that gap, as the dense undergrowth around the village appeared otherwise impenetrable. I walked along the outer edge of the bank, now steps behind Tracy Alton, his radioman, and the platoon corpsman, Roy Potter. I was so focused in the moment, I felt almost as though I was inhabiting a soundproof room. Nearby bomb explosions seemed muffled. I mentally shut out the mayhem around me. We continued single-file as we drew abreast of the gap to the village. The platoon stopped moving forward, pivoting left to face the objective.

The lead element of our column consulted with Alton out of earshot as we waited for the conclusion of a deafening Danger Close airstrike. About 200 meters away, an F-4 aircraft dropped its last 250-lb. bomb and streaked off. A thunderous explosion threw up debris. Smoke obscured the target. A moment later I felt the sting of hot shrapnel strike my nose and cheek. A metal fragment shattered the left lens of my glasses. Instinctively, I went down, not knowing if I had been wounded seriously or not. There was a little blood, but no pain. Doc Potter crouched over me in an instant, assessing what happened. "It's just a scratch," he said reassuringly, as he quickly cleaned the cuts. A small, descending, quarter-inch piece of spent bomb shrapnel had given me a glancing scrape. It could have been much worse. Shaken and embarrassed at my reflexive reaction, I got back up and readied for the assault. I could not see through the broken left lens of my glasses, but was otherwise fine.

We peered into the village, waiting for the go-ahead from Dyer to begin the attack. The village had taken a terrific pounding through the afternoon from arty and air strikes. How could anyone have survived it, I thought? Still, gunfire continued unabated from the unseen, dug-in enemy, directed at Marines elsewhere, not at us. We later learned that the NVA defenders were firing from five-foot-deep spider holes, their machine guns emplaced behind concrete-faced bunkers. On order a minute or so later, the platoon began to step down into the creek bed, inching toward the village still obscured by smoke and brush. The point man, PFC Ardenia Freeman, started walking toward the far bank, no more than five meters from what appeared to be the entrance to the village. Lieutenant Alton stood watching in the streambed, holding his radio handset. I stood near him. An enemy automatic weapon burst raked our right flank from the creek, an estimated 10 meters away. It struck Freeman, who had his head down. He tumbled back and fell. According to Alton's journal, at that moment Doc Potter instinctively—heroically—rushed forward alone, firing his pistol, eliminating the enemy gunner. What courage and presence of mind!

The Marine advance stopped and recoiled. The command group momentarily remained transfixed as we stared down at Freeman, who appeared conscious for a moment, his eyes open, eyelids fluttering, his arms and legs moving as though he might be cycling or swimming. I watched with horror as Doc Potter bent over him and tended to a small, almost bloodless bullet hole near the crown of his head. Freeman lost consciousness and died. I realized then that Lieutenant Alton, who uttered no sound in the immediate aftermath of the enemy fusillade, had lost his glasses. He had dropped his radio handset, holding his arm. He had been hit by the same enemy fusillade, shot through the right forearm. Doc Potter went to work, again without a word, wrapping Tracy's wound. Without direction, the Marines around us stepped back and, now on-line again, fired non-stop into the village with two to three minutes of deafening suppressive fire before falling back up the far bank. Still, we saw no enemy. We received no return fire. At that point, Captain Dyer directed the platoon to rejoin the company, now deployed in a tree line facing the village perimeter. Marines carried Freeman's body.

Doc Potter should have been decorated for valor, but he received no recognition. He performed his duties in that battle just like many other Navy corpsmen and Army medics did in Vietnam every day. His actions at a critical moment doubtless saved countless lives, including Alton's and mine. In the face of danger and almost certain death, he put his life on the line. He had indeed earned simultaneously the titles Devil Dog and an Angel of Mercy.

Darkness, Mayhem

As dusk approached, Captain Dyer ordered the wounded Lieutenant Alton and his platoon to rejoin Golf and Hotel companies, now all crowded in near proximity—too close together—about 200 meters from the village. I learned the company commanders and the battalion command group had assessed the precarious situation and decided there would be no further attempt to flank the village. There were too many unanswered questions about the enemy's strength and disposition. Neither would there be another immediate frontal attack.

Still, the battle would rage throughout the night. We were in pure defensive mode. Marines reported hearing moans from the wounded in the paddy, between our position and the village, pleading for a corpsman. They also heard taunts coming from the fortified village, "Medic, medic," the NVA shouted. Within minutes, it seemed, total darkness descended. The FO team took cover wherever we could find it. I lost contact with Alton and could not locate the company commander. I had no idea who, or which platoon, occupied the immediate, crowded area around me. Just standing up and moving risked possible death by friendly small arms fire. Raub stayed near me, but our battery radio net remained silent, arty support still controlled by the battalion. Flare ships and arty from An Hoa provided continuous illumination over the village throughout the evening, casting grotesque, moving shadows. What was worse, enemy incoming fire or the fear of the unknown?

That night the enemy, familiar with the terrain, kept Golf and Hotel companies pinned down by small arms and mortar fire. A group of NVA probed the rear of our positions, but a small Marine Listening Post drove them back. Withering enemy fire from two directions forced us to hunker down and try to survive the night. At one point, Dyer ordered newly-arrived platoon commander Bill Rogers to move his Marines to an area on our perimeter taking heavy enemy fire, but Rogers refused, explaining to an angry Dyer that it would needlessly endanger his platoon. The captain said nothing more.

Hugging the ground, I began to dig down into what I thought was the paddy floor. Raub did the same. After about thirty minutes of digging, I felt reasonably confident I had excavated an adequate space to provide cover from incoming enemy fire. I discovered to my alarm—and some amusement—at daylight, however, that I had burrowed into the side of a raised footpath rather than digging straight down. I had been unprotected the entire night from enemy incoming and friendly outgoing fire. Days later Lieutenant Alton recorded in his journal: "Puff (a gunship) and flare ships came during the night. Rounds came very close and actually hit one of my men. The rounds sounded like rain thru the leaves." Alton would be medevaced the following morning. I regretted I had no opportunity to see or talk with him after he had been hit.

> That night was the most horrifying I have ever spent. Two companies, Hotel and Golf, were enclosed in an area about 100 by 50 meters facing the fortified village, a stream [and tree line] to our backs. The NVA threw grenades all night long across the stream killing two Marines from Golf and wounding ten. The NVA moved a machine gun behind us and killed two or three more. We were firing into our own lines. I don't know how many were killed by friendly fire. Grenades were going off all over along with incoming mortar fire.

Paralysis, caused by fear, concern over the size of the unknown enemy force, and a dearth of intelligence, had all worked against us. During the night, rumors spread that the enemy might attempt to overrun our positions. We later learned that harassment and probes of our positions had been designed to tie us down while enabling survivors of what turned out to be an estimated two to three companies of NVA (150–200 men) to escape the village to the nearby hills.

With notable exceptions, I witnessed limited command and control through the night. Few dared to stand and move about for more than a few seconds. Still, I noted the bravery of some NCOs and Staff NCOs who moved about and provided the needed leadership and the presence of mind to keep their squads and platoons intact and under some control. Their actions prevented further confusion and panic. Other Marines, on their own, retrieved their wounded under darkness and brought them back to the perimeter. They dug shallow holes for about 25 wounded, incapacitated Marines, providing them some cover. During the nightmarish scene, I observed the courage and calm demeanor of several African American NCOs who moved about providing calm and reassurance. This memory has stuck in my mind for 55 years, though race was not an issue I thought much about. I always adhered to the adage that there were no Black Marines or White Marines, only Marines.

I later discovered I wasn't the only Marine who observed and thought something similar that night. A recently-arrived, terrified White Marine decades later revealed that the actions of his Black squad leader, Corporal

Eddie Lee Weekfall, stood out. Weekfall stayed near and kept reassuring him throughout the night that they were all going to make it. Unfortunately, we would lose Weekfall weeks later—a blow to the gut for us all.

Daylight

Unable to sleep that night, I worried for hours what the morning would bring. Would we renew the assault against the fortified village? Darkness faded; daybreak approached. I learned Golf Company would conduct a frontal assault on the village at dawn through the same paddy where dead Marines still rested. Having now seen death surround me, I thought briefly that I too might be destined to perish that day. Just before daylight, the battalion command group, still overlooking the battle, relinquished tactical control of the assault to the maneuver companies. We would be responsible for calling in our own close air and arty support.

But joy came in the morning. Following 8-inch arty prep fires with delayed fuses to collapse any tunnels or fighting positions, and still more Marine air strikes on the village, Golf Company began the attack. I buttoned my flak vest, for a change, took my M16 off safety, and checked to ensure my ammo magazines were full. We stepped forward in the attack, firing into the village, and were greeted with silence. We received no incoming small arms fire as the company swept toward the objective. The enemy had vanished. We quickly reached the wreckage they left behind and concluded NVA survivors must have fled not long before our attack.

> The following morning, after a night of horror, we finally got to shoot artillery at the village before moving in. The NVA had escaped, our Battalion Commander [I later heard] nearly relieved because he failed to completely envelop the village, allowing the NVA to escape. Our company had five killed and 20 wounded at daylight, Hotel 18 KIA and 43 wounded.

I rejoined the command group and Golf Company began pursuit of the NVA on a well-worn trail from the village to the hills behind it. After an hour into what would be a fruitless chase, we paused. Looking to my right, I observed in the scrub brush, just off the trail, a gravely wounded, uniformed NVA soldier. It was the first time I had seen the enemy up close. Aware Marines might be in pursuit, the NVA must have determined he had no chance of survival and left him. To carry him would have slowed their escape. Although still alive when we saw him, he was unconscious, with numerous severe wounds and labored breathing. The end had to be near. I watched nearby as several Marines and a corpsman gathered round

The author on Operation Essex, Antenna Valley, 8 November 1967.

and stooped to examine him. They consulted and shook their heads. I knew what that meant. Our CP element then moved farther up the trail. About a minute later, I heard a single pistol shot. Nothing more was said by anyone.

Unable to shake the memory, I have thought many times over the years if it was the right thing to do. Was it done out of compassion, expediency, or vengeance? I want to believe, compassion, but I saw none of that in combat. Perhaps there was concern the casualty might be booby trapped. Unlikely, but possible. The NVA sometimes booby-trapped the bodies of dead Marines. Golf Company soon turned around and headed back down the hill to the fortified village. Any likelihood of catching the rear remnants of the NVA retreat had dissipated.

Lieutenant Alton had remained behind with the dead and wounded near the village and was medevaced that morning. He spent a month in-country recuperating. Following a month in Okinawa at Embarkation School, he arrived back in-country at the start of the Tet Offensive in Hue in February 1968. He was assigned this time to another company. Tracy survived the battle for Hue and completed his tour in Vietnam. In addition to the trauma he experienced as a platoon commander, he spent his last years on active duty as a casualty officer back home. He had the thankless duty of informing scores of families of the loss of their loved ones in Vietnam. Surviving the battlefield, the stress back home nearly killed him.

Tracy ultimately recovered and spent a career doing good things in the Veterans Administration, advising and counseling vets on job placement and other issues.

A Surprising Enemy

I learned much later that during the battle, radio intercepts at the battalion command post had picked up enemy transmissions in Cantonese. Chinese advisors had likely been embedded with the NVA during the Marine assault, according to the battalion command chronology. Enemy detainees afterwards reported an NVA regimental headquarters in the vicinity of the battle, one possible explanation for the tenacious enemy defense of the fortified village. The post-mortem chronology revealed additional details of the destroyed village. Trenches and bunkers had been interconnected with adjacent hamlets. One discovered tunnel, 25 meters in length, had an entrance that went down five meters. A second, parallel tunnel extended over 30 meters, with four rooms approximately eight feet by ten feet. Clearly, we had stumbled on a large, underground enemy safe haven.

The command chronology detailed that on 8 November, two days after the battle, Golf and Hotel companies received approximately 38 rounds of incoming enemy artillery large-caliber mortar fire in the vicinity of the fortified village—probably fired at max range at one-to-three-minute intervals. It was a rare and frightening thing to be on the receiving end of enemy artillery. Fortunately, we took no fatalities. I described the incoming days later:

> We took about 40 rounds of 120mm mortar fire on the morning of the 8th to include some teargas shells. One corpsman was wounded and I called in [counterbattery] artillery fire.

The World Through Shades

It was always dark for me the rest of Operation Essex. With the battle concluded, Golf Company began to move deeper into the valley in search of the elusive enemy. I navigated unlevel terrain with broken eye glasses for several days. I later wrote,

> I had trouble of course with my eyesight. The battery could not find my extra set of government-issued glasses. I took [Lieutenant Alton's] discarded glasses, but they soon broke too. I ended up wearing a

> distorted pair the gunnery sergeant had found in the field. God knows who they belonged to, but it was a good field expedient. The glasses made the ground seem closer than it was. I was continually tripping and falling down. The battery advised it sent out a backup pair of glasses on a chopper but they never arrived, finally sending out a pair of shades they found in my sea bag that were not my current prescription.

At first, my defective vision seemed almost comical. A few Marines chuckled as I staggered around, but most did not notice or ask what happened. I grew concerned whether I could be optimally effective, knowing that we had at least ten days in the field ahead of us. Moreover, I would develop a bad case of athlete's foot due to 72 hours of exposure to rain and rice paddy water. I couldn't win for losing, but felt grateful to be alive.

Over the following week, about 50 new replacements fresh off the plane from the U.S. were rushed to the field. Scared, confused, with no grasp of the dangerous environment in which they found themselves, the "newbies" added to the burden for squad leaders who struggled to acclimate, orient, and calm them. One of the new arrivals accidentally shot and wounded a squad leader as we maneuvered against another village. Luckily, the sergeant had been wearing his flak vest and absorbed only a superficial wound to the chest. Medevaced to Da Nang, he spent three days recovering before being ordered to return to his platoon. Shaken to the core, he protested, saying he now had two purple hearts and might get killed if he returned to the field. A psychiatrist spoke with him and after listening to his plea, laughed and told him he would have to return to Golf Company.

A Different Marine Corps Birthday

November 10 is the official Marine Corps Birthday, the date the Second Continental Congress established the Continental Marines in 1775. It is celebrated, according to the Marine Corps Hymn, "in every clime and place where we could take a gun," which I can testify is an accurate statement. That morning, with Operation Essex still underway, we continued through Antenna Valley. Every hamlet the company passed through appeared to have been abandoned long ago. Empty huts contained no signs of life. Numerous unexploded U.S. cluster munitions lay scattered in the empty fields. We took care where we walked, eyes on the ground. To me the cluster bombs appeared toy-like, small round metal balls. While they looked almost harmless, we knew the damage they could wreak. One misstep could take off a foot.

Out of the blue, as we paused for water and a brief rest in one of those abandoned villages, the pilot of an unscheduled incoming Marine helicopter contacted us and asked the company to secure a landing zone for a drop-off. We had no idea what to expect. Minutes later, with the aircraft's rotary blade still whirling, crewmen handed off several large, colorfully decorated Marine Corps Birthday sheet cakes along with two cases of mini bottles of cognac. The crewmen saluted the Marines and the helicopter flew off again, staying no more than a minute on the ground. Perhaps they were headed for another company to deliver more cakes and refreshments. The scene—and the circumstances—were surreal. We did not know that the delivery actually had been planned at battalion before the operation began. The company had been eating C-rations for five days, now this. To be sure, we consumed the cake and beverage without hesitation. I did my part, enjoying a slice and downing a mini-bottle.

While that morning remained quiet for us, almost festive, not far away another Marine infantry company had earlier been locked in a life and death struggle with the NVA in a second fortified village. There would be no birthday celebration there, only death and destruction on a scale that might have exceeded our attack on the 6th.

> Mike company 3d battalion 5th Marines was assaulting a different fortified village in the area and the same thing happened to them that befell our own Hotel Co. The Commanding Officer was relieved the next morning after taking 18 Marines KIA and 50 WIA. After that it was cat and mouse, we hunted and they moved back into the hills.

The command chronology later indicated the Mike Company CO had become disoriented about his location and that of his platoons, thereby losing control of the assault. It looked like a leadership issue. Depleted from its attack days earlier, our own Hotel Company came to the rescue. Were Mike Company's problems more a failure of intelligence, or poor planning by the battalion? Having just taken a beating from one fortified village two days before, had 2/5 failed to provide a sufficient force to envelop a second fortified village? The battalion commander might have found it convenient to blame a company commander from another battalion.

Enemy Platoon on the Move

The day after the Marine Corps birthday, I sat on a hilltop near a huge bomb crater that must have been 20 feet deep and 40 feet in diameter. The company had stopped to rest. During the pause, as usual, I scanned Antenna Valley with binoculars, looking for any sign of the enemy. After several minutes, about 800 meters away near the base of the hill, I detected movement. Gradually, it became clear. An estimated 30 NVA troops in khaki uniforms and pith helmets were moving through the brush, headed for the eastern end of the valley, perhaps to the Que Son Mountains beyond. I spotted a likely enemy officer pointing and giving hand and arm signals as the group maneuvered with caution. The enemy appeared well-trained, seasoned and professional. I wondered later if they were looking for us or trying to leave the valley, knowing we were still there.

I shouted to the captain, "There's a large group of NVA, maybe a platoon, we need to bring fire on them, now" Knowing there would be no time to call in an artillery fire mission on the fast-moving enemy, I asked for M60 machine gun teams and proceeded to direct the fire on the area using tracers to orient the gunners as the CO watched. Within seconds of the opening burst of the M60s, I lost sight of the enemy. After a minute of intermittent fire on the area I could not determine if any damage had been done. I called in artillery without knowing the effectiveness of it.

Water Buffaloes

A day or two later, the company turned back from the far east end of the valley and began to move back west toward An Hoa, the enemy ever elusive, the area calm and quiet. Mercifully, the intermittent rain did not hamper us. Around mid-day, in the middle of nowhere, we stumbled on the unexpected—a small herd of 10 or 15 grazing water buffalo about 100 meters away. Marines were accustomed to seeing a single buffalo, sometimes a pair, occasionally clusters of three or four buffaloes in fields, but not this. We froze in place. Water buffaloes could be dangerous and unpredictable. An adult buffalo stood six-to-seven feet tall and could weigh over 2,000 pounds. They instinctively seemed to dislike us. Whenever we drew near them, the animals would lift their heads, stare, flare their nostrils and sniff the air in a menacing manner. Was it our smell? If so, that day we must have been ripe and put them on edge. We always tried to keep a healthy distance from them. They knew we didn't belong there.

With an eye on the buffalo, which continued grazing, Captain Dyer radioed battalion headquarters, seeking guidance on what to do. The main question seemed clear. Did the small herd belong to NVA military units in the valley? Very likely. After some discussion I could not hear, and a delay of several minutes, headquarters instructed Dyer to kill them—presumably to deny sustenance to the enemy. Our company headquarters element of about ten Marines stood on-line and began to open fire on the animals. The grunts said nothing and expressed no joy in executing the order. I fired two M16 rounds then stopped. I became nauseous as I watched the rounds impact, shooting geysers of water and blood at least five feet in the air with each hit. The slaughter ended after a minute or so. To my amazement, none of the buffaloes tried to run away or charge us. I sadly watched them, one-by-one, topple to the ground after absorbing countless rounds. I turned away and grieved for hours, taking care not to demonstrate any anguish. I thought the slaughter obscene, a senseless taking of life, even if not human life. The scene burned into my memory.

Moment of Panic

A few days later, still with no further enemy contact, we paused for an extended break in an open, hilly area devoid of trees but overgrown with six-foot high grass. The Marines spread out and rested, some catching a few minutes of sleep. I dropped my gear and walked to a quiet area to relieve myself. After a few moments I suddenly became aware: there were no Marines in the immediate area. I heard no one talking, saw no one moving about. I could hear the wind moving softly through the grass. I strained to hear friendly voices. Nothing. In near panic, unaware exactly where the nearest Marines might be, I realized the danger. I could easily be killed or captured by the enemy without any Marine knowing it. I hastened back to my gear—a mere 20-second or so walk, but a seeming mile away, and found Marines quietly milling about. I learned a lesson and dodged a potential bullet: in numbers, there was relative safety. Never lose sight of other Marines in the bush, if possible.

Fallen Squad Leader

Friendly fire. Every grunt feared those words, for good reason. Artillery FOs explained to the grunts time and again the importance of knowing their location on the map before they requested a fire mission. Then there were other types of friendly fire: errors and accidents could kill as well. The company made its way through the valley toward An Hoa combat base near the conclusion of Operation Essex. Convinced now the NVA were in no mood to fight further, we were relaxed, in an upbeat mood, anticipating the cold beer, dry cot, and hot chow only two days away.

Just after daybreak, half the company was already up, moving about, drinking the tasty C-rat coffee, talking quietly, and organizing their gear. Others were still wrapped in their ponchos on the ground trying to get a bit more sleep. I had been milling about for several minutes putting my poncho away. I stood drinking coffee. Out of nowhere I heard a screaming incoming artillery round that sounded like an amplified jet engine. I had no time to react or take cover. I crouched instinctively the split second I heard it. The projectile impacted with deafening force, throwing me to the earth. Stunned and momentarily unable to grasp what had happened, my head cleared and I gradually focused on my immediate surroundings. As I remained on the ground, a few Marines began running toward someone near me, still wrapped in his poncho. He wasn't moving. We gathered round at a respectful distance as a corpsman rushed over, then another, and began to work on Corporal Henry Crigger. The highly esteemed squad leader appeared pale and unconscious. The corpsmen frantically searched to find where he had been hit. They found a tiny entry wound in his back. There was hardly a trace of blood visible. They tried to save him. They put him on a medevac chopper about fifteen minutes later, but Crigger died en route to a medical facility.

Understandably, the beloved 20-year-old's loss cast a bitter chill over the company. Crigger was perhaps the most competent, respected squad leader in the company, the quintessence of calm professionalism. He might have eventually made an outstanding platoon leader. The loss of a Marine brother was always hard to deal with. But how and why did he die in this manner? Where did the round originate? Who was responsible for a senseless death like this? I thought the artillery round had come over the mountain in the direction of An Hoa. My crater analysis confirmed it. I wrote home two days later after returning to the base.

> *A tragic incident occurred on the morning of the 15th. A round fired by my battery killed a Marine in Golf Co. It landed 700 meters from where it was supposed to impact, and 60 meters from me, killing a Marine ten feet away. The concussion knocked me down, I never heard it coming.*

A reported subsequent investigation into the Friendly Fire incident concluded that my own Echo Battery was not at fault, that the round must have been an enemy one. I was not interviewed. It was painfully clear to me—later confirmed—that my battery had fired a pre-plotted H&I round that had gone astray. Something had gone wrong, but there was no accountability.

Fatal accidents happened all the time in Vietnam. Reverberations of such pointless incidents linger for generations. In a 2008 post on the Vietnam Veterans Memorial Fund's Wall of Faces, a Crigger family friend wrote on Corporal Crigger's memorial page.

> Henry, I wish we could have met in this lifetime. You and my Dad were best friends in High School. I met your parents in Abingdon, Virginia, during

Christmas of 2006. They are doing fine, to those concerned. Your Mom took me to a wall in their home and led me to a picture of you. She asked if I knew who you were. I saw your picture so many times, as a kid, I never forgot your face or your name.

I gave your dear Mom a hug while she proudly gazed at your picture and choked back her tears behind a smile. I was humbled to meet the parents of such a fine young Marine. I'll never forget that moment with your Mom as long as I live. I've never met such beautifully spirited people who have the type of love and faith that conquers the darkest of grief and fear. It was a lesson in living without saying a word.

You did not die in vain, my friend. You have only made the lives you have touched stronger. You and your family will always be in my thoughts and regarded with honor, gratitude and respect.

These were heartrending sentiments written 40 years after Henry Crigger died, but they reflect the immediate sorrow we all felt that morning we lost him.

End of Operation Essex

When I returned from the operation with Golf Company, I headed for the battery FO tent, shared at the time with another FO. The heavy, olive, canvas General Purpose tent, stifling in warm weather, still smelled of mildew. It had a plywood floor with some gaps, exposing the ground beneath. FOs slept on cots there when not deployed with infantry companies. Much of the time the tent sat empty. The "front porch" contained a chair and a wash stand—both made from ammo boxes—our comfort items. Soon after arrival, I asked another lieutenant to take a couple of photos of me, one before I cleaned up and rested, and one later. I wanted to record visually the contrast of the two moments as a permanent reminder of the previous 12 days. As it turned out, I needed no such marker. The memory of that operation remains in vivid technicolor nearly 55 years later. That same day I took a photo of a freshly-arrived corpsman whose office tent was a stone's throw away. We became good friends over the next month, but Doc Gary Meridith would not make it home either.

I had no duties that night and retired early after dinner, falling into a deep, uninterrupted sleep. I rose early the following morning and had a generous hot breakfast. I sat on my cot and began to record what I had seen and experienced.

> *It has been 2 weeks since I last wrote. We were out for 12 days. We got back to our base yesterday. What a relief, it was almost like getting*

home, but not quite. It would take 10 sheets of paper to tell you all that happened.

Memorial Service

The frequency of memorial services varied from unit to unit and largely depended on the unit commanders. It is unclear how effective they were for grieving Marines, but this one held special immediacy for me. Our battalion service was held on 26 November to remember the battalion's 31 Marines whose lives were taken 16 October–26 November. The majority of the casualties resulted from Operation Essex. A Protestant and a Catholic chaplain led the service.

I wrote home the same day of the service describing the solemn memorial tribute.

> For each of the dead Marines there was a friend of his who represented him. The representatives would come forward when the battalion commander called out the Marine's name, place a helmet down in two long rows, step back and salute the helmet. Most of these Marines died in Operation Essex, 6-17 Nov. Many were very courageous and a couple will be awarded personal citations for bravery. Just before the service was over, my battery fired three two-round volleys in honor of them.

Brothers in Arms

I don't remember the Vietnam War as an uninterrupted nightmare of death and destruction. Living in a combat zone in Vietnam was not all doom and gloom. I recall intense interludes of humor, laughter, and compassion in the relationships of brothers in arms that existed alongside the mayhem. Humanity reigned, love for fellow Marines endured. A camera captured three Marine brothers at a relaxed moment soon after Operation Essex ended: Sergeant Mark Oakes, Lieutenant Bill Rogers, and Sergeant Bill Adams. I knew them all well. Their lives took separate trajectories once they rose together from the step on a hooch and walked their separate paths. Fate would deal each man a different hand. It was like that in Nam. Here today, possibly gone tomorrow. You might try to maintain an emotional distance from others out of psychological self-preservation, but in the end you often could not. The heavy loss of a brother who served by your side was unbearable, almost beyond comprehension.

Oakes began his tour of duty in September 1966 as a Private First Class rifleman. He extended six months, in addition to his 13-month tour, in hopes that the remaining time on his enlistment contract would be too short for a second tour in Vietnam. It worked for him. He completed his four-year tour in the Marine Corps as a staff sergeant. In an effort to retain him, the Marines offered Oakes an opportunity to attend warrant officer school or to serve as a Marine security guard in an embassy overseas. He opted to return to civilian life. Oakes was a respected, tough, and competent Marine, who, the saying went, had seen some shit. More accurately, as I would learn later, he had seen too much of it. When in the field together, I gave him tutorials on map reading and calling in artillery fire. He told me 50 years later that it helped him immeasurably. Oakes and I were close. I asked him to pin on my first lieutenant bars in Phu Bai in January 1968. He survived numerous grueling battles with the NVA. Multiple close calls took their toll, leaving permanent psychological scars along with physical ones.

Every grunt felt at some point that he might be living on borrowed time. Oakes was no exception. After 13 months in the bush, he was assigned to a logistics role as a platoon guide, ensuring newly arrived Marines were prepared to join their platoon. He oriented them, explaining what they might expect in the field, and provided the materiel needed for them to function effectively in the field. After Nam, he would face decades of depression and anxiety stemming from his experiences. At the urging of his wife and a retired military friend, Mark walked into the VA with them, one on each arm, in 2011. He still has bad days, but has at last received the ongoing support he needed for many years.

Bill Rogers arrived in-country October 1967, a talkative, energetic, and motivated Marine who loved his job and cherished the time with his troops in the field. Bill's goal was to someday take over duties as the company executive officer. He trusted completely his platoon sergeant, Bill Adams, who arrived in-country about the same time as Rogers. Like many other junior officers and enlisted Marine relationships in Nam, the three men became like brothers. Rogers and Adams went into Hue together on 31 January 1968, the first day of the Tet Offensive. Rogers provided senior Marine commanders with early, firsthand accounts of the battle in Hue on runs to Phu Bai. In a firefight at close quarters with the enemy on 9 February, he was gravely wounded by enemy fire. While still conscious, he handed his maps to Adams, who cradled the lieutenant and talked with him until the corpsmen arrived. Not expected to live, Rogers was medevaced to Japan, then to the U.S., and did not return to Vietnam.

5

No Holiday Cheer

Recovery

Marines in Golf Company spent the last two weeks of November 1967 recuperating from Operation Essex. I'm sure all of us were battle-weary and emotionally bruised. An entry in the 2/5 battalion Command Chronology recorded some of the fallout and destruction caused by the recently concluded Operation Essex.

> As casualties arrived from the field their gear and weapons were collected by supply personnel. Items were inspected for serviceability. Serviceable gear was washed and re-issued. Over 150 weapons and approximately 75% of the gear were recovered, reducing considerably what could have been an extremely high combat loss.

My first sustained combat action in Antenna Valley had shaken me. I had not seen many battlefield casualties up close before, had not been enveloped by the sounds and smells of the battle. Yet, I did not fixate on it then. For the moment, I filed the experience away, unaware of how memories of Operation Essex would come in waves years later in my life. At the time, I thought of it as simply an exhausting, tense time, nothing more.

After the battle, the company manned the base perimeter, running local patrols and night ambushes. It was a relatively calm time. Daily life at An Hoa during periods when Golf company had base security allowed me to rejuvenate, reflect, and dream. I took the liberty of imagining a possible future R&R in March 1968, possibly to Australia, but understood the destination was always in high demand. Hong Kong seemed a more realistic second choice. I spent considerable time in the battery assisting with night watches. I enjoyed the hot chow, the dry cot, the never-really-adequate sleep.

> *I am a little more relaxed here at the battery. I've been puttering around learning bits and pieces from the FDC and Exec Pit, all in hopes of knowing more when I return from the field, which may be three*

months more. I have the 8-12 pm watch tonight in the battery, a real killer. I had the 0300-0600 this morning. Could use more sleep, but there is such a thing as getting used to little.

I paid some attention to "housekeeping" duties, finally drawing a valuable, hard-to-acquire rain suit from battery supply to counter the steady downpours. In a letter home, I complained of my new, cheaply-made, government-issue eyeglasses. The plastic frames bent easily. I received a high and tight "lifer" haircut from a local Vietnamese barber. He used hand clippers with great skill and finished with a long, very sharp hand razor on my forehead, nose, the tops of my ears and earlobes. I always thought of what a slip of the razor, maybe intentional or not, could do. Barbers and local villagers who washed and pressed our jungle utilities were allowed just inside the wire at the base. I am sure they divulged to the enemy whatever details of the base they heard about or could see, either voluntarily or under threat. I even questioned, with absolutely no evidence, whether the VC might have occupied portions of the base in underground tunnels.

Whenever possible, I continued to spend time with the Golf platoon commanders, all of whom I considered exceptional officers and people, easier to engage in conversation than most of my battery's officers. I sought their acceptance and they never failed to welcome me when I dropped by their hooch. In the main, we talked of mundane subjects and, amidst laughter, exchanged humorous stories. All the while platoon sergeants and squad leaders paraded in and out passing information and receiving directions. The platoon commanders almost never discussed with me thoughts of their experiences in the field. Was it too painful, too distracting to recall, irrelevant perhaps? We had to persevere and keep positive, the long race still before us. Operation Essex was "yesterday," we still had months to go.

Minor medical ailments in the company could be attended to by the always helpful corpsmen. Days after the operation in Antenna Valley, I developed a plantar wart near the ball of my right foot, making it painful to walk. Corpsmen at the battalion aid station treated it topically with acid for several days before extracting the quarter-inch-long growth. In short order, I was good to go. Battle fatigue and mental stress, however, were more difficult for doctors to identify and treat. Among the grunts, especially, hidden trauma went undisclosed and untreated.

Churning Assignments

The high rate of turnover among small unit leaders negated the experience and knowledge gained by key officers. In late November, both the artillery battery and rifle company COs received promotions to major and received new assignments in their respective battalions. Dyer assumed the S-2 (intelligence) slot in 2/5 and Cates the S-3 (operations) job with 2/11.

A newly-promoted young captain replaced Cates in Echo Battery. Smart but aloof, he made a reasonable first impression, more approachable and open than his predecessor, I thought at first. He had strong, fixed ideas on how a battery ought to be run. On the positive side, he did not question my judgment or second-guess me in any way. He told me early on to prepare to remain with Golf Company for the near future, explaining that he wanted officers to stay longer in the field as FOs before they returned to the battery. I had no problem with that. I preferred life with Golf Company anyway, but the battery required a minimal number of officers to maintain artillery support at sustainable levels. If it came between having officer FOs in the field or pulling them in to keep the battery functioning, battery commanders had to choose the latter option.

The new Golf Company commander, Captain Chuck Meadows, would soon prove an effective and respected field leader. He would earn a deserved reputation for caring for and looking after his Marines. From the start, he impressed me as earnest and conscientious, a good man to boot. My early assessment of him turned out to be accurate—if only more career officers had been like Meadows. Many, of course, put the welfare of their men first, but the more senior a career officer, the less likely he appeared to me to take precautions that could have saved the lives of Marines.

The FO pipeline of lieutenants had begun to slow. The Basic School could not graduate enough artillery officers to replace those killed or wounded. Most newly-arrived arty lieutenants seemed to be directed first to the DMZ, where the 3rd Division remained locked in battle every day with large enemy units sometimes supported by artillery. Fatalities among the lieutenants in 3rd Division ballooned in 1967–68. I learned many years later that of the 38 ground officers killed in action from my Basic School class, 30 had been assigned to 3rd Division. Most of those were infantry and artillery lieutenants.

Uncertainty Ahead

In early December I spent considerable time in the battery taking three- and four-hour nighttime shifts in the Fire Direction Center and the Exec Pit. Then Golf Company received intelligence indicating a potential ominous turn ahead. As a junior artillery officer assigned to the rifle company, I was not always privy to new information. I learned that Golf had received a warning order, a preliminary notice of an order

5. No Holiday Cheer

or action to follow. It kick-started the planning process to allow subordinate leaders and units to maximize their preparation time for what was to come. At some point soon—probably around mid-December—we would move northwest of Da Nang. Something unusual and important seemed to be unfolding. I didn't know what it might be, but I looked forward to it. We had heard talk of a possible move north since October. My morale remained high. I wasted no time, writing home to cancel my earlier request for a bottle of Christmas brandy packed in a box of popcorn. It was against regulations. More critically, we were told no more packages of any kind would be delivered to the field in what was probably going to be a dynamic and uncertain tactical environment. It turned out to be not entirely correct, but I asked friends and family to send no food until further notice, a real sacrifice. I packed up clothing items and my remaining books and shipped them home.

> Today everyone in the battery got M16s. The infantry were the only people with M16s before—now all the other Marines are getting them. They call them "Mattels" after the toy manufacturer. I like mine because of the weight and ease in handling. Never any problems with it either.

My assessment did not mirror that of many grunts throughout I Corps who complained about the rifle's problems ejecting shell casings after firing. Sometime after the grunts received their M16s, the rifles were issued to all battery personnel. I took them to nearby Alligator Lake to test fire their rifles. In the shadow of an imposing string of hills separating the An Hoa basin from Antenna Valley to the south, the makeshift rifle range took its name from its shape. Standing on line and firing their new M16s, my cannon-cockers doubtless imagined for a few moments they were grunts in the boondocks firing at the enemy. Or maybe they fantasized they were back home on a rifle range.

The monsoon had settled in with a vengeance. The rain, wind, and cool weather could chill to the bone. Each night in An Hoa, I pulled my poncho liner up over my head and often slept fully clothed.

> No sun, little break in the clouds, constant rain. Can't take many photos now.

Sudden Death

> 3 December:
>
> Last night a Marine from Golf Company committed suicide—blew his brains out. He arrived during Operation Essex [in November] and was

soon medevaced because of immersion foot. He came back to duty three days ago. A mystery.

I first heard the Marine had probably broken under the strain of combat in Antenna Valley, but decades later I was told a different story. The night of the incident, Marines from the second and first platoons had been socializing, "shooting the shit," "smokin' and jokin'" at one end of a hooch. First platoon Private First Class Robert Wennes entered the other end of the hooch, away from the cluster of grunts. No one paid much attention to him as he sat on his cot. Moments later a shot rang out.

Lance Corporal Barney Barnes described the incident:

> The scene was just terrible, blood and brain matter all over the place, even up to the rafters of the ceiling. Marines were crying and shouting for a corpsman. Everyone seemed to scatter after that. My squad leader Lester Tully and I were standing outside the hooch when the platoon commander approached. He told us that he could not ask any 1st platoon Marine to clean up the mess after they had just witnessed the incident, so he asked Lester and me [from second platoon] to do so. I don't know if we considered it an order or not, but we agreed. We got a bucket of water and two brooms and started cleaning up. Don't know why Wennes did it, some say he received a "Dear John" letter, but I guess no one will ever know.
>
> Years later I was contacted by a cousin of Bob's. He asked if I knew him and I related the story of that terrible night. He told me the family never was told the reason or the details about Bob's death, other than it was nonhostile. By then, his parents had long been gone. The cousin thanked me for sharing the details of that night.

It was the second suicide in the company since July—two of the 382 "self-inflicted" deaths during the Vietnam War, listed in the 2008 National Archives Vietnam Conflict Casualty File.

Not All Wounds Are Visible

A day later, while on a routine patrol searching for the enemy, the company absorbed another, more devastating blow. On a routine Search and Destroy patrol trying to draw fire, make contact, and add to the enemy body count, we failed to see the camouflaged, booby-trapped, U.S. 155mm artillery round hidden in the 15-meter-deep tree line. It was about noontime, hot, humid, and sunny for a change. We were grateful for the warmth. When the round detonated, about thirty Marines had already walked past the booby trap, including me. We had reached an elevated rice paddy about 100 meters away. The deafening explosion forced me to the ground. Kneeling, I looked back as the plume of black smoke cleared and shrill cries of "Corpsman!" spread. The blast left five Marines dead and two seriously wounded. Platoon commander Tracy Alton later noted in his journal that his men had been bunched up going through the dense, hard-to-navigate undergrowth. Four of the dead had catastrophic injuries and died instantly. The dead and wounded were carried up to the paddy by dazed and crying Marines, who laid them down near our command group and left. A medevac chopper arrived not long afterwards.

I could not help but look down for an instant as two of us carefully lifted a 19-year-old casualty onto a stretcher. I regretted it. His uniform was torn from his body, his legs detached mid-hip. His eyes closed, head turned to the side, his blond hair disheveled, he almost appeared from his shoulders up to have just fallen asleep. I wrote home about the terrible incident days later, but fear I might have alarmed my parents.

> I could tell no one really wanted to take him to the chopper. I know he would have been thankful, if he had been alive. Sure, I get scared, but action must be taken in severe circumstances. What if everyone sat around when all hell broke loose? We took booby trap casualties and we will continue to take more. It's one of those inevitable things we can't do much about. Luck and caution mean the difference between becoming a casualty or not.

Of the two wounded, one Marine lost both legs and his eyesight and a Navy corpsman his kneecap.

One of the Marines who died outright was squad leader Corporal Eddie Lee Weekfall, the same Black Marine who calmed a newly arrived White Marine in Antenna Valley weeks before. He had no visible scratch, corpsmen said. When I heard the concussion killed him, I could not believe it. One of the bright stars of Golf Company, Weekfall had been an inspirational influence to us all. We had daily witnessed his enthusiasm, his infectious sense of humor, and his persistent can-do attitude. It had made him an instant leader. Of the five Marines we lost that day, I knew only Weekfall; the others were more recent arrivals. I had any number of conversations with the ever-smiling Weekfall before the incident. He would have been a leader in civilian life if he had made it home. We could not afford to lose such men! But we did lose them, with each passing week. In his journal, Alton described Corporal Weekfall as "an outstanding man, a real friend." Their relationship, and perhaps mine with Weekfall, once more highlighted the bonds so often forged between lieutenants and enlisted Marines.

Among the five fallen Marines one commonality stood out: all appeared to have come from working class families. They graduated from high school, left boot camp, and were assigned immediately to Vietnam.

They were young, aged 18–20, from small towns or inner-cities. Four of the five had fewer than four months in-country. Their brief time of service in Vietnam during late 1967 illustrates the crippling casualties in Marine infantry companies. Although Christmas was only weeks away, the spirit of the season faded some that day.

Combat Loss

Many of us were not trained or mentally prepared for how to deal with the inevitable combat loss of fellow Marines. We were often rushed to Vietnam, individually, to replace casualties and Marines rotating out. We were trained as riflemen or small unit leaders to kill the enemy, not to cope with the emotions stemming from the loss of those who fought beside us. We were left on our own for the most part to face it and deal with it. Some of us had quiet conversations about it. But for the most part, the pain of losing brothers in arms was something we rarely discussed. The fear was, it could be interpreted as a sign of weakness or a character flaw. Repressed mourning over months contributed to unresolved grief when we returned home.

Following the memorial service in November 1967, the uncertainty of life and the loss of Marines I knew driven home, I approached the Catholic chaplain one afternoon to talk. Suddenly somewhat concerned over the remote possibility I might not make it home—I remained confident I would not be a casualty—I sought spiritual guidance on how I might better prepare myself for the possibility. To my surprise and disappointment, the chaplain appeared uninterested. He listened to me, but his comments were short, impersonal, almost mechanical, as if he had heard the same concerns from many others and given the identical response each time. To give him the benefit of the doubt, the padre was nearing the end of his tour. He had only weeks before rotating back home. It is quite possible—even likely—he was worn out or worn down from Nam. I shrugged the meeting off as another "lesson learned" and continued to march. I had, after all, nine months left on my tour and much to prove to myself and fellow Marines.

Back to Phu Lac

The weeks before Christmas were calm. Despite the recent bad days, the mood in the company remained quietly positive. Our casualties in November and early December, however, had begun to affect my outlook

5. No Holiday Cheer

on the war. While in An Hoa, on 7 December we were advised we'd be moving north to Phu Bai after the New Year. We were instructed to send all but a few belongings home if we hadn't already, anticipating an eventual move to the DMZ area.

Days later, the FO team accompanied Golf Company back to Phu Lac to guard Liberty Bridge. Stetson and I spent productive time together. Although we did not directly encounter enemy forces, we called in or relayed several fire missions on suspected enemy targets. I discounted some reports of enemy casualties from recon teams, aerial observers, and local squad patrols. Reporting enemy "confirmed" and "probable" casualties had evolved over time into a Dr. Feelgood game of lies and deception to placate higher commands. I learned from the battery CO that I might be spending another three months in the field—not a big deal at the time—but soon that would begin to change. I previously thought it possible, but unlikely, that I would leave Golf before the battalion moved to Phu Bai. I knew that if I should be recalled to the battery, Stetson could shoulder the job alone. He had proven a good FO, more than competent. The grunts liked him.

Some days at Phu Lac were rife with drama, but it made life more interesting. One afternoon I accompanied Meadows, a Vietnamese interpreter, and a corpsman to the gate of the base. A woman with a leg wound had been brought to the entrance by several other women. They sought medical help. The injured woman told our interpreter that her leg had been broken by U.S. artillery fire. Two corpsmen attended to her, bandaged her leg, and gave her medication before the group left. The incident illustrated a little-told story in Nam: how corpsmen

Lance Corporal Ken Stetson at Phu Lac (6) combat base, September 1967. Forward observer bunker in background.

and medics treated and cared for the local Vietnamese, and sometimes even the enemy, often saving their lives and treating a chronic ailment or preventing a lifelong disability.

In an isolated, freak accident, a Marine tearing down part of a bunker took shrapnel wounds from a grenade that had gone undetected among the sand bags. He had non-life-threatening wounds in his back. I observed:

> Such is life here in Vietnam, Calm, quiet, then violence.

And sometimes death, I might have added. To some extent, I had become conditioned to expect the unexpected and accept it. I had no other option.

More Gratuitous Advice

In mid–December I learned my cousin, Gibbs, had indeed signed up for the Marine Officer program. Earlier, in October, he indicated he had run out of deferments and might drop out of law school and join the Marines. Now he announced he was headed for Quantico. Responding to his request for info on my own OCS experience, I responded with rather pompous, free advice that—decades later—laughably now reminds me of the unsolicited instruction on a different subject provided by the usurper king's adviser, Polonius, to his son, Laertes, in Shakespeare's *Hamlet*.

> Understand that the trials, physical and mental, that one encounters at OCS are so intensely personal that the degree of difficulty for one man in a given area may be another's cup of tea. One man may have trouble with the academic part and find he's one of a few who finds it difficult.
>
> What you are facing is a tremendous challenge. Marine OCS is the most stringent program by far. It is a hurdle that demands all the energies and attention of a candidate. Make up your mind that you will not drop out, no matter what happens. If you are determined to get through it, the battle is half over. Never quit—it's a trait all Marine officers share. The staff wants you to quit. They look for candidates who will stand up to the strain.
>
> I found the first half of the 10 weeks emphasized mental stress. I had a rough time adjusting. Physical pressures were a growing monster. I was pushed to the very limit of my endurance. You might feel like you can't run another step, but you can gut it out if you want it badly enough.
>
> Try not to be noticed. For the first few weeks melt into the crowd and avoid things that might draw attention. You eventually will be scrutinized, but the later the better. The platoon commander and

NCOs like to pick out the weak ones quickly and begin work to get them out of the program.

Never lose your sense of humor. When you get your ass chewed don't let it get you down and don't let them know that they bother you in the least.

Don't drop out of hikes or the runs, because it increases your chances of being eliminated. Expect to lose about 14 candidates from your platoon. Be as calm as you can and try to cultivate a few very close friends. You will get moral support from them and enjoy the weekends too.

For me, the war goes on. I've learned much and still am learning more about the tragedy of war. It is a duty that cannot be ignored.

A Useful Gift

A week before Christmas the company returned to the same village it had raided at night three months earlier. The incursion this time, not so novel as my first experience, yielded no sight of the enemy. The company destroyed a large rice cache and a tunnel.

On 21 December, to my surprise, I received Christmas packages: homemade chocolate chip cookies and a bag of shelled pecans from a grandmother in Arkansas and handmade Christmas cards from a friend's second grade class. Captain Meadows saw the handwritten and illustrated cards and said I should somehow publish them. They would make good reading today. Another gift arrived days later, a 1968 journal from my mentor at the College of Charleston, history professor Phinizy Spalding. As a historian and an inveterate diary keeper himself, he knew the importance of recording momentous events in life. Inside the journal, on page "June 1," was a note with a $10 bill: "enough to buy yourself a drink someday." In putting together this memoir, the journal has proved indispensable. A renowned scholar of colonial Georgia, Phinizy remained a lifelong friend who provided unconditional encouragement and support throughout his life. He passed away in 1994. Unable to attend his funeral due to an unresolvable prior commitment, I felt as though I had lost an older brother or revered uncle.

More Disturbing Reports

Bad news always spread like wildfire. I had limited access to information on leadership and morale failures, but they happened, and rumors abounded. I wrote home on 21 December:

> Two new platoon commanders in the battalion have broken under the strain of combat. One, a new arrival, panicked twice under fire and the second would not go near one of his men who was blown in half on a mine sweep. The Marine hit a booby trap and his platoon commander refused to come up and take charge of the situation. If I were blown up, I'd want someone to look after me even if I were offensive looking.

Did incidents such as these, along with the suicides, reveal serious problems in our resolve and morale? I began to wonder about it. Did it speak to difficulties in OCS recruiting efforts? The shock of the reports, for me, cast shadows of doubts on our effort in-country. Nonetheless, I still believed I was contributing to the war effort. I tried to focus on the mission and worked to maintain my morale.

A Different Christmas

At midnight, it appeared all Marine bases south of Da Nang spontaneously celebrated Christmas with pyrotechnics. Outlines of distant bases were made visible in the darkness. Flares of various striking colors, artillery illumination rounds, small arms and red-colored tracer rounds filled the sky for several minutes. It was truly a wondrous sight. My FO team stood at the entrance of our bunker to watch and listen. For a moment, the war seemed suspended, warm thoughts of home prevailed. Some Marines sang seasonal songs. They could be home, in their thoughts, for a few hours.

Christmas Day 1967 began calmly. No activities outside the base were planned. Sometime around noon we were alerted. A large, noisy gathering of Vietnamese villagers, mostly women and children, approached the base perimeter wire, chanting and waving slips of paper. I later described the scene:

> About 300 people brought propaganda literature along with a labeled—"Peace Christmas Tree." They pleaded for food and protection from artillery fire, which, they indicated, prevented them from working their fields. This is probably true to a considerable degree. They didn't know what the propaganda leaflets read. They were ignorant of our language, as we are of theirs. There is a genuine need for Vietnamese-speaking Americans here. So much could be done.

Our inability to communicate directly with Vietnamese civilians, rather than through our interpreters, created misunderstandings and sometimes led to violence. I accompanied Captain Meadows and two Vietnamese interpreters down the low hill to meet the group at the entrance to the base. I had not seen such a large gathering of villagers since my arrival in Nam. No spokesman stepped forward as their chanted slogans continued. Finally, a peasant woman walked up to hand us the small Peace Christmas Tree—a scraggly specimen about two or three feet tall. She also handed us several neat, legible handwritten notes in English on colored paper. I read and retained three of them.

> Cross over to the side of the Liberation Army, your life will be safe and you'll be sent back to your families.
>
> American boys and girls receive nice Christmas presents, while U.S. bombs and shells kill Vietnamese children.
>
> To all US officers and men!
> The clear-sighted and fair-minded for truth American officers and soldiers do not listen to [President] Johnson to cause crimes in South Vietnam. Praying only you can stop Johnson's dirty, aggressive war. Stand up to struggle for your return together with your family! Let the South Vietnamese people settle their own affairs themselves!
> A merry Christmas and Happy New Year!
> Peace for Vietnam!

As I read the notes and watched the demonstration with some amazement, I began to realize that we were facing an enemy with a sophisticated

VC propaganda notes handed over by demonstrators, along with the Peace Christmas Tree, Phu Lac (6), 25 December 1967.

propaganda capability. It became clear to me, as the protest before us continued, that there were leaders in the crowd. The few farmers, the old men, and women of all ages seemed to key off two younger men in the middle of the crowd, probably local Viet Cong cadres or sympathizers. It was easy to identify them. The local villagers seemed completely unaware or indifferent that they were being used as pawns. After several minutes, with no indication the protest would soon end, I pointed the leaders out to our two interpreters. Captain Meadows stood by silently. I was surprised when, without instructions, our interpreters grabbed the likely organizers and dragged them inside the wire for what they told us would be an interrogation. The crowd hastened away. I worried at the time what "interrogation" might mean and soon began to fear the worse. I did not watch but, from a distance, I could hear the blows and moans. Sometime later, it fell quiet. I didn't see the detainees again. I lacked the moral courage to say or do anything. Was not my silence, in the face of the violence I witnessed, tantamount to complicity? Such lapses during the war would dog me and many other Vietnam vets long after we returned home.

Holiday Ambush

Our company still had not fully grasped that we were battling NVA regular forces with increasing frequency. As the new calendar year approached, the enemy was in full-scale deployment mode, headed for major urban centers and U.S. and ARVN military installations. They were positioning for what would become, in four weeks, the Tet Offensive. Although Operation Auburn was planned to disrupt heavy enemy movements south of Da Nang, U.S. intelligence had not yet determined their objective, beyond the usual general threat to the Da Nang Marine Airbase.

During the late morning calm on 29 December, battalion headquarters alerted us to a deadly ambush the day before involving Echo Company, Second Battalion, Third Marines. Echo had been on loan from the 3rd Marine Division to participate in a multi-battalion Search and Destroy operation led by Fifth Marines. When Operation Auburn kicked off about seven miles east of Phu Lac, the first wave of choppers approached the landing zone on Go Noi Island (called Christmasville) and took heavy ground fire. The aircraft managed to deliver elements of Echo near designated Landing Zone Hawk. An NVA battalion lay in wait for them. The battle spread, including Third Battalion Fifth Marine (3/5) elements, as the Marines fought for their lives, ultimately taking 21 KIAs and 41 wounded. What happened?

According to plan, a platoon of Echo Company had moved toward a designated tree line after the initial landing. After several minutes, an L-shaped enemy ambush trapped the Marines in a kill zone, an overgrown dry rice paddy bordered on two sides by tree lines. A similar scenario and result seemed to happen all too often in I Corps. Undetected by Marines, some of the enemy had crouched in concealed spider holes with camouflaged lids dug into the paddy near the LZ. The NVA allowed a Marine squad to walk pass them. Once the Marines had cleared the spider holes, the enemy rose up and shot them from behind. Within a matter of seconds, at least six Marines lay dead, fallen about 15-feet apart. They had no opportunity to return fire. By the following morning, before our arrival, the enemy had largely broken contact, but remained dispersed in hamlets in the area, according to our intelligence reports.

Golf Company, with my arty FO team, became a relief force. We were helilifted to the site of the ambush, landing in the same LZ as Echo Company had the day before. It was eerily quiet after we exited the aircraft. We slowly made our way toward the identical objective. With the grass about knee high, our visibility of the ground ahead was limited. Suddenly we encountered a haunting sight. Dead Marines lay scattered about in front of us. I attempted to avert my eyes, without success. We walked around the dead Marines and kept moving toward the tree line. I could not help but glance back at the dead grunts. I thanked God I could not see their faces. All had fallen forward, face down. As I recall, their weapons and gear were still with them. They appeared to clutch their loaded M16s, their helmets tilted at odd angles from striking the ground. Thankfully, the bodies appeared undisturbed.

The scene remains a lasting remembrance that periodically flashes into focus. Marines policing the battlefield behind us would have to gather them up, put them in body bags, and evacuate them to the graves and registration unit in Da Nang. There they would be stripped of their uniforms, washed down, prepared for burial, then sent home. Families of the fallen Marines would be notified of the loss in the coming days, I thought. Mothers, fathers, relatives back home did not yet know what I had just witnessed. They would be informed by Marine casualty officers in several days. It didn't seem right, a violation of their dignity, almost an intrusion on their privacy: I knew about the death of their loved ones days before they did.

Unanswered Questions

It occurred to me years later, as I reviewed the events of that day, that the enemy surely must have known where and when the Marine helicopters would touch down that morning. The enemy surely had advance notice of the operation and had prepared a detailed ambush plan. The spider holes were in place and the NVA positioned in the tree line, waiting for the Marines. How? Had they intercepted our advance tactical communications? Possible. It is now known that U.S. forces frequently underestimated the enemy's capability to intercept our unencrypted tactical communications in the field. The NVA could monitor our radio channels. In addition, it was possible that Chinese or Russian advisors and technicians had provided tactical signals intelligence support. Had a senior informant in the ARVN, perhaps, tipped off the NVA? The operation also included several South Vietnamese Army units. Could an informant there have been privy to the sensitive tactical planning of Operation Auburn and relayed the information to the enemy? Perhaps a communist asset had been briefed in detail about the operation in advance and passed those plans to the enemy. We would never know how, but we likely had been betrayed, our intelligence compromised. We don't know how many other Search and Destroy operations were similarly betrayed, leading to untold, unknown casualties.

The Tunnel

I wrote in my journal as we paused for two days in nearby hamlets:

Everyone is apprehensive about the next few days. Two NVA companies supposedly have their headquarters here.

Following the ambush of Marines, the NVA seemed to have vanished. Were they underground in tunnels? I had begun to speculate that the NVA and VC must have extensive underground facilities everywhere they operated. With a so-called New Year's Truce approaching—mainly ignored by both sides—over the next few days Golf Company occupied abandoned huts surrounded by a series of hedgerows. I questioned whether the enemy had used the same structures days before while waiting for Marines to arrive. The smell in the hamlet reminded me of my childhood visits to relatives in rural Arkansas: a mixture of smoke, farm animals, heavy vegetation, and damp earth. Despite my itinerant life growing up, those visits to the delta contained happy times in a place I would always consider "home." The memories did not fit with the dangerous environment now all around me. The company searched for entrances to tunnels in the vicinity that, according to intelligence, likely contained an enemy hospital.

In that very area, months before, an industrious Golf Company squad leader entered a tunnel without another Marine present. He quickly realized he could not turn around in the tight confines. He moved ahead hoping the tunnel would widen enough to turn around. But it appeared to be a trap, logs protruding from the walls, preventing his efforts to get out. He later estimated he spent about 45 minutes attempting to turn around. He finally managed to do so, but not before panicking, desperate for fresh air and freedom. More than 50 years after leaving Vietnam he still suffered recurrent nightmares of being trapped.

Shadows and Baseplates

The damp chill seeped in while we awaited further orders. I couldn't get warm. Cold rain set in on New Year's Eve, the day I turned 23 years old. I had an opportunity to observe the grunts in Golf Company work as they patrolled, searched, and did other things that grunts do. Despite being worn down with fatigue and sleep deprivation, they seemed superhuman in their energy, resilience, and focus on mission. Wearing torn and dirty uniforms, boots often needing replacement, they remained energized and positive.

Back home, in the view of some Americans, the Marines with me and others like them who did the fighting in Nam, might not have been considered the "Pride of the Nation," as President Franklin Roosevelt once called those giants from another generation, poised to invade Nazi-held Europe on D-Day. Public opinion had begun to turn against the war in Vietnam. Portions of the public began to blame those who served as the actual cause of the conflict. Whatever Marines in Nam thought personally about the war in 1967–68—and some, I'm sure, viewed it as futile—they always looked after one another. They fought and lived for one another. They showed they would also die if needed to save the Marine who fought alongside them.

Steady harassment by an elusive enemy the next few nights—occasional incoming small arms fire and thrown hand grenades—set us all on edge. We worried, could it be prelude to a larger attack? Threatening enemy activity around us required illumination to assist in detecting possible assault formations and to discourage probes of our perimeter. Aircraft flares filled the night sky for hours at a time. The artificial light had some downsides, but provided a measure of relief and confidence. Better to deal with eerie, moving shadows under bursts of illumination than stare into total darkness, where an active imagination could run wild.

I listened to the strange, almost animal-like whooping of the descending baseplates of dying flares. The terrifying whistles grew louder as they descended toward earth. How close were they? Where would they land? There would be little warning before impact, if close. Small parachutes slowed their velocity, but I already knew the falling metal could kill. Indeed, two months later, in Hue, an illumination flare would also kill a Golf Company corpsman. I reflexively folded my arms over my helmet and hugged the ground, making myself as small as possible. I could not help but think of the first day of my arrival in the battery and seeing Lieutenant Wilk's caved-in helmet. The baseplates impacted the ground with a loud, metallic thud. Some sounded close.

What Does Valor Look Like?

Doc Gary Meridith would be remembered and greatly missed when Golf Company 2/5 fought in Hue, now two months away. Whenever a Marine needed one in combat, a Navy corpsman always seemed to magically appear, including, or especially, on the most dangerous fire-swept battlefield. Moreover, corpsmen often played a dual role—that of a healing counselor and confessor when a grunt needed to vent or to seek advice.

On New Year's Day 1968, we began a slow return in good weather and under clear skies to the company combat base at Phu Lac through an almost empty landscape. We had been in the field for six days. We looked forward to reaching An Hoa, the old refrain remained an alluring constant—hot food, a dry cot, a shower. With the memory of the deadly NVA ambush days earlier, stark images of fallen Marines still vivid—overwhelming—I shot a series of prep fires. It was called reconnaissance by fire, firing on tree lines ahead of the company's cautious move across rice paddies to minimize any risks. We all felt safer—and were safer—after watching a white phosphorous marking round followed by a target erupting from volleys of a "battery three, fire for effect": 18 rounds of 105mm high explosive rounds fired by six howitzers from my battery at An Hoa. "Get some!" someone shouted. This was how artillery support was supposed to work, low risk to the friendlies, deadly suppression of any enemy who lurked in tree lines.

An hour before nightfall on 2 January 1968, we moved into another small, empty village. We ate C-rats and put out early warning listening posts and small ambushes ["stingers"] as darkness fell. My FO team set up a radio watch for the evening. An hour or so later a loud explosion rocked the quiet stillness around us. Small-arms fire rang out in the vicinity of one of our defensive ambushes, placing everyone on alert. I described what happened that night a few days later in my journal.

5. No Holiday Cheer

One of our stingers [night ambush] ran into trouble. Doc Meridith was killed, the troops say, when he reached down and tried to throw away a grenade that landed amid the 8-man stinger. Three Marines were wounded by fragments.

Rather than lunge away from the grenade, what might have been an instinct for some, Meridith had picked it up and tried to throw it away. The grenade detonated before Doc could release it. He absorbed most of the blast. A Marine Listening Post in the vicinity saw seven enemy and called in to say they were going to throw grenades, open fire, and return to the perimeter.

Doc's death disturbed all of us. But as usual, we had no time to mourn. The suppressed anguish we all experienced at various times would emerge, perhaps years later in various forms, for many of the Marines. The operational tempo remained relentless. Marines rotated in and out. Often a grunt might be medevaced for some reason unknown to others and not return at all. Nothing might be said about it. The sudden, unexplained disappearance of wounded or sick Marines deepened the sense of mystery

Doc Meridith, standing in front of the Forward Observer officer tent, An Hoa, December 1967. Meridith's tent, with flaps up, is in the background.

and uncertainty. Others rotated home, their tours ended, without a goodbye. Few of us asked questions. We were left to our own thoughts or to worry about what might have happened to our buddies. After making my journal entry about the incident, I shoved Doc's loss deep into my subconscious. At the time, I might not have thought much more about it after his body was taken away. But the memory of the event and recollections of my interaction with Meridith would re-emerge years later without any prompt.

The grunts considered 21-year-old Meridith, who had a year or two of college, a wise, older brother, someone they could confide in. Although he had been in-country just six weeks before we lost him, his valued gentle, calm, and caring manner left an irreplaceable void. I discovered with great disappointment decades later, as his memory began to seep to the fore, that his selfless act—like that of corpsman Roy Potter in Antenna Valley six weeks earlier—had gone unrecognized. Meridith did not have to accompany the Marines to the ambush site, but I'm sure they welcomed his presence. He did not have to stoop, pick-up, and attempt to throw the grenade. He did it to save his Marines. That's what valor looks like.

6

Calm Before the Storm

Uncertainties

4 January 1968 journal entry:

> *After seeing the Colonel [newly arrived Lt. Col Ernest Cheatham] on the evening of the 3rd I am all set and looking forward to the job. Spent quite a bit of time in the Combat Operations Center [COC] bunker learning the ropes—no fire zones, color codes and the like. I haven't relaxed for 30 minutes since coming in from the field. The reason is partly due to unrest and nervousness stemming from having a new job, partly that it is so time-consuming and interesting.*

When I arrived at An Hoa with Golf Company, the battery XO directed me to clean up and report to the 2/5 command bunker as acting artillery liaison officer. I had not anticipated the assignment. The regular liaison officer had left on R&R to meet his wife in Hawaii and would not return until sometime later in January. I looked forward to the challenge and opportunity. Golf Company had no planned operations, but I thought Stetson could handle any unexpected support.

By that time, I had become aware of an emerging, periodic blue funk. I thought the mood stemmed in part from physical exhaustion. I was surely not alone. Now over four months into my tour, despite no longer considered a new guy, I had not grown any more accustomed to death and destruction than I had during my first weeks in-country. In fact, I seemed to react more to it. Had I not seen enough, with each passing week, to dull the anguish? It didn't work that way with me, and I doubt it made it any easier for others. From my optic, it was all about the trade-offs. At what point did the effect of mounting casualties outweigh the absence of a clear mission I could believe in? I began to question how long I could deal with the strain. Of course, I would keep going. I had no other choice. That approach—power through the adversity—is what got me through previous mental obstacles. I hoped it would carry over to my remaining tour in Nam. The difficulty of coping with dignity and resolve, hiding ever-growing doubts about our progress in the field, was an issue other Marines doubtlessly experienced. But it was not something we could talk about or work out with others. We all had to put one foot in front of the other. Each passing day brought each of us that much closer to leaving the war. Around me, short-timer calendars appeared on helmets, flak vests, C-rat cartons, and in journals. Like the popular expression of the day, we rocked on. The Animals' 1965 anthem "We Gotta Get Out of This Place" had special resonance for many in Nam.

Then there was my ever-present guilt. At some point, I knew I would leave Golf Company behind for the battery. On one level, I now yearned for it. But how could I leave the FO team with a clear conscience? The battery was a safer environment than the incessant grind in the bush with Golf. The grunts faced ambushes and booby traps, day-in, day-out, some for 13 months. For most of them, there was no way out: opportunities to leave a rifle company were few. Comparing an enlisted grunt's options with mine as an arty officer seemed almost obscene—five or six months in the field at most for arty officer FOs, 13 months for an enlisted grunt. Where was the equity? I thought of Lance Corporal Stetson. As a trained artillery Scout Observer, not a cannoneer in the battery, he had few options as well. Would he be destined for a full tour in the field, or would he have a chance to return to the battery or be reassigned elsewhere? I didn't know. But in early January 1968, I was still technically an FO assigned to Golf Company. One day at a time—I couldn't afford to tie myself in knots with worry. I would sub for the next few weeks, expecting to return to Golf Company as FO.

Life in the Command Bunker

The first day of my new, temporary assignment I met the four corporals from my battery I would be working with, all experienced in liaison work. They stood daily, sometimes intense, six-hour watches and staffed the battalion command bunker 24/7. They were all accomplished. Rodgers was quick-witted, smart, and helpful. Although he would leave Vietnam in a few weeks, I would see him once more at a Parris Island recruit graduation ceremony in 1969. We exchanged warm greetings there before he left the island with a relative who had graduated from boot camp. Nicholson was effective, a little zany, somewhat absent-minded. He resembled Charlie Chaplin in appearance and was "salty"—blunt with all ranks of Marines—and competent. Salty was okay, you saw it a lot among enlisted Marines who had been around for a while and knew the ropes. Officers and senior staff NCOs usually left a good, salty Marine alone. Fuller was sharp, a little arrogant, from California. He considered himself a ladies' man and wanted everyone to know it. He liked to entertain all who would listen with stories of his alleged conquests back home. McGuiness was a good Marine who knew his job cold. Street-smart, to his credit, he preferred and always took the 2400–0600 watch. He enjoyed the midrats, usually "horsecock"—a time honored, naval service culinary tradition of plain bologna sandwiches, sometimes with cheese and without mayo or mustard, retrieved from the mess hall during the graveyard watch.

I would work the daytime, and some of the nighttime, watches with them and be on-call round the clock. At other times I would stand watch at the battery, a ten-minute walk away.

Not Winning Hearts and Minds

Late on 8 January I stood watch in the 2/5 command bunker. CAP Marines called in an urgent fire mission. "Friendly" but often undependable Vietnamese Popular Forces, co-located with the CAP, reported observing "300 VC on the move." From my experience, the enemy didn't move together in numbers like that. The pumped-up battalion intelligence and operations officers present in the bunker, both senior to me, wanted to fire on the target right away. I urged caution, thinking any knee-jerk response to the report, in the absence of further corroboration, invited possible disaster. A fire mission gone wrong could end up killing civilians, friendly PFs, and Marines. I recommended we first determine the reliability of those who requested the fire mission. Were the Marines simply relaying the fire mission without verifying the location and existence of the target? The description of the target seemed too good to be true, hundreds of enemy troops in the open? Sitting ducks? At first glance, who wouldn't want to believe it and want to engage them?

Pressured by senior officers, and without a persuasive counter-argument other than "let's be cautious," to my later regret I agreed to seek clearance to fire the mission. Doubtless like the senior officers present, I wanted to avoid becoming an object of derision, perhaps having my ass chewed out by the battalion commander for saying no or for being accused of passing up out of prudence a golden opportunity to strike the enemy. After the inevitable delay, higher-ups approved the fire mission. If 300 VC in fact had ever been near the PFs, enough time had now elapsed that they would have moved well out of the target area.

I relayed the mission to Echo Battery, which proceeded to fire 12

105mm rounds on each of four targets. That was a lot of metal downrange. I waited for a damage assessment from the CAP Marines who called in the fire mission. Minutes after the battery's "Shot, out," the CAP radioman screamed an urgent "Cease Fire, End of Mission." Hours later, while I was still on duty, the CAP reported an unspecified number of friendly villagers had been killed and wounded. The incident caused me acute remorse. I felt I had been pressured to initiate the fire mission by intemperate senior officers. But, in the end, it was I who gave the green light to the battery, I was also responsible. I recorded the event in my journal the following day:

> Today was hectic with the worry of last night's incident. Learned six children were injured, three died later. Six friendly PFs were killed, nine wounded. The German [Red Cross] doctor was busy working on them this morning. It's a tragedy about the children, but a fact about war, that death cares not about innocence. I talked briefly to the colonel, who sided with the decisions of last night [to fire the mission]. He thought it must have been a stray round or a gun shooting wrong dope.

The colonel's comment amounted to bullshit. I refrained from explaining to him the details and dynamics of what occurred in the bunker the night before. It would have done little good. Lieutenant Colonel Cheatham would always have his foot on the accelerator. He brushed off the incident without further discussion. He seemed unfazed over the Vietnamese civilian casualties, concluding the mission-gone-wrong as simply another by-product of the war. The battery likely did not fire the "wrong dope." His comments were the first indication I had of his general disregard for artillery and collateral damage to the Vietnamese populace. But since no Marines were killed or wounded, there would be no investigation, no accountability. Reflecting further on the incident two days later in my journal, I asked how the U.S. could hope to win the hearts and minds of the Vietnamese when we were killing them, intentionally or not. From my ground-level, but imperfect, ill-formed optic, I mused:

> There must be sanity in a war like this. As many civilians as possible must be kept alive and propagandized by pro-western thought. This is still a "limited war" and will remain so—as will I believe, every conflict the U.S. gets itself into in the future.

It wasn't only the casualties gnawing at me, but also my evolving view of the rationale for the war. I still clung, barely, to the hope that in time we could win it. I was not yet ready to admit the war a lost cause, but I would inch, bit by bit, in that direction. I was knee-deep into the morass.

Doubts, But Staying the Course

In a rare exchange between us, almost five months into my tour, on 9 January I responded to one of my father's few observations of the war—that it appeared to him the communists were getting desperate to negotiate a peace. He thought they must be losing on the battlefield. I responded:

> Dad, at times I wonder who is more desperate [for peace], the VC or us. What tangible progress has been made? We are still sniped at and harassed 2,000 meters from our perimeter. Still, we step on booby traps and mines. It is frustrating, for me, beyond the point of helping the Vietnamese. They seem largely disinterested. I try to do my best to help my fellow Marines. That is the best I can do. I feel sorry for the innocents in the war, but, in reality, women and children are capable and have been known to fire rifles and plant mines.

By that time, I had determined I was working, first, to enable the Marines I fought alongside to return home alive. That was my chief motivator—just as it seemed prevalent among many, if not most, other Marines. Securing tactical objectives directed by higher headquarters, paid for in Marine blood, and abandoned within hours, seemed obscene, a betrayal of the grunts doing the fighting. The repetitive Search and Destroy operations where enemy ambushes triggered bloody battles, equated to nothing less, I thought, than trading Marine lives for often-exaggerated enemy body counts. Grunts were used as bait to initiate fighting so we could trumpet at the end of the battle the number of enemy dead. Ground elements like Golf Company could care less about enemy body counts. Alleged enemy casualty figures might have resonated with higher headquarters as proof of progress, but they rang hollow with those doing the fighting and we knew them to be mostly exaggerated.

The numbers of Marines killed and wounded in an encounter was now what mattered to me, and, in the end, the mounting, relentless casualty toll was a major factor in turning the public back home against the war. Journalists covering the war reported what American combatants experienced in the field. Their reports, arguably, were not the principal factor the American public soured on the war. It was the mounting casualties that anguished families back home. It was not a good feeling to continue fighting for a cause I wanted to believe in, but one which I began to doubt was worth it as the days passed. Eight months to go.

Preparing to Leave for Phu Bai

The monsoon had settled in, near-constant rain. My journal entry, 11 January:

> *Our battery commander returned from Phu Bai. He says the living conditions in Phu Bai won't be bad. Mud ass-deep.*

That sounded fine with me. Getting out of mine-plagued, booby-trapped An Hoa would be a blessing, even if the mud was ass-deep in Phu Bai. Another benefit: a large base like Phu Bai offered plenty of cold beer, hot showers, a large PX—a few of the niceties of life in a combat zone. We all seemed to look forward to a change in scenery, literally and figuratively. Operations around An Hoa, dominated by enemy booby traps and mines, had affected morale. We knew from stories we heard that operations north of Da Nang would bring us closer to meeting the NVA on the battlefield. That was fine, let us meet the enemy face-to-face, I thought.

Flare-up in the FDC

That same afternoon, I took a break from duties at the 2/5 command bunker to visit the battery Fire Direction Center and observe activities there. I sloshed ten-minutes through the red mud and puddles from the battalion command bunker to the battery. The FDC was a 12×15 foot sand-bagged bunker with an entrance covered by an olive canvas tarp to prevent light getting out at night. The covering blocked sunlight from coming in during the day, leaving the interior dark, cramped, the air humid and stale. Marines working the FDC were a tight group, often shirtless because of the heat. They were well-trained specialists and considered themselves a rather elite group, somewhat "brainy." They looked down on the "knuckle-draggers" who manned the gunline.

The FDC was a well-oiled machine that crunched out the data required to destroy enemy targets. A radio operator received fire missions on a squawk box speaker, which could be heard by all present. The bunker contained two large firing charts set on folding wooden tables dimly lit by two generator-powered lightbulbs. Coleman lanterns served as backups in case the generator failed. American Forces Vietnam Radio was always tuned in for news updates and the latest hit songs. The tone was normally relaxed, filled with light-hearted banter, stories that strained credibility, joking, boasting, and laughter—too bad I didn't record a casual 30-minute audio of activity there. Once a fire mission came into the FDC, however, the tone turned deadly serious. Lives often hung in the balance. One chart operator plotted target data provided by the Marine calling in the fire mission. The second chart operator verified the data to be sent to the guns. As the first chart operator plotted, then barked out the gun data—first the gun deflection (the direction of the guns), then the quadrant (elevation of the tubes required to hit the target), the second chart operator would call

6. Calm Before the Storm

Fire Direction Center showing the Firing Tables used to compute gun data, Echo Battery, An Hoa, 1967 (courtesy Martin Dunbar).

out "check" (gun data verified) or "hold," which prompted a re-plot by the first chart and extra attention by the Fire Direction Officer, or FDO.

The FDO had the responsibility of confirming the computed data, including the number of bags of propellant, or "charge," required to ensure the artillery rounds could reach a distant target. During daytime, the FDO relayed the data to the Exec Pit, where the XO or officer on duty relayed it to the guns and fired the battery. During nighttime hours, if the Exec Pit was unmanned, the FDC duty officer would relay the data directly to the gun chiefs. A gun chief would repeat the deflection and quadrant and wait for the word to "standby ... fire," then repeat the sequence to his crew. Then "boom," the round was off.

Shortly after the I arrived at the FDC to observe the afternoon of 11 January, we received a fire mission. While FDC personnel worked to compute the gun data, the recently-arrived battery commander, doubtless alerted by activity he saw on the gunline, entered the bunker and stood silently watching the Marines work. Intense, the CO wore a permanent scowl, often critical of junior officers. I always thought he seemed to be concealing some self-perceived inadequacy. I stood silently to the side, watching the scene. After the end of the mission, he lashed out at the FDO, a quiet, affable officer. Raising his voice and demeaning Lieutenant Harley Hamm in front of the troops, the CO accused him and the FDC personnel of unprofessional conduct and using improper procedures as they worked over their firing charts. I thought the comments unjustified—a blatant display of the bullying and poor leadership I had seen before. Following his rant, the CO stared at me for several seconds, as if to gauge my reaction, perhaps deciding whether he should include me in the tirade. He declined, turning his attention back to a deflated Hamm. He left the FDC, which had grown quiet.

Dilemma

In mid–January, 2/5 and Echo Battery had made final preparations for the move north to Phu Bai; 2/5 would replace Second Battalion, 26th Marines, which would then shift north to Khe Sanh and the DMZ area. Echo Battery would replace Bravo Battery, First Battalion 13th Marines. The evening before departure for Phu Bai on January 13, I packed my gear in the FO tent. My few remaining belongings were stowed away under my cot in a rubberized, waterproof "Willy Peter" bag.

I gathered my thoughts on what might be in store in the coming days. The regular liaison officer, would soon return from R&R. I had enjoyed two weeks in his absence, a good break. The interlude had provided an inside look at the grunt battalion operational nerve center. My impending return to the field as FO had now begun to seem a bit of a drag. I began to question how much longer my luck in the bush might last:

> *I'll probably go back as FO for a bit longer. The future is actually uncertain. I'll expect to go out to the field again just so I won't be disappointed.*

I realized my view of the bush had changed somewhat. For two weeks I had enjoyed the relative safety and "good life" in a battalion combat base (hot chow, a dry cot, plenty of water to drink and to wash with) and an occasional beer. I thought I could adjust to it. No one incident triggered these thoughts. It was rather an accumulation of events and experiences internalized and processed over time. Although I had completed almost half my tour, the road ahead suddenly began to look much longer. Similarly, as much as I valued my FO team and the camaraderie of the grunts,

I had begun to look forward to something different. Was I simply suppressing a wish to escape the relentless perils of the field? Probably. I hated to admit that might be the reason. Would I have felt that way had I been convinced the war was actually being won and that what we were doing in Vietnam was worthwhile and appreciated by the Vietnamese and the American public? Perhaps.

Banter with Staff NCOs

The night before the flight to Phu Bai, I enjoyed a beer with two senior Staff NCOs, the battery first sergeant, who liked to organize poker games on paydays, and Golf Company's Gunnery Sergeant Pierce, a Native American from Arkansas who would give anyone the shirt off his back. Both were World War II vets. The Gunny had been with us when we raided the NVA village the previous September. The comic relief the two provided helped me leave the war behind for a few hilarious minutes. As I listened, they outdid each other with jokes and profanity. Occasionally glancing to see my reaction, they recounted bawdy, hilarious tales, none of which I took as factual. They were in a good mood and succeeded in impressing a skeptical young boot lieutenant, if that was the intent. They certainly had a captive audience. I remarked later in my journal:

> Staff NCOs have got to be the funniest people alive.

Yes, they could be very funny. You might laugh with them, but never dare laugh at them. With the respect they received up and down the chain of command, they could make or break a tour for a junior officer or enlisted Marine. They often had the ear of the CO and other senior officers and could influence daily decisions that impacted individual Marines and the unit, for better or worse. Good Staff NCOs were like gold in a combat environment, team builders and able to keep enlisted Marines focused. Poor or lazy ones could be disruptive, damage morale, and hamper mission efforts.

I had limited exposure to Staff NCOs before arriving in Nam and only a rudimentary grasp of their critical importance in the chain of command. It was, in my view, an unfortunate flaw in the Marine officer training syllabus during the late 1960s. In the Basic School it had always been the repetitive "What now, Lieutenant?" Yes, the lieutenant bore the responsibility of his unit's performance, but he needed assistance and support from lower-ranking, often more experienced Marines. Help from NCOs and Senior NCO was critical to success. Basic School doctrine encouraged junior officers to go it alone too often, to shoulder any burden, without due thought to how the enlisted team around him could help achieve the mission. Our training ignored how inclusivity in decision making could be a force multiplier. Inexperienced lieutenants would learn that lesson the hard way, after arrival in-country. I know I did. After my beer with the senior staff, I retired to my tent to make final preparations for the next day. In my journal, I noted:

> Don't know what Phu Bai brings, good I hope, or better at least.

Gear now packed, all I had to do in the morning was put on my boots, eat, and mount up. I was, as usual, bone-tired, but lifted by the laughter shared the previous evening and by the excitement of the anticipated flight the following day. I found it difficult to fall asleep. After a few minutes an 8-inch howitzer several hundred meters away sounded off, firing an occasional H&I over my tent. I could now relax. I had grown accustomed to the noise and could only get into a good sleep when the large cannons made themselves heard. As it turned out, the much-anticipated move to Phu Bai would not foreshadow anything good. Hey, this was Nam, better to limit expectations. Unknown to us, the Tet Offensive lurked just a couple weeks away.

Chaplain Demers

Up at 0500, I hurried to the Combat Operations Center to check on last minute preparations for leaving. The battalion staged near the airstrip

The author near the runway tarmac at An Hoa, awaiting helilift to Phu Bai, 14 February 1968.

6. Calm Before the Storm

that morning, happy to be leaving An Hoa, a hell hole, land of booby traps, they called it. Any destination would have been better.

Lift-off was delayed to 0900. A squad returned late to base from a night ambush, delaying the departure. It was always hurry up and wait, or so it seemed. Some Marines took the occasion to catch some Zs. Others, like Lance Corporal Stetson, sat quietly and talked. What lay ahead for them? Rumors proliferated.

At last, I boarded an Air Force C-130 aircraft with the command group. I sat alongside the battalion's new Navy chaplain, Father Richard Demers. At 6'4" and 250 pounds of muscle, Demers had a towering intellect to match. This gentle giant had once been a diocesan priest, but became disillusioned from having to advise parishioners on issues—such as marriage—with which he had no personal experience. He viewed it as hypocrisy. A monsignor understood this restless, inquisitive priest and recommended service with the military. The lure of adventure proved too hard for him to resist. He chose to leave the safety of the U.S. to serve with Marines in Nam. Many of us, I am sure, longed for those small comforts he voluntarily left behind. After giving him five weeks of introductory training for chaplains at Parris Island, the Navy rushed him to Vietnam. He arrived in Da Nang in the backseat of a Marine F-4 fighter aircraft.

Sitting on the floor of the plane, Demers and I engaged in an intense conversation. We proceeded to talk—rather, yell—nonstop over the loud

Chaplain Demers in his hooch, 1968 (courtesy Christopher Demers).

noise and vibrating aircraft during the 35-minute flight to Phu Bai. The topics of conversation are hazy now and not that critical. What memory remains? I had not known, or would know afterward, a more enthusiastic or positive man in Nam than Chaplain Demers. At that stage in my tour, I had begun to conclude just about everyone seemed to regard their remaining time in-country with some dread. Many appeared to be counting the days left. But now, Demers appeared, literally out of the blue, energized, excited about his job. His enthusiasm was infectious. My contact with his predecessor had been a disappointing experience, making it even more refreshing to talk with a man of God who took the time and interest to listen, acknowledge, and respond to what I said. If he exuded positive vibes about his job and our mission in Vietnam, why couldn't I? We walked off the aircraft together but did not have an opportunity to talk again in-country. We would meet again a couple of years later at Parris Island.

Demers in Action

As it turned out, Father Demers proved without a doubt that he would do anything for his Marines. He walked beside them in the field, a pistol on his hip, although I am sure he never used it—he valued human life. He administered aid and comfort to those who suffered from damaging physical and psychic wounds of combat. Years later, I found he had access to a stash of mini-bottles of liquor. He would sometimes offer one to wounded patients. On at least one occasion, he had to be reminded by the battalion surgeon that casualties with head wounds should not consume alcohol. For gravely wounded Marines who were Catholic, and for some who were not, he administered or offered Last Rites, often while crying.

All the while, Demers urged Marines not to abandon their faith, especially those who had fallen friends or buddies. They could not know that as the months passed, however, Chaplain Demers was gradually losing his own faith. During the Tet Offensive, Demers consoled a lieutenant who had just delivered dead and wounded Marines to the medical battalion in Phu Bai. The lieutenant years later recalled that he had become dazed, nearly paralyzed, from shock after seeing a captain he knew being prepared for embalming. Although the lieutenant was conscious, he could not speak or move, temporarily immobilized. Neither could the lieutenant recall what Demers told him. He only remembered that the chaplain had placed his arm on his shoulder, saying words that did not really register, but that didn't matter. The calming gesture and the tone of the chaplain's voice are what the lieutenant remembered, providing remarkable solace and comfort. For months afterward, Demers kept encouraging the same officer not to blame God for the loss of his Marines. In retrospect, now, I wonder—was he trying to convince himself?

Chaplain Demers would receive a meritorious Bronze Star for his service in Vietnam. His citation could not have been more descriptive. It reads in part,

> He not only brought cheerful hope to the injured, but also assisted medical personnel in rendering first aid to casualties. Actively participating in his unit's Civic Action Program, he was instrumental in establishing harmonious relations between Marines and the local populace, thereby contributing significantly to the accomplishment of his battalion's mission.

Only recently did I discover that Chaplain Demers experienced a crisis of faith and conscience in Vietnam. He returned home disheartened and disillusioned. He no longer felt he could function as a priest. He had grown up believing in the sanctity of life. In Vietnam he had concluded that human life was not respected. He was shaken to the core by the carnage of war. Whereas he had earlier urged Marines not to blame God, in a terrible twist of irony, he now questioned how God could have permitted so much human destruction. Eight years after his ordination, at his request the Catholic Church released Demers from his vows.

After leaving the priesthood, Rich Demers married and raised two sons. His wife had lost her first husband, a Navy helicopter pilot, in an accident off the Vietnam coast. In connection with MBA studies at the University of Chicago, he and his young family left for Ghana, in West Africa, in 1976. They spent two years helping locals organize small-scale sugar cane factories. In 1978, he returned home and took a leadership role in a business career and civic affairs.

Over the years his family attended churches of various denominations. In time, Demers gravitated back to the Catholic Church after the pope invited former priests to return, but his move was driven more by cultural familiarity than religious conviction. Demers felt he had left part of himself in Vietnam, according to a family member. He loved the Vietnamese and considered them innocent victims of violence. At one point during the Tet Offensive, he visited an orphanage in Hue and managed to provide the children and Catholic priests food and medical care. Living out the respect he held for the people and those who suffered from the war, he returned to Vietnam several times years afterward for brief periods to teach English to children.

Richard Demers had trouble adjusting to normal life back home. No one job seemed to satisfy him. He appeared to have lost his optimistic outlook on life. The Vietnam War seemed to have hindered his ability to be happy. And, like substantial numbers of other Vietnam vets, myself included, he did not seek or receive the counseling or therapy that might have eased the awful burden he carried. Still, people continued to be drawn to him. Demers died twenty years ago, but he lives on in the memory of many of us who knew him. In January 1968 there must have been something most unusual, perhaps mystical, about the charismatic Father Demers. He made a huge impression on me. He provided inspiration and hope at a critical juncture of my tour. More than fifty years after that brief, casual talk on an aircraft—in route to what would soon be one of the fiercest and most iconic battles in Vietnam—Demers remains one of the best and most memorable people I met in-country. Thank you, Father Demers.

Phu Bai

After arrival in Phu Bai, I stowed my gear in the designated hardback hooch I shared with two other lieutenants. The plywood quarters seemed luxurious in contrast to the transient FO tent and open-air sleeping accommodations I had enjoyed the previous five months. As I unpacked that afternoon, I listened to "Woman, Woman," by Gary Puckett and the Union Gap on Armed Forces Radio. I never liked the song, other than the brass sections. It fell solidly into the "easy listening" category that had begun to take hold in American music culture. Nevertheless, women were often on my mind, the gentle sex, scornful of war.

Journal entry, 14 January:

> *Looks like I will be going back to Golf Company for a while. I believe I have learned as much as possible as an FO.*

In truth, I now had begun to loathe a return to the field. In intermittent rain, I trudged through sticky mud and explored my immediate surroundings at the enormous Phu Bai air field and base for an hour. Passing the expansive Post Exchange, I stepped inside for a quick look, overwhelmed by the merchandise for sale, especially the electronics. To me, it resembled what I imagined a well-stocked stateside PX might look like. Afterwards I ran into Frank, an OCS and arty school classmate who seemed to have won the luck of the draw and so had earned my envy. He had been assigned to a large-caliber artillery battery upon arrival in Nam and would serve no time in the field as an FO. Moreover, he had received his silver first lieutenant bars shortly after our mutual 1 December date of rank. My promotion warrant had not yet surfaced in my battery.

Over 500 lieutenants graduated with me from the Basic School, but

I can recall seeing no more than a handful in Vietnam, and then only in passing for brief conversations. The war seemed to swallow up and spit out some of us. But I cheered up when I met another TBS classmate days later. Jay Oelsner had attended artillery school with me. We were assigned to the same gunnery homeroom and became good friends. We took a short, extracurricular speed-reading course together while at Fort Sill. I enjoyed Jay's humor. His unyielding joie de vivre and intelligence impressed all who knew him. Jay survived his tour, but died in an automobile accident weeks after he returned home from Nam. He would be the first post–Vietnam service casualty of my Basic School class.

Turning Point

Uncontrollable events often dictated someone's course, or fate, in Nam. An assignment here, a decision made by someone there, perhaps an action you—or someone else—made on the spur of the moment. Good judgment helped one's prospects for survival, but luck—good or bad—reigned supreme. I tried to take reasonable precautions. I heard a few

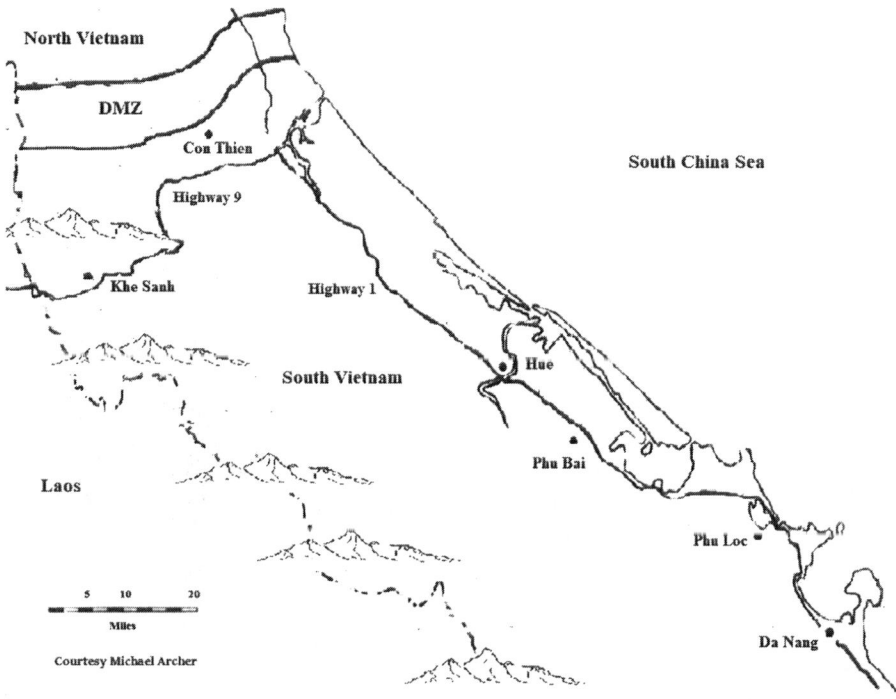

Map of Northern I Corps, graphic by Michael Archer.

Marines exclaim that God had a plan for them, whatever that was. It was up to the Big Guy.

The regular artillery liaison officer returned from R&R on 15 January. I helped him in the battalion operations center and then visited the battery. I noted in my journal,

> Parts of the battery dribbled in today. Took a morning visit there and talked with [trusted XO] Marty Dunbar.

Dunbar had become a respected mentor—knowledgeable, calm, judicious and wise, always willing to listen and advise. He noted to my hidden delight that I might be assigned to work with the battery's four 155-towed howitzers once the guns arrived from An Hoa, rather than return to the field with Golf Company. I replied, "I hope so," with a solemn, straight face, attempting to hide my relief at the prospect. The battery CO seemed to confirm it days later, informing me I should prepare for an eventual return to the battery. He provided no timeline. In the interim, he said, I would technically remain Golf's FO.

It did not work out that way. Unknown to me at the time, my FO days with Golf were over. Such was fate. The Tet Offensive would soon begin. Stetson would accompany Golf Company into Hue as the FO. It would be Ken Stetson who would give his life for his country and I who would long deal with the aftermath. I would remain in the battalion as the second arty liaison officer. In a critical decision that might have determined my destiny, about the same time I spoke with Dunbar, the battalion CO announced he wanted two arty officers assigned to the headquarters

Lieutenant Martin Dunbar, a Sunday morning, near Highway 1, April 1968. Marty could not recall how he obtained the baseball glove.

command group, one to accompany the battalion CO in the field during planned tactical operations in the Phu Bai vicinity. The other liaison officer would man the battalion ops center.

Nothing but an Illusion

For several days I basked in the relaxed, casual routine at Phu Bai, but as each day passed, I sensed the almost otherworldly experience was just a mirage. I understood life in Phu Bai masked reality. For me, the real world did not include living, or acting, a seeming carefree life inside a large, relatively secure base. It was the war, outside, over there, in the bush, with all its dangers. I did not join the Marine Corps to sit on my ass. Yet, still enjoying the stateside-like environment, on the 16th I hung up my jungle boots, polished my garrison boots despite the occasional downpour, and ventured to the post exchange. I spent $4.50 for a shoulder holster for my .45 pistol and purchased a small footlocker made of beer cans at a Vietnamese concession. The resourceful Vietnamese crafted wonders with beer cans, some useful, some deadly.

> *Tomorrow, I plan to go bridge hopping on Route 1 to check Golf's outpost responsibilities. Sgt. Oakes gave me lifer's haircut.*

On the 17th, after a hot breakfast, I slogged again through the deep mud to join Golf platoon commander Lieutenant Bill Rogers, and Sergeant Adams, his platoon sergeant, at the jeep we were to take south along Highway 1. Rogers stood talking with Gunny Pierce. Golf had responsibility for guarding the bridges south of Phu Bai. Before we left, Ken Stetson showed up unexpectedly to see us off. In fresh, clean utilities, he looked rested and in good spirits, smiling and joking along with the rest of us. For some reason, I snapped a photo of him—three days after his 22nd birthday. Exactly one month before we lost him in Hue. I think it must be the last known image taken of Ken and reveals his personality. I would take only a handful of photos in Vietnam after that one. Nearly seven months of my tour remained.

The trip south proved uneventful as I listened from the backseat to Rogers and Adams—brothers in spirit—talk incessantly. Small-vehicle and motorcycle traffic flowed normally and there were numerous pedestrians. Absence of traffic flow anywhere along the highway would have indicated a likely enemy presence in the area. We returned to Phu Bai that afternoon after talking with the squad leaders whose Marines were assigned to guard the bridges. That night a group of us watched "Who's Afraid of Virginia Woolf?." I disliked the exaggerated, hysterical portrayal

Lieutenant Bill Rogers, letter writing, Phu Bai, mid-January 1968.

of a marriage falling apart due to alcohol abuse. But what the hell, at that point I agreed with the theme of The Grassroots song: live for today—who knows or cares about tomorrow? That was the spirit of the times. We all drank too much beer and rolled the dice for who would pay the tab.

Mounting Tactical Alerts

The weather remained uncomfortable, cool and breezy, rain intermittent, the sky leaden. The sun rarely appeared, filtered through the cloud cover. Soaking rain would continue for weeks. I couldn't shake the damp chill. The gloomy weather seemed to presage something ominous ahead. I took a photo of the dark, moving rain clouds. The image reflected an unsettled feeling, my own gloom, about the unknown events that lay ahead. The socked-in weather would prevent close air and artillery support in Hue and other battlegrounds during the Tet Offensive. For Golf Company, the approaching fight would be held in drizzling rain, at close quarters, in an unfamiliar urban environment.

On the positive side, on 18 January we enjoyed for the first time hot water for showers; the following day, most of the battalion would move south along Highway 1 on a brief operation to provide security to the Phu Loc District headquarters. Intelligence indicated significant enemy movement there. The arty liaison officer, Barry, would accompany the battalion command group and three rifle companies. Golf Company would remain behind to provide base security. As the assistant liaison officer, I would also stay behind with the battalion XO and other headquarters elements in the combat operations center, assigned to help man the battalion operations center.

Tet, the Chinese New Year, drew closer. On the 21st, the war began to creep toward Phu Bai; the base went on high alert. For several days, intel reports—blinking red—indicated an acceleration of enemy movement and activity throughout I Corps. The NVA began to rocket the base, nothing heavy to start with, just harassing fire. With each alert, though, tensions mounted. Helmets and flak vests became mandatory after nightfall, when most of the rockets arrived. Concern rose over a possible ground attack against the base.

Journal entry:

> Had the 2400-0600 watch. Hit the rack soon thereafter. Up at 0930 to eat breakfast—four eggs, sausage, toast. Back to the rack for another hour. Asked Rodgers to drive me to the PX to have some film developed. Took an hour nap at 2100. An alert drove me back to the operations center where I ran out the clock reading Par Lagerkvist's novel, Barabbas. Disappointing. At 0230 had to go with an engineer out to the Seabee platform and remove 2 dud 105mm artillery rounds from the proximity. Will blow them tomorrow.

Encountering PTSD

Since our arrival in Phu Bai, Sergeant Oakes—the Golf Company guide, responsible for logistics—had made himself a helpful presence as we set up the COC. I tasked him with useful errands connected with setting up and running the COC. Seeming to have time on his hands, Oakes welcomed the requests. I had worked with him in the field for several months earlier and appreciated his field savvy. He was a talented Marine NCO. Had he been pulled back to the rear for the last few months of his tour as a reward to a weary, deserving Marine for a job well done? Very possible, if not likely.

I had become aware that Oakes seemed to be dealing with some trauma. I observed it in his expressionless stare. I thought perhaps he had been broken by some horror in the field. I briefly pondered if it might be what I then called battle fatigue. While he sometimes could be animated with a keen sense of humor, at other times he wore a distant stare, what I would recognize in later years as PTSD. I sensed Oakes was deeply wounded in spirit. It seemed clear to me that he was seeking emotional support, a helping hand, someone he could trust and with whom he could talk. All grunts experienced trauma of one sort or another. Some handled it better than others. Aware of his invisible wound, I did what I could to help him.

"I Knew We'd Be Moving"

On 22 January intelligence indicated a likely impending escalation of enemy attacks on Phu Bai.

> *There is a big scare tonight about the possibility of a mortar attack, flak gear and helmets are mandatory from 1830 on.*

The artillery battalion operations officer visited the COC and wanted on-call defensive fires ready to go. The night remained calm.

The following day Lance Corporal Stetson delivered an hour-long class on how to call in a fire mission for 40 Golf Company Marines. It coincided with an alarming intelligence report: the likelihood of a general widespread enemy offensive before Tet, on or about 3 February. In my journal I played the role of an experienced armchair strategist. What did I actually know? Not much. I had absolutely no access to high-level strategic intelligence and no inkling of what was about to happen in the weeks ahead:

> *Last night the battalion XO made everyone don flak gear and helmets for fear of a mortar attack. Before the Asian New Year, there is a large offensive planned by the VC—reason being, they want a victory to bargain with when peace talks are made. I'm really not expecting anything to come of the talks.*
>
> *Technically I am still in the field [the officially designated Golf Company FO], but will not be going out often with the company. I like liaison work and feel I've done enough as FO. My man Stetson is fully capable.*

Then this, the consequence of the recent intelligence.

> *On returning from evening chow, I learned that 2/5 will be moving very shortly from Phu Bai to the south, God knows where after that. This place looked too much like a staging area to be permanent, and it turns out, I was right. I knew we'd be moving.*

6. Calm Before the Storm

The temporary glow of garrison duty now receded, the prospect of engaging the enemy likely. Golf Company security elements on Route 1 were mortared that night. The base defense coordinator called twice for extended arty illumination on the perimeter.

On the 24th the battalion and its command group returned to Phu Bai. Plans were announced. The entire battalion would soon decamp to the area south, near Phu Loc. Stepped up enemy activity raised concerns the NVA might attempt to interdict Highway 1. That night, Hill 230—manned by Marines as a defensive element west of Phu Bai base—was hit by the enemy and required illumination. The battalion CO and the 5th Marines complained loudly that the clearances to fire in support of the company there took too long. I was pushed to get clearances faster. After dinner, I turned in and slept a couple hours.

> *At 2400 Rodgers woke me up and said it was time for watch. He said that someone had stolen the Mighty Mite jeep about 2130. He was understandably shaken.*

I wasn't too concerned. The jeep could not have been lost. Someone had "borrowed" it, perhaps after a having a few too many at the club.

The operational tempo accelerated. After midnight the 26th, Phu Bai received enemy mortar rounds but no casualties. Hill 230 also took incoming mortar rounds. Three days later I learned I would accompany the battalion on an extended operation near Phu Loc, about ten miles south of Phu Bai. The battalion command post would be set up in an abandoned railway tunnel near the Cai Do Peninsula off Highway 1. I accompanied the battalion command group, with three rifle companies, leaving Phu Bai on 30 January. Golf Company—now attached to the First Marine Regiment—with Stetson the acting FO, would stay behind in Phu Bai as base security.

For various reasons, that journal entry, on the eve of the Tet Offensive, was the last notation in my journal. In the months that followed, I lacked the energy, motivation, and leisure to pick it up again. Writing would be too painful. The accumulating deaths of close colleagues and friends, along with the demanding duties in the artillery battery, left little to no opportunity to collect my thoughts or to defend my rationale for fighting in the war.

Hue—Late January

As January ended, the stately city of Hue remained almost untouched by the war. The former imperial capital was a major cultural center and home to powerful Buddhist religious institutions. French engineers had deemed the Imperial Citadel, bounded by 15-foot thick walls, almost impregnable when they completed construction in 1820.

Tet approached. U.S. intelligence seemed unaware of the danger just a day away. It had tracked the movement of the crack 4th and 6th NVA regiments to the mountains west of the city, but no attempts were made to attack or interdict them, according to Eric Hammel's *Fire in the Streets*. The 3rd Marine Division headquarters had been deployed to northern Quang Tri province. Elements of the 1st Marine Division backfilled it in the Hue region. The closest Marine combat elements were positioned in Phu Bai. South Vietnamese commands in Hue were minimally manned. The 1st ARVN Division occupied the northeast corner of the Imperial Palace complex. On the more modern, southern side of the west-to-east flowing Perfume River, which divided the city, a small, mainly Army contingent occupied the fortified MACV complex, a former hotel. The installation sat on Highway 1, which cut through the eastern portion of the city.

7

Hue

The Tet Offensive

In a December 1967 speech Ho Chi Minh called for intensified communist efforts to win the war on the battlefield. He published a pre-Tet poem provided to Viet Cong officials and North Vietnam diplomats alluding to a forthcoming decisive battle.

The Johnson Administration reacted with concern using World War II imagery. The president seemed to grasp the threat of an imminent enemy offensive. He announced Hanoi was preparing "kamikaze attacks" in Vietnam. Joint Chief of Staff Chairman General Wheeler chimed in, delivering a speech claiming, "we are winning the war." But he added a caveat: it was possible the communists could attempt a last, desperate offensive like the Battle of the Bulge. General Westmoreland also sounded the alarm—U.S. intelligence reports indicated stepped up VC reconnaissance of potential targets in Saigon. He cabled Washington that communist forces had planned a countrywide effort to win the war.

In early 1968 intelligence indicated NVA units were on the move. Marine units like ours were shifting north to protect Khe Sanh and bolster other key combat bases in Quang Tri province. Our assumption for the past two months, based on occasional intelligence gleaned from higher headquarters, pointed to the possibility that my infantry battalion, 2/5, would wind up at the DMZ. The prolonged fighting in the DMZ had thinned out frontline units of the 3rd Marine Division.

On 30 January, the 2/5 headquarters group set up a command post in an abandoned railway tunnel near Phu Loc, south of Phu Bai, just off Highway 1. We prepared operational maps and installed needed communications equipment. There would be room in the tunnel for our personal gear and we would be protected from the elements, as well as from any enemy fire. But within hours, we would receive intelligence reports we found hard to understand.

Earlier that day, a Marine lieutenant led a routine convoy run from Da Nang to Hue. He had a few minutes to visit the Citadel and had his photo taken there by another Marine. Little did he know—he was likely walking among North Vietnamese and Viet Cong regulars wearing civilian clothes who had already begun to infiltrate the city.

A U.S. press release in Saigon reported an enemy order to attack lowland cities, including Saigon. Now predicting widening enemy attacks before or after Tet, Westmoreland ordered a redeployment of troops from mountainous border areas in the west to positions closer to Saigon. U.S. Ambassador Ellsworth Bunker and Westmoreland reported that communists could break their earlier-announced Tet truce. Westmoreland cabled Washington that the siege of Khe Sanh had reached a critical stage and could represent a turning point in the war. All U.S. military units were placed on maximum alert on 30 January, bracing for what appeared to be an approaching enemy offensive.

I was unaware of the disturbing detailed intelligence pointing to an imminent enemy offensive. Communist troops had moved within striking distance of more than 30 cities and large towns. The siege of Khe Sanh had begun 20 January, drawing the full attention of U.S. commanders to that remote base near the Laotian border in northern I Corps. North Vietnam had celebrated Tet on 29 January, a day earlier than elsewhere. On 30 January attacks began prematurely at Nha Trang, followed by strikes in two cities in I Corps and five in II Corps.

In the dark, early hours of the following morning, the NVA took over Hue. The extent of the attack in the imperial city came almost as a complete surprise to U.S. forces and pointed to a dire intelligence failure. Two fresh NVA regiments of about 5,000 regulars, with battle-hardened VC units, now occupied the entire city. One regiment took over the historic Citadel north of the Perfume River, the other occupied the southern half of Hue. Without an awareness of the situation other than fragmentary reports that parts of Highway 1 had been attacked, that morning the 1st Marine Division's Task Force X-ray in Phu Bai ordered Captain Meadows's Golf Company to proceed immediately to Hue, with other available small Marine units scattered in and around Phu Bai. Their mission: relieve the besieged ARVN base inside the Citadel and bring out the commanding general.

Golf Company Alert

Golf Company squad leader Barney Barnes recalled the hours before the communist takeover of Hue and the ensuing confusion. On 30 January

7. Hue   151

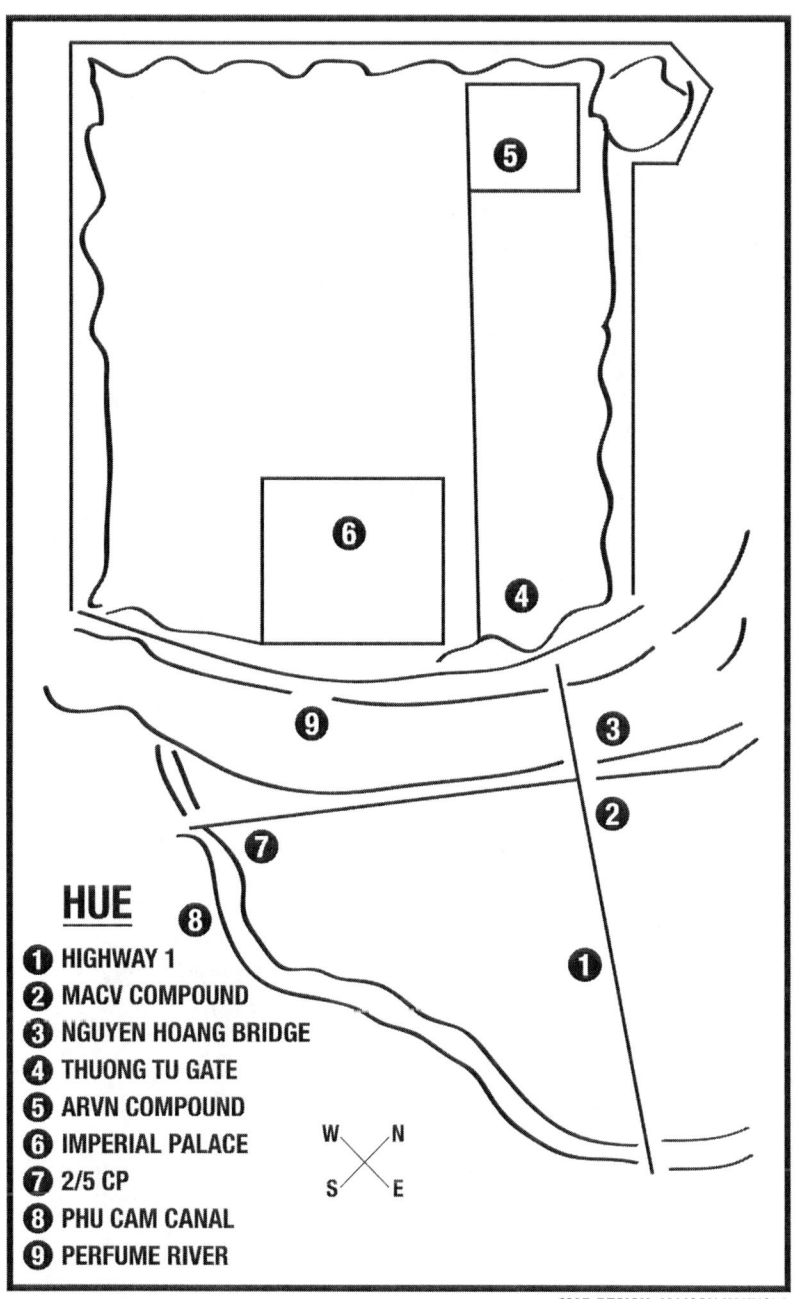

Map of Hue, graphic by Allison Kaukola.

Golf Company was the only infantry company assigned to Phu Bai, the "palace guard," under the operational control of First Battalion, First Marine Regiment (1/1), which had the overall mission of base security. The other companies of 2/5 were spread out miles along Highway 1 stretching south from Phu Bai to the Hai Van Pass, just north of Da Nang. Golf received orders to conduct a night march to Hill 230 west of Phu Bai. After dark, the company left Phu Bai base and arrived shortly after midnight the 31st. They tried to dig in defensive positions, but the rocks made the attempt futile. They adapted as best they could. Barnes remembers:

> Sometime around 0330 [31 January] several rockets streaked over our heads and landed in Phu Bai. Capt. Meadows called in the apparent location where the rockets came from to the 1/1 Command Post in Phu Bai. Golf remained on full alert the rest of the night. At daybreak the company left the hill and returned to Phu Bai.
> Arriving at our tent camp, we stowed our gear and went to breakfast. Rumors started making the rounds: An Hoa base was hit very hard and that we were flying back there to fight. No one was glad to hear that news. We did not want to go back to the "booby trap" capital of Nam. Then it was changed—we were going to Hue instead.
> We were elated, we had heard the stories about how Hue was a beautiful and modern city. I looked at my camera and realized I only had 12 shots left on my roll of film. With no time to go to the PX and with Hue being a big city, I was sure I could just buy some more film there. We were only going to be gone a couple of hours anyway.

Perilous Ride

Golf left Phu Bai about 1400 by convoy, unaware of what awaited. As they drew closer to Hue, Barnes saw no children playing, no normal activity. He grew suspicious and alarmed at the absence of what normally would have been a crowded road full of people. The company had just come off bridge security south of Phu Bai and knew what normal traffic patterns looked like. When U.S. military convoys passed through, "kids would come out of nowhere, gathering along the roadside hoping to get some food from Marines on the trucks." Now on Hue's southern outskirts, Golf Company started taking distant rifle fire. They headed for the MACV Compound, passing a burned-out ARVN Tank.

> Ten days later, on February 9, my squad would be ambushed on this very spot. That is the day we lost Tony Threet [KIA] and John Wayne Rowden [KIA], who were in Lester Tully's squad. John received the Silver Star for his actions that day.

As the company approached the city, it took heavier sniper fire, wounding the .50 caliber machine gunner on Barnes's truck. The convoy stopped. Under steady fire, Marines jumped off, helmets flying in all directions. Each Marine grabbed whatever "steel pot" he could find.

> We could see the NVA firing at us from across the paddies. We just didn't know what size force they were. We saw their gun positions and the NVA running around like ants, they were so far away.

Proceeding to a traffic circle, Meadows stopped again and took a map off the wall of a gas station, the only map of Hue available to Golf Company. The other side of the traffic circle led to a causeway, a long stretch of elevated road about 400 meters in length, rice paddies on either side, with Hue just ahead. Along the way, Golf came upon Alpha Company 1/1.

> They were pretty well shot to heck and back and I knew then, we all knew, that the intel that we received back in Phu Bai was nowhere near accurate. What we had been told about "a few NVA in Hue" was not correct, there were a whole bunch of them.

The causeway left the Marines exposed to enemy fire from the west side, but the raised berm afforded good cover. Golf proceeded under sniper fire toward MACV on foot, reaching the compound about 1600 hours. About two hours of daylight remained. (Ironically, and perhaps intentionally, today the MACV is now a Retirement/Nursing Home for NVA soldiers.) While the company rested outside, Meadows went inside for a short time then re-emerged. Calling for all his lieutenants, Meadows informed them Golf's mission remained: proceed to the 1st ARVN Division Compound and escort their commanding general back to Phu Bai.

Approaching Ambush Corner

Heavy sniper continued as the company proceeded toward the Citadel and an adjoining commercial area exposed to sporadic sniper fire.

> It was my first time to actually see NVA soldiers. I've always said that one of the blessings of that first day was that we did not know how large a force they were and how small a force we were in comparison. Was I scared? Yeah, I was, heart pounding, rapid breathing, adrenalin rushing, flat out fear. Fear of the unknown, but we didn't have time to think or dwell on it, we just reacted to the best of our abilities to overcome and carry on and try to accomplish our mission.

The company approached the Nyuyen Hoang Bridge that spanned the Perfume River. Second Platoon under Lieutenant Steve Hancock led the way and began to cross it. Two ARVN tanks sat parked at the southern foot of the bridge. Barnes climbed up on one tank and asked the occupants if they could lead Golf across the bridge. Terrified, aware of the overwhelming NVA force now in the city, they refused.

> Looking back, I wish now that I would have commandeered one of those tanks. Before becoming a grunt, I had been a Track Vehicle Repairman. I could have driven that tank across the bridge.

Barnes's squad crested the midpoint of the bridge and began to descend the slight incline toward the Citadel. An NVA machine gun opened up in a bunker at the left end of the bridge. Two Marines in front of Barnes were hit and went down. Barnes directed his squad to the right side of the bridge, out of the direct line of fire of the enemy machine gun. He crawled forward to identify its location. A Golf machine gunner opened up to counter the NVA weapon, but was killed and the assistant gunner wounded. As the NVA dueled with another Golf machine gun, Barnes and a second squad leader, Corporal Lester Tully, crept up close to the enemy bunker on the left walkway of the bridge. Tully stood up and hurled several grenades into the bunker as Golf Marines provided cover fire, killing all five NVA. Tully would receive the Silver Star for his act of heroism.

Ambush Corner

Lieutenant Mike McNiel's platoon took over the lead. McNiel recalled he had only 19 men, about half strength. His Marines turned a corner and headed cautiously down a street toward Thuong Tu Gate, which led to the Citadel. McNiel recalled he had three machine gun sections and one rocket launcher team. The area appeared deserted, eerily quiet. Not one civilian had been seen since before the company approached Hue. One of the squads moved slowly toward the gate on the left, or west, side of the street. A few trees were interspersed on the sidewalk. Peering ahead, the lead Marines had a seven-foot wall on their left. Another squad, with McNiel near the point, advanced on the east, commercial side of the street. Metal security grates barred entry to the shops. Both squads approached a moat in front of the gate.

Suddenly, as a North Vietnamese flag was hoisted on a flagpole atop the gate, at least one, probably more, automatic weapons opened up on the Marines. Withering machine gun fire swept both sides of the street. Corporal Lucas, only weeks from rotating back to the States, fell on the left side of the street with a fatal wound to his side. He tried to wave away corpsman Donald Kirkham, who, facing almost certain death, ignored the

7. Hue

Lieutenant Michael McNiel, An Hoa, December 1968.

warning and began to crawl to him. A moment later he too was struck, in the neck, by an enemy volley and died. In front of them, Private First Class Bill Tant took cover behind a tree. Captain Meadows paused at what would be called Ambush Corner, out of the line of fire pouring down the street from the gate. He had only moments to assess the gravity of the danger, weighing whether to push ahead with the company. He quickly sensed the threat, making it impossible to execute the orders given to him. He held up the Marines behind him.

On the commercial side of the street, the only cover was a one-foot-deep setback that led to the entrances of various shops. In the opening volley of enemy fire, a Marine in front of McNiel was hit in the stomach. McNiel stepped forward under fire and picked him up. Attempting to backtrack and return to the corner would have been tantamount to suicide. Instead, somehow McNiel, with one free arm, broke through a metal grate and ran through the shop to an alley that led back to Golf Company. The wounded Marine survived.

The firefight lasted five to ten minutes, but time stood still for the Marines, a nightmare blur. With several of his Marines on the street pinned down and unable to move, Meadows directed his men clustered near the corner to throw smoke grenades into the street. Under cover of the haze, an unknown Marine, not in the company, commandeered and drove a local truck down the street, exposed to enemy fire, and stopped. Meadows himself retrieved fatally-wounded machine gun team leader Lance Corporal Gerald Kinny, from McNiel's squad, and carried him back to the corner. Tant helped load the remaining casualties onto the truck and the vehicle backed down and around the corner.

At this point, Meadows radioed that he was withdrawing to the MACV compound. He had seen enough to know that any further attempt to enter the Citadel would be suicidal. He had taken enough casualties. He began to realize that the NVA now likely occupied the entire Citadel, and perhaps the rest of Hue, in overwhelming force. It had been a ferocious six hours since Golf left Phu Bai for what seemed to be an easy, if not routine, mission. Barnes describes the end of the nightmare this way:

> We loaded our 5 KIAs and 44 WIAs with covering fire of a US Army Quad 50 [four .50 caliber machine guns], and began our journey back across the bridge. We arrived at the MACV Compound around 1900. Tully's squad and mine set up for the night in a park, which ran along the river bank [near MACV]. It was a long, long night. We were scared and since we had been told not to bring chow, hungry too. I broke out the only thing I had, a pack of Chuckles Candy and shared them with Lester.

Tant recalled collapsing on a cot in a room in the MACV compound used by officers. He fell into an immediate deep sleep and lay undisturbed for hours. At one point he overheard Army officers discussing the unfolding situation in Hue. An Army colonel said, "Based on everything I've seen so far, it beats anything I experienced in World War II."

Tet Shockwaves

While Golf Company would fight for its life during the first few days of Tet, we in the battalion CP south of Phu Bai struggled to comprehend the scope and size of the surprise enemy offensive. Fragmentary radio reports from Hue sometimes confused and shocked us. I listened to encrypted radio transmissions summarizing the fighting, finding the reports tough to digest. Alarm turned to disbelief and back again. We had known an enemy offensive might be in the works, which I had detailed in my journal, but little more—no specific locations, no times, no idea of the scale. Marines around me in the railway tunnel also expressed repeated consternation and confusion. I made an effort not to reveal any negative emotion or make critical comments to those around me. I tried to project an upbeat, professional composure while keeping my thoughts private.

Reports of attacks on U.S. and RVN bases and population centers began to arrive. They too sounded grim and confused. Then we received intelligence updates of street fighting in Hue. "You've got to be kidding, what the hell is going on?" I muttered to myself repeatedly over the next few days. My shock slowly turned to anger—first towards the enemy and then towards our own apparent intelligence failures. I found situation reports describing the massive enemy force now holding the city hard to believe. Bullshit, I thought. Impossible. How could it happen? Hadn't we been winning the war? Hadn't our leaders back home told us victory had been within reach? Now this.

As it unfurled, the Tet Offensive marked a decisive turning point in the war, a seismic psychological shift. Reports of coordinated enemy attacks on U.S. bases throughout South Vietnam and the rising death toll during the Tet Offensive effectively extinguished any remaining optimism I had of an eventual military victory over the VC and NVA, at least on my watch. The enemy displayed a boldness and commitment I had not expected. For months, there had been a growing gap between the progress the Johnson administration had trumpeted to the public about the war and what we were experiencing on the ground. That now looked like the PR ploy it had been from the start—to shore up public support for the war, despite the stalemate. Now our own U.S. forces in Nam seemed, in part, to have been duped into believing victory was within our grasp.

I had bought into the notion of inevitable victory over the communist forces throughout my year of training, even as I understood after I arrived in-country that we faced a resourceful, tough enemy. I had observed not long after my arrival in August 1967 that others around me, in fact, also harbored questions about the conflict. When would it end? Not during our watch, it now seemed. What would victory look like? Defeating the enemy seemed ever elusive. The answers were far above my pay grade. Now with the Tet Offensive underway, from my optic, the victory I had once hoped was attainable, perhaps through perseverance, had now begun to fade.

Although the widespread Tet attacks set U.S. forces back on our heels for a short time, the offensive ultimately failed militarily, destroying the VC's ability to fight effectively going forward. We also dealt a grievous battlefield defeat to the NVA. The South Vietnamese people did not join communist forces and overthrow the Saigon regime. Despite the positive tactical outcome, the Tet Offensive provided further evidence to me that we had not at all crippled the communist forces' will to fight. Yes, as always, we would crush the enemy on the battlefield, but the shock of the enemy's surprising attacks lingered, weakening public support for the war back home. Mounting U.S. casualties would further erode support for the war. In-country, we continued to focus on mission and fighting the good fight, but our morale had taken a hit. At the time, I paid little to no attention to U.S. media commentary on Tet. A TBS 3-67 survey conducted in 2016 found that 77 percent of our classmate respondents thought U.S. media reporting on the Tet Offensive had a negative effect on our morale in-country. They also found the reporting accurate.

Awaiting the Call

Some of us waited in the tunnel for the call to join the battle in Hue after most of the battalion joined the fight. On 3 February 1968 the 2/5 Forward command group with the CO, primary staff, and three companies left for Phu Bai, then continued to Hue. As the assistant artillery liaison officer, I remained with what became the battalion reserve. It included the battalion XO, some headquarters elements (the "cats and dogs") and Echo Company. We were charged with assuring the security of Highway 1 between Phu Bai and Da Nang.

As information on the battle in Hue trickled in during those first few cold, wet days, it was the old refrain: I could never get warm. I listened to Armed Forces Radio, with its non-stop music completely detached from the war, and its news updates: periodic accounts of battles raging in other areas of Vietnam. Certain pop songs still trigger specific memories of that anxious, uncertain time and place for me. Two indelible "classics" played on Armed Forces Radio as those bleak, confusing days as the Tet Offensive unfolded. Listening to them, I sensed two Americas had begun to emerge. The songs came from different cultural places, perhaps emblematic of the political divide emerging back home between those who supported the war and those who opposed it. But I dug both tunes. The moody, ominous-sounding Box Tops song "The Letter," to me captured the uncertainty, gloom, and possible impending doom caused by the war. Released in September 1967, soon after I arrived in Vietnam, the song spent four weeks at #1, and was the ranked #2 of all pop songs in 1967. *Rolling Stone* magazine includes it in a list of the 500 greatest songs of all time. The other classic, released in December 1967, was the zany and happier "Simon Says," by the 1910 Fruitgum Company. It's message: don't worry, be happy.

More News from Hue

In the tunnel, the feeling of helplessness and confusion hung in the air. Stetson and Golf Company, I learned, were in the thick of it. Yet there

I sat, far from the battle. I wanted to be there with them. Fragmented reports from Hue in the first few days changed to more fulsome descriptions of the battle. The detail, while not all that encouraging, indicated some progress and helped to ease the uncertainty. I found time to write home on 4 February:

> Our month-long operation [south of Phu Bai] has been suspended for an indefinite period of time. For the past week we have not been fighting a guerrilla war, but a conventional one. Our battalion has been fighting in Hue and along Highway 1 between Phu Loc and Hue.
>
> Golf Company went north to Hue about five days ago to take the city held by an unknown enemy force of unknown strength. Golf never got into the Citadel. Only later did it become evident two enemy regiments held Hue and the Citadel and the Imperial Palace complex.
>
> Golf Company went up with 168 effective troops and yesterday morning [3 February] had 88 men still in the field. Foxtrot and Hotel are in Hue now with the forward CP. I am in the rear CP acting as Fire Support Coordinator—near Echo Battery. The rear CP and Echo Company, our remaining infantry unit, are not yet committed to Hue.
>
> We are south of Phu Bai. Phu Bai has been rocketed 8 times in the past 5 days. I was there during one of the attacks when we received four 140mm rockets.
>
> Last night was completely quiet, no units were in contact and no mortars fired at friendly units. We are [preemptively] firing artillery at a hill near us today [to clear brush and undergrowth that might conceal ethe enemy]; it is 494 meters high and towers right above us. It would be an excellent enemy mortar position.

That same ridgeline would be used by the NVA to deadly effect several months later, mortaring Echo Battery on the reverse slope to avoid direct counterbattery fire. Trying to sort out the earth-shaking events around me, I speculated on what the NVA strategy might be. My superficial take on the battle revealed how little I understood the complex strategies of both the communist and U.S. forces.

> The NVA could be launching the [Tet] offensive for two reasons. Either they actually believe they can defeat us in conventional warfare or they are trying to tie us down in the south for a gigantic push across the DMZ. Many seem to think the reason for all this is so they would have a bargaining element at the conference table. They are looking for a success.

Assault on Hue Central Hospital

On 5 February, 2/5 was ordered to take the NVA-fortified Hue Hospital complex. Lance Corporal Barnes recalled the enemy had forced the eviction of civilian patients and used the rooms and beds to treat their own wounded. Around 1500 hours, Golf Company started the attack on the main building of the strongly defended complex and engaged in a meter-by-meter battle with the NVA. While taking no fatalities during the initial assault, the company had five WIAs. Around 1600 the Marines managed to reach the interior of the main building. Although most NVA appeared to have fled the complex, for the next hour or so, Golf began the tough task of clearing each room. The Marines found four dead NVA inside and 25 or 30 wounded. The Marines thought additional enemy still remained in the hospital. An operating room contained fresh blood-soaked sheets, bandages, and other medical supplies. The NVA had clearly used it.

On a stairwell between the 1st and 2nd floors, a platoon sergeant passed two nuns on their way down the stairs. They bowed, and he bowed in return. When he looked up, he was staring at a pistol. The "nuns" were two NVA soldiers. One, with the pistol, tried to fire it, but it jammed. He threw it at the platoon sergeant and the NVA ran down the stairs toward the ground floor. The platoon sergeant, visibly shaken, alerted the Marines. The nuns reached the courtyard, their habits billowing in the wind, their Ho Chi Minh sandals barely touching the ground. Barnes and other Marines pursued them, but they quickly disappeared.

Progress

South of Hue in 2/5's reserve headquarters, news of fighting in the city had brightened as the days passed. On 6 February I wrote once again, wearing my grand strategist's hat. My optic still stemmed from a limited, superficial understanding of the ongoing Tet Offensive.

> The battalion has done very well for itself in Hue. The pictures of the fighting there are probably crowding the newspapers. I wanted to go there. It is a better place to fight than in the rice paddies. The Communist offensive, I feel sure now, is ebbing. They could have struck while the iron was hot and assaulted Khe Sanh and the DMZ. Still, the entire 1st Marine Division is tied down to the point where if a Communist drive threatened our positions near the DMZ, I doubt whether any Marines could come to their aid. I think the NVA are attempting to come to the conference table with a spoil to bargain with. I'd rather

think that than the possibility that the communists sincerely believe they can win a permanent military victory.

I was wrong, the communists were pursuing an eventual military victory, perhaps not in the short-term as they had planned, but on the expectation that the Tet Offensive would weaken American resolve in the longer term.

> I should become the official Arty Liaison Officer within a month. It is a trying job but, I hope, will be a rewarding one. Our battalion commander, Lt. Col. Cheatham, is a go-getter, at times too rash, I think.

Big Ernie, as he was nicknamed, stood well over six feet tall, weighing over 200 pounds. He had played defensive tackle with the Baltimore Colts and Pittsburgh Steelers. I would soon discover Cheatham could be an unrestrainable force of nature, a master of intimidation with Marines under his command, and an excellent field tactician. He barked at me—rather, at his artillery support—several times during the fight for Hue. Cheatham would receive the Navy Cross for his leadership in Hue and retired a lieutenant general.

Stand-Off in a Tunnel

After spending all of the 5th and the morning of 6 February clearing and taking back the many buildings of the Hue Hospital complex, which occupied a full city block, Golf Company prepared for its next objective, the Provincial Prison. The company found that NVA troops had escaped from the hospital, falling back a block farther west to the prison. Golf cleared, one by one, the structures between the hospital and the prison.

Barnes and several other Marines secured a building near the main prison building and waited for orders. He looked out the back window of the house and saw at least three NVA in a prison guard tower. He asked a Marine carrying a grenade launcher if he could hit the tower. Three rounds were fired, two of which hit the target. Later that evening, the Marines found two dead NVA there. After nearly three hours of constant pounding by our mortars and 106mm recoilless rifles, NVA resistance at the prison collapsed and the surviving defenders fled. Golf launched a final assault and found very little opposition. Counting the NVA in the guard tower, 36 enemy lay dead.

As the Marines scoured about, Barnes and another Marine found a hole in one of the prison walls with an NVA pack and a carbine rifle nearby. They widened the hole and crawled in. Once inside, they found a tunnel that branched off left and right from the entrance. They first crawled to the right, shining a flashlight ahead. Running into a dead end, they proceeded back to the entrance and began crawling to the left. Continuing about 30 feet, out of the pitch dark, they heard, "Don't Shoot. Me no NVA. Me no NVA." Barnes turned off the flashlight and flattened out on the ground, estimating the voice was about 30 feet down the tunnel. He tried to talk to the unseen person, but the response was the same, "Me no NVA, Me no NVA." Barnes tried to assure him that he was not going to shoot him, but that he needed to surrender. He did not want to fire his M16 in the cramped space. Five minutes of back and forth resulted in no progress. The Marines backed out of the tunnel and informed Captain Meadows, asking the CO to send an interpreter. Once the ARVN soldier arrived and assessed the situation, he refused to assist. Infuriated, Barnes had no other choice but to continue to clear the prison, thinking the company command group would resolve the situation.

The following morning, Meadows called for Barnes. On his way, Barnes was a nervous wreck. "Was he in trouble? What did he do? Was it the previous day's tunnel incident? What? What? What?" is all he could think about. Reporting to Captain Meadows, he learned the answer:

> The CO asked me how long I had been a LCpl. Squad Leader. When I replied, "since the middle of November, Sir," Meadows said that I was doing an excellent job and from this day on, I would be a Corporal Squad Leader!! Days later, when I was being interviewed by a news reporter, I was told that the guy inside the tunnel was indeed an NVA, a platoon sergeant. When I told the reporter about the incident and our dealings with the ARVN interpreter, I was told that he could not report that [the interpreter's refusal]!

Chasing the NVA

In a day-long operation south of Phu Bai on 7 February, Echo Company 2/5 and our reserve battalion command group pursued an NVA unit of unknown size during a steady, chilling, light rain. The NVA's mission had likely included cutting Highway 1, stopping the supply lifeline traffic from Da Nang to points north. Had the enemy accomplished a prolonged shutdown of traffic, it would have complicated efforts to resupply Marines engaged with enemy main force units in Hue.

The hunt followed a Marine ambush earlier that morning that killed six NVA in full combat gear walking casually down a trail toward Highway 1. By the time the command group and I reached the ambush site, Marines had stripped the corpses in search of any intelligence that might identify their units. They placed the bodies side by side to intimidate and demoralize the enemy. I understood the action might have had some possible tactical purpose or value, but it still seemed unjustified, unnecessary, and immoral to me. I recoiled at the disturbing sight of the bullet-riddled bodies. The dead appeared larger in stature than the friendly, diminutive South Vietnamese paramilitary Popular Forces I was used to seeing farther south. I wondered for a moment if the dead might have been Chinese military advisors, but they were more likely fresh NVA recruits—perhaps ethnic Chinese—sent south for the Tet Offensive.

Passing through the ambush site, we tracked the fleeing enemy for at least an hour at a quick walk, sometimes running. The NVA made no effort to turn and fight back. We must have been no more than minutes behind them. And they must have carried some of their dead and wounded with them as they fled: we found no additional bodies. The enemy had been well-equipped, prepared for the Tet Offensive. We stopped momentarily at times to retrieve discarded new equipment and ammunition. In a desperate attempt to evade Marines in hot pursuit, they left behind bloody bandages, torn clothing, unpacked mortar rounds in wooden boxes, AK-47s stored in cosmoline grease, B-40 rockets, assorted other ammo, and any materiel that would have slowed down their frantic escape. Eventually their trail petered out in the steady light rain. We returned to the railway tunnel empty-handed, but encouraged we had foiled probable NVA plans to cut Highway 1.

Horror in Hue

Perhaps the most compelling, graphic eyewitness account of what happened to the Hue populace during Tet has been written by a female Vietnamese journalist based in Saigon at the time. *Mourning Headband for Hue: An Account of the Battle for Hue, Vietnam 1968*, is written in a breathless, stream of consciousness style. Only recently translated into English, it is not for the faint of heart. Nha Ca arrived in Hue on the eve of Tet, late January 1968, to visit her parents and siblings. She was caught up in the vicious fighting for four weeks, unable to escape the battle. She returned to her husband and children in Saigon at the end of February 1968 and immediately began to write about what she saw, heard, and experienced. Some of her writing appeared in a Saigon newspaper weeks after the battle for Hue. Her book is an unforgettable account of innocent civilians caught up in war.

Unknown numbers of grunts returned home from Vietnam with permanent memories of seeing or experiencing similar atrocities to those that Nha Ca documented so vividly. What some of them saw in Hue haunts them to this day. Below are two such stories, personal recollections of

Barney Barnes, on bridge security duty, Highway 1, south of Phu Bai, January 1968. The Battle of Hue lay just ahead (courtesy Barney Barnes).

Barney Barnes. The events he describes occurred about 13–15 February 1968, around the time I arrived in the city. I was unaware of the events at the time, although they took place no more than about 500 meters away from where I was billeted with the battalion command post.

Barnes recalls:

> The railroad station was the first time that I witnessed the complete ruthlessness and total disregard for life that the NVA held, and the atrocities that they committed [in Hue]. Just after crossing the bridge and entering the railyard we saw a huge pile of dead bodies. There were at least 30 or more, mostly civilians that the NVA had massacred and just left to rot. The stench of the decaying bodies was terrible, so my squad was assigned by our lieutenant [a temporary replacement] the task of burning them. He had just arrived from another company in the battalion.
>
> I don't know if this order came from higher up in the chain of command or if it was the lieutenant's idea. It really didn't matter at the time, because the smell was so terrible and the sight of the piled-up bodies was so horrific,

something had to be done. We got three 5-gallon cans of diesel fuel and poured them over the bodies and lit it. All the while the lieutenant was snapping pictures with his camera and making jokes about the situation, which I thought was totally uncalled for. Those bodies burned for two days.

In another incident (shortly afterwards), Barnes and his squad had searched and cleared a house near the station. He went out the back door to look around.

To my horror, I found the body of a very young Vietnamese woman, probably in her twenties, lying in the backyard. The NVA had stripped her and cut her from her pelvis all the way up and pulled her skin back and off to the sides and laid her unborn baby beside her. A truly shocking image that remains with me even today.

The discoveries marked the first time that Golf Company had new replacements sent in. These new guys were more or less thrown into the thick of it without much instruction or teaching. I'm pretty sure that they arrived at Phu Bai one day and were off to Hue soon after that. So, for the most part, they learned on the run.

While at the Railway Station, Golf enjoyed its first chance to bathe and shave since mid-January—in the nearby Phu Cam Canal. Barnes reports,

It was here that the Company Gunnery Sergeant ordered us all to write home and let our parents know we were OK. I tore off the back side of a C-Rat Meal box and used that as a postcard and sent it home.

Hue, At Last

I finally arrived in Hue with the battalion reserve the afternoon of 14 February. We had been waiting two weeks to join the fighting and received a 12-hour notice before leaving. I had had enough of life in and around the tunnel. I wanted a piece of the action in Hue. We stayed on high alert as we traveled north; our jarring journey in trucks traveling at high speed on the pot-holed road was mercifully uneventful. Since Tet began, NVA troops had attempted to shut down traffic at various points on the highway. Our small convoy skirted Phu Bai then navigated a bleak countryside of endless rice paddies on both sides of the road as far as the eye could see. The devastation inflicted on the city after two weeks of fighting became evident when we reached the southern suburbs—few buildings appeared untouched by the fighting, rubble strewn everywhere. Stretches of city blocks lay in partial ruin, the streets empty. Where had the people gone? A faint stench hung in the air. We drove through empty streets to the Hue University medical school faculty apartments, close to the railway station and the Perfume River that separated the city from the Citadel and Imperial Palace complex.

The battalion command post had been set up on the second floor of what had once been a well-maintained apartment building. It seemed secure enough, I thought, as I dismounted from the bed of the deuce-and-a-half truck, a 2½ ton workhorse. A low-walled courtyard around the multistory building provided some additional security, but the upper levels of the building were exposed to potential sniper fire.

As I ascended the steps to the mostly empty building, I could hear intermittent small arms and machine gun fire in the distance. Without electricity, the apartment lay in ruins, plaster chipped off the walls, any furniture that had been there destroyed or taken out. To be sure, no housecleaner had reported for duty that afternoon, and the former occupants were nowhere to be seen. I walked through an open door into what appeared to be the former living room, now emptied of everything, a cluttered billeting space for headquarters personnel. No one there, I entered another—the former kitchen—containing windows on the far wall that overlooked a levelled neighborhood.

Amidst the debris, a piece of civilization stood out, untouched, on the floor. Marines had been walking over and around it for days. Partially covered by shards of broken glass, plaster, and splinters of wood, lay a clean, hardback copy of Hemingway's *The Old Man and the Sea*. I picked it up, reverently, and placed it on a counter. I did not want it damaged. To me, the book represented a symbol of hope in a savage war. An indestructible symbol of man's better nature had survived, untouched by upheaval and death.

What had become of the educated professionals who once lived there, I wondered? Once I saw the book, I had instant respect and admiration for them. I wished I had known them. I also mourned for them. Had they been rounded up and killed during the first hours of the city's occupation by the NVA? Perhaps they had been forced to treat the enemy wounded. I hoped they would be able to return to their apartment, but had strong doubts that they had survived. I walked back out into the quiet living room. I would occupy it, along with about fifteen other Marines, for the next two weeks. We all slept on the floor, each pile of gear marking a small staked-out temporary living space.

I kneeled down and began to remove items from my pack, discovering to my alarm that I was now without a camera. In the thick of what would later become regarded as a landmark battle of the Vietnam War, I would be unable to make a visual record of any of it. Words would have to suffice. Sometime after I left Phu Bai with the battalion weeks before, my compact Yashica camera had gone missing from my bag of belongings. I had made a habit of not carrying the camera around with me. It was something else to look after, so I kept it in a small, waterproof bag. I tried to shrug off the disappointment. It wasn't the time or place to dwell on the loss. Besides, as the battle evolved, I would not have the stomach to take any photos in Hue. Nor would I be motivated to take many more images after that for the remainder of my tour. What bothered me was a nagging question—had a fellow Marine stolen it? I didn't want to think so.

Hours after my arrival, I wrote:

> I am in Hue now. Last night we got word the battalion reserve would leave this morning for Phu Bai and that we would be in Hue by early afternoon. It happened, and I'm glad. Finally got here.
>
> The battle for the city is not all over or near completion. We have fairly well succeeded in securing the southern half of the city. Hue is divided by a river. On the northern side six battalions of South Vietnamese are battling the NVA. Everyone here doesn't expect this battle to end for two weeks at least.
>
> My battalion has lost a great many Marines, including junior officers. Hotel Company today was without an officer; a gunnery sergeant was leading the company. Foxtrot Company has had one officer killed, one wounded. My old company, Golf, has lost two wounded lieutenants.

Stetson in Hue

The officer FO pipeline appeared to diminish and dry-up as the months passed. The Marine Corps had been unable to produce the required numbers of junior artillery officers to replace those killed, wounded, or rotated back home. The pressing need for junior infantry officers to replace casualties resulted in a reduction in numbers of TBS officers who would have been assigned to other military occupational specialties, such as artillery. In addition, a worsening recruiting climate back home for the junior officer pipeline resulted in unfilled quotas. Arty lieutenants arriving in Nam seemed to have been rushed north to backfill those killed and wounded. To fill the gap, enlisted FOs like Stetson began to lead FO teams.

In early 1968, I had left Golf Company on the expectation I would soon return to the field. It didn't happen. The battalion commander wanted two arty officers. Another lieutenant was unavailable to take over my duties as FO in Golf Company. Stetson stepped up. I had full confidence in him. I had one concern, but could do nothing about it. An arty lieutenant had the rank to deal with grunt officers as an equal. A lieutenant

FO could shield his team from watch duties with the grunts. The FO teams had their own arty net watch. In addition, an arty lieutenant could advise when and how to employ artillery without being directed by grunts who might have little experience themselves in calling in arty fire missions. As a lance corporal, Stetson would be subject to pressure from grunts of higher rank. His inclination was to help and accommodate others when needed or asked. I hoped he would not be taken advantage of by grunt officers. In Hue, Stetson had called in night time illumination missions, and perhaps some high explosive fire missions. But for the most part, he fought essentially as a rifleman while the battalion gradually pushed the NVA located south of the Perfume River—street by street—into the western suburbs of the city. I would see him for the last time three days after my arrival in the city.

Precision Destruction Mission

The morning of 17 February, elements of First Battalion, Fifth Marines (1/5) were pinned down, struggling to breach the 20-foot high, 15-foot thick Citadel wall. In a futile effort to assist them, I was directed to attempt a rare eight-inch howitzer Precision Destruction artillery mission. The cannon was the most accurate artillery piece in the inventory. Its 200-pound High Explosive projectile could inflict great damage and had the technical capability to hit a point target with consistency. The objective that morning? To destroy enough of the wall to enable Marines to enter and engage the NVA defenders. But any attempt to breach a section of the wall amounted to mission impossible. I considered the fire mission a desperate measure, an effort I knew could not be successful. I thought at the time it amounted to a probable folly conjured up by senior officers, somewhere, to make it appear Task Force X-ray was making every effort to support the assaulting Marines. I did not object to the mission when I received it, but feared it might endanger attacking Marines pinned close to the outer wall. Neither was it likely the attacking Marines welcomed the fire mission. Some of them were reportedly dug-in less than a hundred meters from the wall.

I took a small vehicle, with a driver for security, to a point near the Perfume River, overlooking the southeast corner of the Citadel. I could not see the pinned-down Marines. Informed they were sufficiently distant from the Wall, but unaware of their exact location, I called in the Danger Close fire mission on the arty radio net. I held my breath and silently prayed when I heard the battery relay, "Shot, Over," on the radio. The driver and I crouched down behind our vehicle. Moments later the artillery round screamed down to earth about 1,000 meters away. It appeared to impact just short of the wall, spraying some attacking Marines with rock and concrete, but not seriously wounding any of them. A small correction in the gun's deflection or elevation might have resulted in a second round striking the wall, but I received an immediate, "Check Fire, End of Mission." I breathed easier. Numerous direct hits on the thick wall would likely have done little to damage it enough for the assault to reach the Citadel.

Last Meeting with Stetson

I returned to the 2/5 headquarters compound, relieved I did not have to conduct further missions with Marines so close to the target. As I stepped out of the vehicle in the courtyard of the CP, I saw a shirtless, wounded Marine lying alone on a stretcher about twenty feet away. I walked over and looked at him in disbelief. It was Stetson. "What happened?" I blurted out. Pale, but conscious and lucid, he looked at me and managed a weak smile. Stetson said he had been shot. He pointed to a small entry wound to his upper right abdominal area. He had been cleaned up and was not bleeding. In a muted, but clear voice he said, "Don't worry, lieutenant, I'm going to be all right." Standing there, I could say no more, neither did he, as he turned his head away from me.

Seeing my anguish, he had tried to calm and reassure me. Typical of Stetson—always thinking of others. I only hope I provided some measure of comfort to him in return. As I stood by unable to talk further, within seconds, it seemed, a Marine driver and a Navy corpsman appeared and placed Stetson in a truck. I watched, dazed and silent, as it sped away to the helicopter landing pad. After several minutes staring at nothing in particular and unable to move, I became aware of my surroundings and slowly walked up the stairs to the battalion CP. I stood alone in a darkened room trying to process what I just seen. I found it difficult to think. It was all a blur as I dealt with the anguish. I wanted to cry out in despair and grief. I later learned Ken survived the short flight to Phu Bai, but died soon after arrival at the medical aid station, trying to dictate a letter to his wife, Jan. Someone later told me Ken did not get beyond a couple sentences. I don't know what happened to the note; Jan did not receive it.

Over the years I have thought countless times of my last meeting with Ken Stetson. Divine Providence must have enabled our encounter. Can mere chance explain our minute together?

Courtyard, Hue University Medical School, Faculty Apartments, February 2008. The entrance to the Second Battalion, Fifth Marines Command Post, is visible. The palm tree is the approximate location of my final meeting with Lance Corporal Stetson on 17 February 1968.

Conversation with Captain Meadows

Hours after I saw and spoke with Stetson for the last time, I could respond if spoken to, but little else. My actions and reactions seemed mechanical, on autopilot. I wept inside. I wanted to scream out in anger, but did not. Any display of emotion would have been unacceptable. Marines, especially officers, could not cry out. So, I stifled deep mourning and guilt that lingers to the present day. It happened. I had to accept it. Had I not been assigned to battalion headquarters as the second arty liaison officer, I would have gone into Hue with Golf Company at the start of the Tet offensive. It could have—maybe should have—been me, not Ken, who leaned out a window and took a shot to the gut.

That night, after a battalion planning meeting for the next day's operations, I intercepted Meadows before he left the command post. Unshaven in over two weeks, his utility uniform soiled like all the other grunts, he looked exhausted. He had experienced the loss of dozens of casualties in his company. Meadows understandably had critical things to do then. We were in the thick of an epic battle. Under clear strain himself from weeks of street fighting—but being a compassionate officer and a good man—he gave me a few moments. He paused and looked at me when I approached him. We spoke before he descended the stairs of the apartment.

I told him, given Stetson's death, I was available to step in as FO with Golf Company, if he needed me. I had no idea what his response might be, nor did I consider at the time that I could not unilaterally suggest any such reassignment without having the prior approval from my own artillery chain of command. Still, I felt compelled to volunteer, it was the least I could do. I experienced disappointment, mixed with relief, from Meadows's response. He looked straight at me without expression as I managed to get my words out. What did he see, I have since asked myself? Did he think he saw fear—maybe a coward? He replied that he appreciated the offer, but he did not need an FO at that stage of the battle. Meadows then took a few moments to tell me how well Stetson had acquitted himself during his time in Hue. It came as no surprise to me. Always optimistic and looking to help his fellow Marine, Stetson volunteered to take much-appreciated radio watches for the grunts, Meadows recounted. Our brief meeting then ended and the captain hastened to return to his company.

Dissecting this exchange many times in recent years—near obsessively—I have wondered, what were the thoughts behind the captain's response? Did he think he had no need of an arty FO? I prayed that was the reason. Or did Meadows not respect my FO skills in the field? Or, perhaps, worst of all, did he decide to tell me what I hoped he would? I had an opportunity to revisit this important, but confused, memory with Meadows in a 2008 visit back to Nam and again in 2009 at a reunion, but did not raise it. Perhaps I did not want to hear the answer he might give, but honestly, as I recall, it just never crossed my mind then to ask.

For decades I had wrongly blamed Meadows, in part, for Stetson's death. I have questioned—with some bitterness over the intervening years—if Stetson's presence with the grunts in Hue was needed. Was it critical? From the onset of the fighting, there were constraints and limits to the effectiveness of artillery support in an urban environment. Mortars were effective, but not so much large caliber artillery, as the fighting raged at close quarters. Angered that his death could have been averted, I thought Stetson had served in Hue more as a grunt rifleman than as an FO. But over time I have come to accept the doctrine and tradition that dictates every Marine is, first, a rifleman. The FOs deploy with the infantry units they support and if they become riflemen while doing so, it goes with the turf. Some FO lieutenants I knew in training at Fort Sill had been killed in the field as well, fighting much like the grunts they supported—they were Basic School classmates, lieutenants Hank Norman, Charlie Ryberg, Dennie Peterson, and Ted Edwards. Given what happened to Stetson, it has been difficult for me to accept it was his duty to be there with his grunts. I'm sure Stetson must have understood and accepted this. After conversations with several Marines, more than 50 years later, I have pieced together information on what might have happened the day we lost Stetson. I had to know.

Firefight in a Colonial-era Villa

An entry in the 2/5 Command Chronology for 17 February 1968, the day Stetson was killed in action, reads:

> From 1047h until 1705h 2/5 Marines were plagued with incidents involving sniper fire, automatic weapons fire and B-40 rockets, 60mm mortars and 82mm mortars. 120 rounds of 81 mortars were returned on suspected enemy mortar positions. 2 USMC KIA, 20 USMC WIA, 10 NVA/VC KIA.

That brief entry was by any standard an understatement. The abbreviated notation indicates what had to be a major firefight, but there was much more detail to know other than these sterile casualty numbers and the terse description of the fighting that actually took place that day. The two fallen Marines noted in the chronology were Golf Company's Corporal David Warner and Lance Corporal John Lewis. A third Marine, killed in the same firefight, had not been included in the report because he was a Marine attached to the company, an artillery FO. Lance Corporal Ken Stetson was KIA the same day. For decades I had not pursued the details of that fearsome firefight that claimed Stetson's life. I had been told the day I saw him for the last time that he had been shot leaning out of a window firing his M16 at the enemy when he was struck in the abdomen by an NVA soldier firing an AK-47 from a Spider Hole, a hidden fighting position. I had left it at that. But in 2021, I pursued additional information on events concerning Stetson's death.

About mid-day Captain Meadows and Lieutenant McNiel moved southwest from the Hue railway station through a cane field, toward a wooded area. Unknown to them, a tree line ahead obscured a heavily defended NVA command and control center for the enemy's tactical operation in Hue. An ambush and intense firefight ensued. Warner and Lewis were both shot and killed at the outset, near a colonial-era villa. Seven other Marines were wounded at the villa. According to information provided by Private First Class Tant, before the ambush McNiel (who, during the firefight, took a round to his flak vest, over his heart, and survived) was approached by an unidentified Marine (likely Stetson), with his radioman (likely Raub). The Marine reportedly told McNiel that Meadows had directed him to provide artillery support to McNiel's platoon, if required, as his platoon advanced toward the tree line. In the ambush and ensuing firefight, those two Marines—almost surely Stetson and Raub—had taken cover with other Marines, including Tant, on the ground floor of the villa.

As the firefight developed, Stetson was hit when an NVA rose and fired from a Spider Hole, Tant said. Stetson returned fire and reportedly killed the enemy soldier. After helping carry Warner and Lewis to the street for evacuation, Tant rushed back to Stetson's aid and put him on his back. Conscious and lucid, Stetson told Tant—who was a wiry 130 pounds—that he was too heavy, that Tant couldn't manage it. Tant said yes, he could do it. He proceeded to carry Stetson, who held on to Tant's suspender straps, about fifty meters to the company CP. Following initial triage from a corpsman, Stetson and other wounded Marines were rushed to the Battalion Aid Station. Subsequently, I saw Stetson in the courtyard and had the opportunity to talk with him moments before he was taken away and medevaced to Phu Bai. Raub, now without Stetson, maintained the artillery battery frequency for the remainder of the operation. He was wounded sometime near the end of the fight for Hue and I never saw him again.

O.K. Steele

It's remarkable how fragments of a conversation at a certain time can linger for a lifetime. I stumbled through the next few days, shaken by Ken Stetson's loss. During that period, I had a memorable encounter with the newly-arrived battalion Executive Officer, Major Orlo K. Steele, known as O.K. Steele. Steele was a warrior, and like Captain Meadows, a compassionate human being. My long-remembered exchange with him took place near dusk one evening, in his jeep. I had accompanied him on a reconnaissance of the mostly secure area around the battalion headquarters. I cannot recall if he asked me to go with him or if I was directed to ride as security. Not far from our headquarters, Steele asked his driver to stop the vehicle. We sat in silence for a minute or so at an intersection between the battalion CP and the Perfume River. It was quiet, getting close to twilight. The streets were empty. Steele turned to speak to me as I sat in silence in the back seat of the jeep. In a casual manner I had not experienced dealing with a senior officer since OCS, he asked how I was doing. He inquired about my background before joining the Marines and listened attentively as I spoke. We talked a little about the operation in Hue. A short time later we drove back to the CP.

The brief exchange made a profound impression on me. What a great leader. During an epic battle, a senior officer took the time to talk with a lieutenant trying to hide his grief. Over the years, I've wondered about the conversation. Maybe Steele just thought he needed to get away for a while. Had he asked me to accompany him at someone's advice, perhaps Meadows? Or was he just passing time, the more likely possibility. How and why was I there with him? Regardless of Steele's motivation, I consider our meeting a genuine, simple act of human kindness.

In 1987, while on reserve duty at Camp Lejeune, I saw then Major General Steele leaving a building. I intercepted him, saluted and greeted him, and stated who I was. "We were in Hue together," I noted. He remembered me, or at least he said he did. "Of course," he replied, with a smile. He paused to talk for a few light-hearted moments, as his aide and driver stood by. He then entered his staff car and drove off. Steele punched all the right tickets in a distinguished military career. A graduate of Stanford University, after Vietnam, a CO of Marine Barracks 8th and I in Washington and CG of Second Marine Division. He was decorated for valor for his service in Vietnam

Unexpected Notice

Sometime about mid- to late–February, as the fighting in Hue proper began to subside, my battery informed me that I had been selected to fill a quota to attend a one-month battalion embarkation course in Okinawa in March. I was directed to report to my battery in Phu Bai no later than 26 February, proceed to Da Nang, then board a military flight to Okinawa to attend the course, which would begin in early March.

I learned through talking with others who had completed the course that students were actually not expected to load their battalion's equipment on a Navy ship without expert assistance. Professionals who specialized in embarkation would take responsibility. That was a good thing. Attendees viewed the course more as an extended R&R than anything else. Why I was identified to attend is unclear to me, but I was between assignments, the most likely explanation. It was time for me to leave the field with the grunts and return to the firing battery. Others I met in Okinawa noted they too were between assignments when they filled the same quota. I would return to my artillery battery upon completion of the embarkation course.

Another Night Move

By 24 February the NVA had been pushed out of the close-in western suburbs of Hue, headed for the mountains. Our intelligence indicated an NVA battalion had dug in south of the city to slow any Marine pursuit of enemy main forces in retreat and determined to inflict as many casualties as possible before attempting to evade our pincer movement. In the early morning hours that day, 2/5 would execute an unusual, risky, night movement from the Hue University area to the southwestern outskirts of the city. The objective: interdict and destroy fleeing NVA fighters trying to reach the hills west of the city. When I first heard about the planned Search and Destroy op, I thought a dreaded battalion night maneuver sounded like far too much of a gamble.

Hours before daylight, I experienced a reflexive anxiety of the unknown, the shadows, and the unseen, as I saddled up, placing a full, 30-pound pack on my back. I thought back to Golf Company's bold night movement months before. At that time, it seemed miraculous that we had surprised a number of NVA troops billeted in the village early that morning. Maybe we would have similar success. But that had been a company operation; a more complicated battalion night tactical move seemed a different order of magnitude, with much more room for error, perhaps more vulnerable to detection by the enemy.

We began to move out about 0200 hours. I had not slept earlier. Surely, I thought, all of Hue would hear us moving through the quiet, empty streets. As the headquarters group got underway, I cringed hearing what seemed deafening noise of equipment banging, boots kicking stones and crunching debris. A few dogs began to bark. I feared the clatter had to alert any enemy still hidden there. I thought of the sure mayhem that would result if the battalion were taken under fire. Despite the racket, we encountered no hostile resistance, a fear calmed.

The daring and effective nighttime movement must have taken any NVA or VC left in the area by total surprise, I thought, as fear of an enemy ambush subsided. But perhaps not. As the enemy's main force scrambled to get out of Hue, I worried, small enemy cells might be left behind to delay the advancing Marines. They might hesitate to oppose a large Marine force on the move, but be inclined to take on a smaller group of Marines.

I had no idea of the tactical and logistics planning that had preceded our night move. From the 24 February 2/5 Command Chronology:

> A jump Battalion Aid Station was established to support a Search and Destroy operation. At the primary BAS in Hue, walking wounded [from the battalion night move and subsequent encounters with the enemy] could be put in holding wards for 24–48 hours and returned to their respective companies.

The Command Chronology noted that official manning levels of the battalion during the month in Hue were in the (implausible) high 80 percent range. Five different memorial services had already been held at the company level, when time allowed, earlier in the month. True, fresh casualty replacements had been pouring into Hue, but all without any field experience.

The Beauty of Vietnam

We crossed the Phu Cam Canal that divided the city proper from the sparse southern suburbs. Demolished buildings gave way to empty, damaged huts as daylight broke. The companies fanned out and began to arrive at designated checkpoints. Following a stop for water and a breather, Cheatham directed the Air Liaison Officer and me—along with our radio operators and a rifle squad as security—to set up on Hill 103 (103 meters elevation) to observe the battalion's planned sweep to the west. We were to call in artillery and air missions on any enemy we spotted attempting to flee the battalion's advance.

Our casual climb up the hill proved uneventful, although I learned years later that the NVA had used the summit for surveillance during the first days of the occupation of Hue. We were fortunate it had not been booby-trapped. Reaching the top, the squad set up a defensive perimeter. Soon the sun broke through, drying out uniforms soaked by steady drizzle for three weeks, and providing welcome warmth. We took advantage of a relaxed several hours filled with humorous banter. It helped soften the intensity of the battle that the grunt squad had already experienced in the city. They were dog-tired but alert and energized.

In Nam, I was struck repeatedly by the country's breathtaking beauty. The summit offered a panorama of the surrounding area. It would have been a striking spectacle under peacetime circumstances, but still an awe-inspiring sight despite the scattered devastation. Indeed, Nam during the war was a country of stunning contrasts—savage fighting among incredible lush vistas, quiet beauty juxtaposed against ear-splitting violence. At some point early on in my tour, dazzled by the promising splendor, amidst ferocious fighting, I swore I would someday return to what would be a peaceful country, absorb the scenery, and know the Vietnamese better. Forty years later I returned.

Close Call

After several hours scanning the area with binoculars, we observed no enemy, only an occasional glimpse of our maneuvering companies. Our idyllic interlude ended with instructions to rendezvous with the battalion command group as soon as we could do so. Days later I described the ensuing events:

> Before I forget, day before yesterday I nearly "bought my lunch" as they call it here. On the morning of 24 February, the air officer and I and our radios and squad security setup on a Hill 103 to observe the battalion's advance.
>
> We were called down at 1400 hours. Our planned route traversed a large cemetery, an area we assumed would have been secured earlier by the battalion. Wrong. We moved down the hill in single file, following a winding footpath. When we reached the bottom, headstones of raised graves extended on both sides of the path.
>
> Going up a trail, an automatic weapon opened up 30 meters in front of our point man and fired a burst up our ranks, but luckily hit no one. My radioman took cover behind me out of earshot.
>
> We scattered on each side of the trail behind the graves. How we avoided casualties from the initial burst of fire seemed like a miracle. The incoming fire was steady and had us pinned down. To my alarm, the Marine carrying my radio had bolted in one direction and I in the other. He was then about 15 meters behind me. Over the incoming fire, he could not hear me to transmit a fire mission.

Unable to move, I could hear streams of rounds buzzing inches over my head. The enemy machine gunner appeared to have identified my location. The fire now came in short bursts, the gunner apparently conserving rounds. Hugging the ground, I dared not try to look over a headstone to locate the source of the fusillade. The squad with me could not move either as fire raked the area, preventing any suppressive, return fire. At such close proximity to the automatic weapon, unable to move or identify its position, we stayed where we were for what I estimated was about five to ten minutes. The only way out, I concluded, was to call in artillery as soon as possible.

Luckily, the squad leader's radioman, on the battalion net, had taken cover within shouting distance. Through him I called in a Danger Close fire mission. I had no idea of the size of the NVA element blocking our path. I could not determine if we faced just one weapon or more than that, but knew our response must be one of overwhelming force to eliminate the threat. I placed the initial white phosphorous marking round about 100 meters from our position, in the area I thought the enemy would move once the fire mission began. The radioman repeated my request for fire, sent first to the battalion commander's radio then relayed to the firing battery in support. I feared the relayed fire mission would add critical minutes to the battery's response time, but clearly understanding the urgency, the supporting battery's Fire Direction Center notified us, "Shot, Over," in no time at all.

> *After 20 minutes of screaming (I've lost my voice) I finally succeeded in getting a mission called in. The first marking round was immediately on target and I Fired for Effect. We fired WP after HE [High Explosive rounds] and, under a cloud of white smoke, got out. I dropped a total of 40 WP and 70 HE rounds. I hope that was the last fire mission I'll have to call in.*

The enemy fell silent. Given the destruction of the area generated by the artillery rounds, I doubt they could have survived. Dense smoke from the WP rounds masked our movement for several minutes. We hurried to the battalion command group without wasting a moment. Miraculously, we managed to evade the ambush without a casualty.

Within minutes we had reached the battalion CP. Not a word was said by Lieutenant Colonel Cheatham or any of the battalion staff. I had not expected a warm "welcome home" committee. I understood the command group was occupied in the moment, focused on pursuing an enemy frantic to escape. But the deafening silence at our return seemed to underscore what I had come to sense was the battalion commander's disregard for the artillery support he received. I did not call in another fire mission with the grunts. But I have taken pride that the results of this last, harrowing one—with lives on the line—was, by my standards, near-perfection.

Blowback Back Home

Let us return to the immediate aftermath of the 1968 Tet Offensive. Within days after it began, other than the continuing battle in Hue, it had become evident the enemy offensive would fail. Nearly all attacks were quickly repulsed by U.S. and South Vietnamese troops, damaging the Viet Cong's infrastructure and, due to combat losses, its ability to sustain future attacks against ARVN and U.S. forces. The South Vietnamese populace did not rally to its cause. A Viet Cong secret report captured months later concluded its military successes were limited. A separate communique assessed that the offensive was a good start, but further efforts were required to attain victory. The near-destruction of VC main force units would mark the nearly full transition to North Vietnamese regulars.

Despite its failure to achieve its battlefield objectives, the communist offensive put the Johnson Administration in a position of having to further justify its policy in Vietnam. In a February press conference, President Johnson stated the offensive had been a total failure. General Westmoreland, however, requested the deployment of 200,000 more troops to Vietnam. When the request was made public, it stirred fresh opposition to the war. The Administration balked. Chairman of the Joint Chiefs General

Earl Wheeler offered Westmoreland only the 82nd Airborne Division and the 27th Marine Regimental Landing Team. Westmoreland accepted them. Previously planned deployments of U.S. forces in South Vietnam would reach nearly 550,000 by the summer of 1969, but then decline.

The repercussions of the battle in Hue rippled through the American public. Influential journalist Walter Cronkite visited Hue during the late stages of the battle and commented that the war appeared to be a stalemate. It was a resounding U.S. military victory in the imperial city, but the costs were high—220 U.S troops and 400 South Vietnamese troops killed, an estimated 5,000 NVA and VC, and as many as 6,000 civilians killed, an estimated forty percent of the buildings in Hue destroyed.

A Harris Poll taken in mid–February revealed a short-lived surge of support for the war in the immediate wake of Tet attacks. But a Gallup poll taken about the same time found half of the public disapproved of Johnson's handling of the war, 35 percent approved, the rest were undecided. While the Tet Offensive marked a crushing military setback for communist forces, and the VC virtually decimated as a fighting force for an extended period, the Johnson Administration concluded there was a limit to the continued escalation of the war. Plans for a gradual reduction of U.S. forces, the Vietnamization of the conflict, and a search for a negotiated peace would begin.

I viewed the Tet Offensive as a clear turning point in the war, stunned the enemy could muster such a wide show of coordinated force. Previously I had hoped we could win the war, but now I thought victory a longshot, probably out of reach. Along with that, I understood I was likely living through a critical period in the Vietnam conflict. Facing another six months of concealing growing despair, I wanted my tour to be over.

8

Decompression and Reflection

Dash with Wounded Marines

I began to make my way from the field south of Hue the afternoon of 25 February. I would overnight at the battalion command post, followed by a night in Phu Bai at my battery, then proceed to Da Nang to board a flight to Okinawa. Hue appeared secure at the time, but the NVA south of the city continued to fight. The enemy would inflict casualties on 2/5 and our advance enough to allow most of the NVA to escape. Earlier that day we had overtaken and engaged with a unit of unknown size. As Golf and Hotel pressed the attack, I was released from the field, hopping an ammo resupply truck headed for Hue.

We first stopped at the Jump Battalion Aid Station at the edge of the battlefield. I found a group of corpsmen and the primary battalion surgeon working feverishly over six fresh casualties. Some were wounded more gravely than others. All required triage and immediate evacuation to the primary Battalion Aid Station in Hue, manned by a newly arrived doctor from the States. I stood aside some distance, but within earshot, watching the surgeon work on one of the badly wounded Marines. After a few minutes, the doctor shook his head in frustration. I heard him tell a corpsman there was little he could do for at least two of the casualties. I recoiled when I heard it. What did he mean? Were they beyond saving or did they require more advanced medical aid than he could give them? I didn't know, but feared the worst. "Don't throw in the towel," I wanted to shout. "Save them! Let them live along with the others!" At the time, I thought it unjust, the doctor cruel for having said it. Could the wounded Marines hear what he said? I later came to understand, however, that he had little choice but to focus on those he knew he could treat there.

A few minutes later I sat in the bed of the deuce-and-a half truck with the wounded. I avoided looking directly at them. All appeared alive, a couple unconscious. I ached to hear their moans. As we began to roll toward Hue, it occurred to me that if ambushed on the way, we would be effectively defenseless. I assumed the driver had a weapon and I had my rifle and pistol. During the fifteen-minute dash to the main Battalion Aid Station on a rough dirt road, one of the badly wounded Marines, with multiple fragmentation wounds to his face and arms, suddenly sat up. It startled me, as he had earlier appeared to be unconscious. Pale, his head and face pock-marked with numerous black-colored, small shrapnel wounds, he turned his head and stared at or through me, wild-eyed with fear, and asked, "Am I going to make it?" It seemed to be an almost rhetorical question directed, perhaps, at no one in particular. How did he summon the strength or willpower to ask?

Without hesitation, I tried to calm him. "You'll make it, don't worry," I replied in a self-assured voice. I wanted my words to calm him, but did they? I'm not sure they even registered. Perhaps he could not hear me. I flashed back to my last exchange with Stetson days before. If I had had the power to cure and prevent anyone from dying, I would surely do it. He reclined again, closed his eyes, and remained quiet until we reached Hue. Arriving at the battalion CP, I jumped from the truck to avoid getting in the way of the casualties as corpsmen worked to clear and treat them. I hope they all made it.

The following morning, the 26th, I boarded a small, three-truck convoy bound for Phu Bai. Again, we were on our own. Luckily, we reached the base without incident.

Unanswered Questions

Sergeant Bill Adams died hours after I left the field that day, killed in action at the end of the fighting in Hue. The loss of this 26-year-old Marine came as a blow to the gut to all of us who knew him. We all had the utmost respect for him. Adams received a posthumous Bronze Star with Combat V. I knew Adams and watched him work, a flat-out charismatic, inspirational Marine. Whenever I saw him, he struck me as super-charged, naturally animated, always smiling. His demeanor must have come natural for him, no pretenses. He radiated an inward grace, oblivious to the dangers he faced. I have wondered if Adams would have remained as motivated as his tour progressed. Time in-country had a way of eventually grinding most people down, but Adams stood out as a possible exception.

Two former platoon commanders in Golf still grieve his loss more than fifty years later. Bill Rogers remembers him fondly. His recollection testifies to the close, enduring bonds between some enlisted Marines and junior officers. Such relationships were not uncommon in Nam—brotherhood, forged in combat. On 9 February, two weeks before Adams died, he had held Lieutenant Rogers after Bill took multiple AK-47 rounds to the stomach and groin. Rogers handed Adams his map, a gesture that highlighted the transition of leadership of the platoon. They talked quietly until a corpsman arrived and administered morphine. Rogers eventually received a medical discharge and returned to Arkansas to help run his family farm.

Rogers remembers Adams:

> He had earlier served five years in the Army, then joined the Marines to fight for his country in Vietnam. He was married with a young son. He and I became good friends, not just Marines who worked together.

Lieutenant Stewart Brown, who took over platoon commander after Rogers, worked with Adams just two weeks. Brown still finds it difficult to control his anguish over the loss of his platoon sergeant:

> It has been an emotional struggle for me to put together this remembrance of my platoon sergeant, Billy Adams. Writing about him is difficult. Words seem inadequate. I feel I was not his equal. I think he was a better Marine than I was, a better Marine than almost any other I knew.
>
> My last conversation with him was under enemy fire. We had discussed when leaving our night position that morning that we had a lot of open ground to cover before arriving at Hill 42, our objective. My platoon was severely depleted by that point. We numbered about 20. Losses on Hill 42 over the next two days would leave us with 13 Marines when we returned to Hue city.
>
> On the day he died, I traveled with a squad in the lead, then my radioman and me, followed by another squad, with Sgt. Adams and his squad in the rear. I separated from him in battle for a number of reasons. My next highest-ranking Marine was an E-3 Lance Corporal, so I figured spreading the leadership out was important. That speaks to my high regard for Adams. He inspired and steadied those he directed.
>
> We also traveled apart to reduce the chance of the loss of both of us at once. I had to have Sgt. Adams in a position to provide leadership in the event I went down. As we approached Hill 42, I told Sgt. Adams to lag behind me with his trailing squad should our lead elements encounter a dug-in and concealed enemy force, as we had the day before. I wanted to have at least a few Marines not pinned down and able to maneuver. If needed, I knew Adams would maneuver and attack with the trailing force to try to free us up.
>
> Now nearing Hill 42, we were directed to pass through Hotel Company in front of us. Our goal was to join Hotel in the attack. I wanted to coordinate with Hotel Company before passing through. That's when I last talked to Sgt Adams. By radio, I directed him to lead our platoon just short of the crest of

8. Decompression and Reflection

the hill in front of him. My exact language was for him to move to "that berm up there" and wait.

I was with Lt. Harvey, the Hotel Company CO, when I received a radio transmission. Adams was in contact with the enemy on the reverse slope (beyond the crest of the berm), just about 25 meters away. I then heard that Sgt. Adams had been hit. Adams might have misunderstood where to stop, a possibility which has long tortured me. Why did I use the word "berm"? Why didn't I just tell him to stop short of the crest, or top, of the hill?

On the other hand, Adams might have advanced to the other side of the hill, the reverse slope, out of a super-abundance of bravado and courage. Perhaps he felt the urge to move on, to surge forward, to engage the enemy. I don't rule out there being a misunderstanding. But it is just as likely that his courage and aggressiveness propelled him over that hill. He was brain dead when I next saw him.

Sgt. Adams was hugely entertained by combat. I have said many times he was courageous to a fault. That is not to say I thought he was reckless. He just didn't let fear impede him in any way and relished the opportunity to take it to the enemy.

In the end, we all moved under fire and did our jobs, though not as happily as Sgt. Adams. He learned urban warfare quickly in the weeks before when we fought in Hue. He had become proficient in supporting arms and fire and maneuver. He was "career" all the way. He was a warrior in the truest sense.

Defining what set Adams apart from other Marines, he cherished his subordinate, fellow Marines, but had no hesitation using them to kick the enemy's ass. Chesty Puller used to say sergeants are the core of the Corps. The best of them live the warrior's life and impose it on their men. This was Billy.

Some years ago, at a reunion memorial service, we were asked to write on a blackboard the names of our Marines who fell in Hue. I was the sole source of knowledge on several Marines who had only lasted a few days in combat and probably the only person who could name every platoon KIA from memory. I wrote a number of names, but saw Sgt. Adams's name had already been written there.

This was the first time in our reunions that we discussed the personal stories of our fallen Marines. Enough time had elapsed to allow us to talk about it. We adjourned to the refreshments. All of us wanted to huddle and discuss Billy, recounting episodes of his bravado, his courage, and how he was killed. He had become almost a myth. It was so gratifying—comforting—to realize after so many years that my feelings toward him were universally shared.

Stewart Brown left the Marines after he was wounded and medevaced from Vietnam months later. Receiving a medical discharge, he became an attorney in private practice then later served with distinction as an Assistant U.S. Attorney in Georgia.

Arrival at Phu Bai

I felt immense relief when I reached Phu Bai the afternoon of 25 January, accompanied by a strong sense of guilt. I had to bail before the battle south of Hue had ended. Leaving the battalion still engaged with the NVA, before the Search and Destroy operation had concluded, did not sit well with me. Add to that my concern over how my departure might have appeared to others—perhaps the sniff of cowardice that some—or, more likely, I—might have attached to the departure. On the other hand, when a Marine needed to meet travel deadlines when transitioning out of the field—for R&R, to rotate back home, or for some admin reason, such as embarkation school—he typically dropped everything and left. Marines normally understood when someone had to leave the field for any valid reason.

I learned upon arrival in Phu Bai that my former radioman, Raub, had been wounded, but not seriously. Had he been hit in the same ambush as Stetson?

> *Poor Raub, my radioman, is still with Golf. He also grew close to Stetson. He's lost now and I want him back in the battery as soon as I can. He's been in the field too long and wants R&R in Australia.*

Conversation with Battery CO

After talking with the battery commander the next day about what I experienced in Hue, and receiving encouragement from him to proceed, I drafted a Bronze Star citation for Stetson. I did not have an exemplar to follow, but the CO said he would endorse it. At this point, I had experienced few direct dealings with him. I had been with the grunts most of the time he commanded the battery. I had little reason to doubt his word or to distrust him. I had witnessed how he treated some battery officers, but gave him the benefit of the doubt. He appeared less critical and sarcastic toward me than he did with other officers. I never figured out why. Perhaps it was because, as an FO, I was not under his thumb.

Although the award for Stetson was richly deserved, I am certain now that my draft did not meet the award guidelines or format. Citations for personal valor required eyewitness endorsements from other Marines, often difficult in a fast-moving combat environment. The CO could have worked with that, but unknown to me at the time, he had only days left in the battery himself. I learned months later that nothing came of the draft award. The award nomination died in place. Enlisted Marines often did not receive the recognition they deserved. Most acts of daily valor in the field went unrewarded, especially those of enlisted Marines assigned to infantry units and support units with the grunts. "Uncommon valor was a common virtue," Admiral Chester Nimitz stated, referring to the Marines fighting on Iwo Jima. The same could be said of the Marines I observed in Vietnam. All too often, it appeared to me, the paucity of decorations awarded to enlisted Marines contrasted with those received by career Marine officers. It struck me as a possible matter of "me-first" at the top of many command structures. Senior career officers seemed to do a good job looking after each another.

First Reflections on Hue

Before leaving Nam for Okinawa, I began to rerun in my head the previous two weeks. My initial potential positive experience as an arty liaison officer had soured over two months. Dealing with a high-strung battalion commander who had little respect or appreciation for artillery stung perhaps more than anything else.

> *I felt I was doing some good, but no one else gave us [artillery liaison] encouragement. I am glad to get out. In most ways it was a thankless job. There was a lot of unnecessary pressure from Lt. Col. Cheatham. He was always jumping on our back, wanting artillery quicker than was practical, and calling the regimental commander asking for immediate fire. We were never consulted, always told how to use artillery. Our FOs didn't have a chance to call in their own artillery. That's what happens when you get enlisted FOs—they can't really object to the grunt commander's use or misuse of artillery. I'm looking forward to embarkation school.*

I summarized the battalion's losses in Hue on 26 February:

> *We've taken 421 casualties—45 KIAs, since 1 February. [The battalion Command Chronology cites 65 KIA and 421 WIA in February 1968.] In Golf Company alone, 150 casualties. The battalion keeps getting replacements, but the inexperience! My relief in the Fire Support Coordination Center [also called the Combat Operations Center] has never been an FO, he just got in-country and admitted he hates the job. The FSCC is a job that almost demands FO experience in the field.*

I received an update days later in Okinawa that Golf Company suffered 208 casualties (dead and wounded) in Hue. Although the complement of a Marine rifle company was about 200 on paper, due to the high casualties and the inability to put replacements in the field quickly enough, infantry units in Vietnam in 1968 often operated at half that strength, sometimes less. Barney Barnes noted he knew only a handful of Marines in Golf company who went through the battle of Hue without getting wounded.

Another Golf Company Marine recalled years later that Captain Meadows once told him the company had gone into Hue the end of January with 167 Marines but had lost 24 KIAs and had 197 wounded in the battle (a total of 221 casualties, compared to the 208 number I noted on 26 February 1968, with two days remaining on the operation). Some were wounded two or more times, which explained the high numbers. Casualty numbers also included many newly-arrived Marines. Around 12 February, rushed replacements began to arrive in the company. In the heat of combat and without time to learn the ropes from those more experienced, a considerable, but unknown, number of them were killed or wounded.

The cumulative casualties weighed heavily on me. I wrote for the first time of the searing shock of losing Stetson.

> *I'm going to wait until I get to Okinawa before writing LCpl. Stetson's wife. Stetson is the big blond kid you see in some of the pictures. I suppose I know him better than anyone else here. We were together from the day I got to Vietnam until I left Golf Company on 4 January.*
>
> *Stetson was a remarkable man—besides an outstanding FO, he was the bulwark of the company in that he never was depressed, always doing things for people and never a complaint. I had quite a few close, personal talks with him. He had no ambition to go to college; didn't talk much of his family life.*
>
> *Well, that's it for now, until Okie in a couple of days. When I return from Okie in April [the CO] said I'd be coming back into the battery, probably as the Fire Direction Officer.*

Public Reaction to Tet

Americans back home had begun to grow war-weary. By the end of March, communist forces had begun to withdraw from Khe Sanh and had been beaten back from their objectives during the Tet Offensive. These were clearly tactical military victories for U.S. forces. Spinning the narrative, Westmoreland drew analogies between the failed Tet Offensive and Germany's last-ditch, failed effort to stop the Allied offensive at the Battle of the Bulge in 1944. He proclaimed that the situation in South Vietnam had stabilized and returned to normal. But war weariness had become evident at home and, I sensed at the time, had begun to affect Marines. The public wasn't buying the good news. In the wake of Tet, major news media outlets revealed a strategic administration plan to raise troop levels by more than 200,000. On 20 March a Gallup poll reported a new wave of public pessimism about the war. On 22 March Johnson announced the eventual replacement of Westmoreland and his reassignment as Army Chief of Staff. A Harris poll three days later showed 60 percent of the public believed the Tet Offensive had either been a standoff or a defeat for the U.S. cause in Vietnam. A 30 March Gallup Poll showed a 63 percent public disapproval of Johnson's handling of the Vietnam War. The following day the president announced he would not run for re-election.

Halfway to Paradise

I arrived at Camp Hansen, Okinawa, on 1 March, the day before scheduled check-in. Course attendees would likely experience a mix of guilt and delight. I certainly did. While we would enjoy hot food, rest and a respite from the war, our fellow Marines left behind in Vietnam were missing the opportunity to decompress and share the same small creature comforts. We also had time to ponder our eventual return to Vietnam and what the future held. I took a room in the transient BOQ. School didn't start until 4 March so I enjoyed a three-day R&R. I ventured outside the base and had a steam bath. Who would have thought an 80-pound woman walking up and down my back could have been so relaxing?

> It's great here! Hot water when you want it, great food at meal times and the [officers'] club. I am certainly fortunate in getting this. People who have just finished the Embark School say all the work can be finished in class. The night and weekends are yours. Believe me, it is a very good feeling to be able to enjoy the little pleasures and comforts of life again.

I bought an expensive camera and used it weeks later to photograph a series of local street scenes in Naha City, the capital. Those were the only photos I took with that camera. I secured it in my locked seabag in a Marine storage facility before leaving Camp Hansen for Vietnam, thinking of the incredible images I would take with that state-of-the-art 35mm camera.

The transient BOQ was only a five-minute walk away from the club, a gathering place for Marine officers traveling to and from Vietnam and for those who attended courses at Camp Hansen. Anyone who lingered there a few minutes was sure to see someone he knew. I noticed the subsidized booze sold there was ridiculously cheap, marveling at the cognac for sale at $3 at bottle. The assistant club manager was a TBS platoon mate at Quantico, among the first infantry officers in TBS 3-67 to arrive in Vietnam. Within a month after arrival in-country, he had been severely wounded near the DMZ as a platoon commander for First Battalion Ninth Marines, known as the Walking Dead. The temporary club assignment enabled him to recover and receive the medical care he needed. He would go on to spend an illustrious career in the Marine Corps, retiring as a general officer.

Lieutenant Joyner

Early in the embarkation course I met Lieutenant Steve Joyner, the XO of a 3rd Division infantry company near the DMZ. I did not understand at the time I met him that I was trying to cope with Ken Stetson's loss. Steve and I took a taxi one Saturday to check out the local culture in Naha. It was an eye-opener for us both. Looking back on that time, and after reading, many years later, an account of his positive reactions to Okinawans in a letter to his grandfather, I could relate to Steve's keen interest in other cultures. He noted in a letter I read years later that old Vietnamese men reminded him of his grandfather back home. Thanks in part to my service in Vietnam, immersion in cultures not my own would become a lifelong interest for me, as I am sure it would have for Steve—if fate had not intervened, who knows where his interests might have taken him? Along with his time in Vietnam, his interest in the wider world surely would have grown and perhaps would have had an important influence on whatever he decided to do with his life.

Joyner was an extrovert, charismatic, a friend to all who met him, an optimist with a rich sense of humor. His never-met-a-stranger personality drew people to him before he joined the Marines. Devotion to the welfare of his troops had marked his time in Nam. Unknown to me then, Steve was also a deeply spiritual man. Humble and self-effacing, he frowned on the gratuitous use of profanity and would call out those using it if he thought it excessive or inappropriate.

A former junior college All-American who played under head coach Don Coryell, defensive coach John Madden, and graduate assistant Joe Gibbs at San Diego State, Joyner stood out as a key linebacker in the Aztec defensive scheme. Teammates said when he walked off the football field, he left all aggression behind. His father's sudden death when Steve was a college junior prompted a change in direction. Football began to recede in importance, being the bread winner for his mother became a top priority. Encouraged by former Marines in the San Diego State athletic department, he began to think about Marine Officer Candidates School. He signed up in spring 1966.

His transition from big man on campus and football celebrity to

8. Decompression and Reflection

Marine Corps lieutenant came with heavy costs. Like all junior infantry officers in Vietnam, he had to contend with leading battle-hardened, exhausted Marines facing crippling casualties in a war that had grown gradually unpopular among those who served and with Americans back home. His Marines were at times confused and disappointed by media reports of diminishing support back home for those who did the fighting in Vietnam. They wanted to return to "the world," and they expected their officers to minimize risks to the extent possible and avoid decisions that would needlessly place them in harm's way. The consequent blowback he received from some superior officers took its toll on Steve's self-confidence.

In Okinawa, Steve and I had far-ranging talks about Vietnam, our families, and the future. In a combat environment, we would not have had that opportunity to share concerns.

We were both troubled by recent experiences, but hesitant to discuss particulars. We soon established a bond of mutual confidence, however, secure in the belief that our discussions would not be shared with others. I sensed that the optimism Steve usually exhibited, while genuine and a natural product of his character, also masked something more puzzling about him. I detected an unease in his remarks about his experiences, but I could not identify the reason for them. Had he turned against, or doubted, the value of the war, like me? I probed to find out, without success.

At some point, I felt comfortable enough to tell Steve about Stetson's great personal qualities. Steve listened carefully and patiently. He understood my pain. I knew he had experienced something similar, but I was unable to learn what it might be. He tried to reassure me with encouraging words and our need to move on, to continue to march—duty. While I finally unburdened myself during our stay in Okinawa, Steve remained guarded about his own concerns. The few comments he made, left me with the impression that he intended to leave the Marine Corps after Vietnam. Maybe that was what I wanted to hear. I learned 50 years later, from his administrative records, that Steve had applied for a regular commission just weeks after he returned to Vietnam from Okinawa. He wanted to remain in the Corps for a career.

I eventually learned what appeared to disturb him in Okinawa. During research for *Promise Lost*, my biography of Joyner, I interviewed one of Steve's longtime friends, who also spent time with him in Okinawa. The friend explained that based on Steve's comments to him, he believed Joyner suffered anxiety over leading men in combat. Steve had expressed concern that his missteps on the battlefield, a questionable decision made here, a misreading of the combat environment there, might lead to the deaths of his Marines. Joyner doubted his abilities, likely stemming in large part from disrespectful treatment by one of his company commanders. That critical piece of information doubtless explained the disquiet I had noted many years earlier.

Political Awakening

While in Okinawa I began to follow the 1968 presidential primaries in both political parties. I found myself favoring candidates who criticized the war. One night, after hearing Otis Redding's "Dock of the Bay," I listened to a news bulletin that Robert Kennedy had declared his candidacy. Elated, I wrote home:

> Today I heard the news of Kennedy's entry into the race. I was a bit surprised. I don't believe he can wrest support from LBJ. I like Kennedy's stand on the war. He is progressive. [For the same reason] I like Rockefeller over Nixon.

I had evolved from a cautious supporter of the war during my first couple of months in Vietnam, to a blatant, but private, critic; I now wanted to support anyone who would bring the war in Vietnam to a close. The change was liberating for me, but I could not talk about it with others. We all had to remain publicly apolitical. I began to track Kennedy's campaign day by day over the next few weeks, hoping he would win the Democratic Party nomination. I liked his statements on the futility of the Vietnam War more than anything else. He struck me as inspirational and articulate. During his brother's presidency, I disliked him. But now, I thought he exhibited a compassion toward all fellow Americans and an idealism that had grown out of deep personal grief. Unknown to me at the time, Steve Joyner had also taken interest in Kennedy's entry into the Democratic primaries. In a letter to his sister that I read many years later, he asked what she thought of Robert Kennedy. Did the question stem from mere curiosity, or something more than that?

Vietnam Intrudes

I ran into two Marines transiting Okinawa on their way home, Golf Company's Sergeant Mark Oakes and the former Echo Battery CO. As previously noted, I had suspected in Phu Bai that Oakes suffered from combat trauma. In the conversation we shared in Okinawa, I found it odd that he expressed no relief over the completion of his tour and his return home. He spoke in a monotone, the PTSD now more evident. In a photo I took of him, he found it impossible to conceal his obvious depression. He headed home to what would be an often-painful post–Vietnam life. He would find it difficult to find his footing, living without needed medical help for 40+ years. He was fortunate to have a loving and supportive family and friends on his difficult journey.

In Vietnam, my battery CO had been a veritable Mr. Hyde who made life difficult for his lieutenants. Now at Camp Hansen on his way home, he transformed into a Dr. Jekyll. He could not have been more personable and friendly, offering enthusiastic kudos on the job I had done, exclaiming my work would be recognized. I thanked him, but wondered why he went out of his way to tell me. Why hadn't he provided the same encouragement in-country?

Meanwhile, my recent experience in Hue intruded on my life in paradise:

> *What a rotten operation that was—in more ways than one. People outside the battalion blame the leadership in part for high casualties, claiming the troops were not trained or ready for fighting in the streets. But 2/5 learned and adapted quickly and it was not the battalion's fault in my opinion.*

Writing Ken Stetson's wife Jan was a priority. I was eager to explain to her Stetson's positive impact on the Marines who worked with him. Forty-five years later Jan, remarried and with a fine family, provided me a copy of the letter I sent to her from Okinawa. It read in part,

> *We [Ken and I] had several long conversations over the months. We were as close as an officer and enlisted Marine could be. I had great respect for him. His death is a personal loss to me. He was professional, a Marine with no pretensions, an uncommonly good person. He was an ideal combat Marine.*
>
> *He was a generous spirit, bigger than life. The Golf Company commander in Hue mentioned your husband's exemplary conduct during the strain of combat, how he stood watches for his fellow Marines and did his best to lighten the mental and physical burden of others without regard to his own comforts.*

Return to War

The month in Okinawa sped by sooner than I had hoped. Vietnam awaited. As Steve Joyner had reminded me earlier, we had to keep going, we had a mission to accomplish. We would return to Vietnam, Steve to his company near the DMZ, and I to my artillery battery about 70 miles away. We would exchange letters once, but I did not see him again. Without dread, looking forward to what might lie ahead, both genuinely upbeat, we wished one another well and pledged to keep in touch. I felt rejuvenated, prepared to complete my tour. Steve talked about taking R&R in July and meeting in Australia. "Sure, let's do it," I replied. I did not discount the possibility during our conversation, but I soon concluded that a week of R&R following a month at embarkation school would not be advisable. How would it look to fellow Marines? Steve would rejoin Lima Company Third Battalion, Fourth Marines, and assume his former job as executive officer. My forward observer days behind me, I would join Echo Battery north of Da Nang as a battery officer. I had valued my time in Okinawa and had treasured the opportunity to know Steve Joyner. His friendship left a lasting impression, crucial in the formation of *Promise Lost*. The book is a heartfelt thank you, a tribute to a friend's quiet acknowledgment and support, an ode to a brother Marine who understood—and experienced—the same self-doubt and sense of loss and grief.

Upon arrival at the Da Nang military terminal, I watched in surprise and fascination as Armed Forces Television re-broadcast President Johnson's memorable speech announcing he would not run for re-election. Servicemen gathered round the TV to watch with interest but without discernible reaction. There were no cheers or loud negative comments—but neither did anyone express disappointment. I would argue, those serving in Vietnam at the time assumed Johnson's announcement would have little to no impact on their destinies. Still, I welcomed it. In my own world, maybe I discerned a dim light at the end of the tunnel. At the same time, I respected the courage Johnson demonstrated in informing the American public he would not run again. He realized it was time to fold his cards. He appeared sorrowful about the war he had conducted in Vietnam. To me, his decision not to seek re-election was clear recognition that continued escalation of the war was not the path he should have taken earlier or should take going forward. I began to wonder if there might be hope for an eventual end of the conflict, sooner, not later.

The announcement on the air terminal loudspeaker directed that passengers returning from Okinawa should proceed to board their flights to in-country destinations. Yes, I looked forward to a new beginning in my tour as a battery officer. I had no feeling of impending doom, no reluctance to return to Nam. I wanted to pitch in and do whatever might be needed to get through the next six months.

9

Echo Battery in Action

Post-Tet Stalemate

While the communist offensive failed, American public support for the war weakened. Planning for an eventual drawdown of troops in Vietnam had begun. We were inching toward the door, fighting all the way. Peak troop strength in-country rose to its maximum, 543,000 in April 1969, then began a slow decline.

Echo Battery seemed to move into the enemy crosshairs. Second Battalion, Fifth Marines, the battalion we supported, was charged with securing Highway 1 between Da Nang and Phu Bai. The April 1968 Second Battalion, Eleventh Marines, command chronology stated that the battalion's four firing batteries provided support to expanded Fifth Marine Regiment operations. Frontline firing batteries would move with greater frequency to support increasingly mobile rifle battalions.

Shaky Welcome

When I returned to Echo Battery—located near Phu Loc, about a kilometer west of Highway 1—at the beginning of April 1968, a new CO smiled and greeted me cheerfully, a good start. He was a pleasant, hands-off officer, a welcome change from his predecessors. He would leave the battery in three months, however, punching his command-time ticket like other career officers, moving on to greener pastures. I would follow the customary progression of forward observers in Vietnam at the time—several months in field with the grunts, followed by a return to the firing battery for the remainder of the tour. I was assigned as assistant executive officer to Lieutenant Dunbar, with collateral duties as motor transport and supply officer. The new work motivated me. I wanted to pitch in any way I could.

Dunbar extended a sincere welcome, pleased to have me back in the battery, but I received an initial cold reception from a couple other officers. As I unloaded my gear upon arrival, someone said there was no room in the officer's hooch, I would have to find other accommodations. What other accommodations? There were none. I winced at the remark, one I anticipated I would receive after a month in Okie. What I read as a frosty reception might have been a construct of my own sense of guilt. While my return to Echo Battery disappointed on a personal level, I could hardly blame the officers. Resentment of the month I spent in Okinawa probably played a part; I had enjoyed a month in Okinawa. I could not allow their behavior to affect me.

A commanding officer is responsible for promoting morale and team-building. He sets the tone for the work setting. In a combat zone—with a divisive war back home an ever-present distraction—building an effective mission-driven management team became all the more critical. In this case, stronger leadership could have helped. The ice gradually melted. The day-to-day task of operating a firing battery in combat conditions would draw us together. We were all in the same boat. Every man had a job to do, we had to rely on each other.

I slept on the ground the first night outside an old French concrete bunker. The following day, using discarded wooden ammo boxes, I built a six-foot by four-foot lean-to sleeping space against the rear wall of the bunker, a small target for any enemy incoming fire. I stacked a platform of empty ammo boxes to sleep on and had room to stow gear at the foot of the "bed." What other luxuries would I need?

The concrete bunker contained two rooms, the FDC and Exec Pit. It was steps away from my spartan quarters. It had one entrance. The first space held the Exec Pit, with a landline, radios, and room for a duty communicator and officer on duty. An adjoining, windowless second room accommodated two firing charts and their operators. Kerosene lamps kept the chart room and Exec Pit workable round the clock.

Echo in Action

Echo Battery's six 105mm howitzers and two 155mm towed howitzers were located in a broad geographic bowl, a mostly flat area surrounded by hills. A high ridgeline separated the battery from heavily travelled Highway 1, about three kilometers to the east. Lower and more distant hills encircled the battery in other directions. In the distance we could see the likely effects of Agent Orange, extensive areas of dying or dead trees at various spots. A small hamlet in the valley stood about 2,000 meters to our north, but we rarely saw or interacted with the inhabitants. The villagers

9. Echo Battery in Action

kept a respectful safe distance. On occasion, a few boys would approach our perimeter selling small items, but the locals largely avoided contact with us. For that reason, we were reasonably good neighbors.

Echo had always enjoyed a solid, deserved reputation for providing effective artillery support to the grunts. I grew acquainted with the gun section chiefs and their four-to-five-man crews. The section chiefs of each cannon were all experienced, battle-hardened Marines. Each man ran a highly disciplined and motivated team. Any problem Marines were moved promptly to noncombat units elsewhere. I had always judged battery personnel as proud, stoic professionals; now I could experience their work as an insider. Early on, I spent time on the gunline observing, without interfering or over-supervising their work.

Cannoneers took their craft and mission seriously. All understood the critical importance of fast, reliable, accurate support for the grunts and recon teams that needed arty now, not later. With each fire mission, they knew Marine lives might be on the line. They understood survival in the bush often hinged on how soon and how accurately gun crews could put artillery rounds on target. It was all about pride—striving to be the best, most responsive battery in Vietnam. That motivation drove the cannoneers in Echo and doubtless all the other Marine batteries in-country.

I learned much from and about the various howitzer crews, not only by spending time talking with them, but through interaction on headphones during fire missions and H&I fires. When firing the battery from the Exec Pit, I could overhear what a gun section chief told his crews and their responses to his orders. Rapport and morale-building often resulted from our normal conversations and from sometimes humorous exchanges during fire missions. The general tenor always remained serious and professional.

Fire Mission, Echo Battery, An Hoa, December 1967.

Unfortunately, protocols to prevent hearing loss in artillery batteries did not exist. There was no ear protection available in the supply system. That came at a cost: at least one Marine in the battery had to be medevaced after being rendered almost totally deaf and unable to hear directions from his gun section chief. There was reported scattered use of cigarette filters as crude ear plugs. One night, as I walked the gunline during a fire mission, a cannon about 30 feet away discharged a round over my head, leaving a painful ringing in my ears hours afterward. It's a popular joke among Vietnam vets to look at a vet's ears for hearing aids once they learn he was a cannon-cocker.

Drug Use

In mid–1968, drug use in frontline combat arms commands like Echo Battery was almost unheard of. In the field, especially, Marines relied on each other to stay alive. Common sense dictated that drug use by anyone would violate that trust and endanger fellow Marines. Sometime after rejoining the battery, I heard a rumor that one or more of our Marines on the gunline had purchased marijuana joints from a local boy. It sounded plausible. Vietnamese living near U.S. combat bases always sought ways to profit from the presence of Americans, and many times they succeeded. We knew, too, that marijuana and drug use in general had become more popular back home and that it would only be a matter of time before experimentation with various drugs would reach combat units. We heard occasional rumors of drug use in rear echelon units. We were always alert to the possibility, but we never confirmed that Marines in our battery had actually used marijuana. I walked the gunline at night without ever smelling the weed's pungent odor. Many years later, however, I learned to my surprise that during the same period, Marines in some rifle companies near the DMZ openly used drugs, even in the field. The enforcement of directives against drug use ultimately fell on small unit leaders.

Fragging

"Fragging," like drug use, became a high profile issue the year after my departure, a symptom of an unpopular war and the gradual breakdown of discipline in our armed forces in Vietnam. Murdering fellow servicemen with hand grenades became a notable problem by 1969. One of my TBS classmates, Lieutenant Robert Rohweller, died from a fragging incident in April 1969, ending a promising career of a superlative infantry officer.

At least 100 servicemen died from fragging during the Vietnam War, including 37 officers in 1969 alone, according to Peter Brush of Vanderbilt University, in a HistoryNet essay. From 1969, when statistics were first kept, to 1972, documented and suspected fragging incidents reached at least 900—a likely undercount. The motives for fragging varied. They included perceived harassment of subordinates by a superior NCO or officer; actions by a senior officer or NCO thought to endanger the troops; attempts by officers to control drug use and discharge normal command responsibilities; and the enforcement of standard military discipline. An increase in racial tensions has been cited as a contributing to the problem. I would add the growing realization that the war was unwinnable and that the U.S. was exiting the conflict, also damaged morale and contributed to fragging. Reflecting on the breakdown of discipline as the war began to wind down, former Marine Commandant P.X. Kelly observed that there was a dramatic difference in the Marine Corps between when it went in to Vietnam in 1965 and when it exited in 1971.

Fire in the FDC

One morning in early May I had finished a breakfast of C-rats and had shaved using my helmet as a bowl. I had listened to Merrilee Rush sing "Angel in the Morning," a song that reflected new "liberated" values back home. I stashed my shave gear away and went inside the FDC. In a letter home I described an unusual, dangerous incident that occurred later that day, following an enemy mortar attack on the battery.

> One of my men was filling a Coleman lantern in the rear room when the lantern somehow caught fire. He tried to pick it up and run outside but tripped, spilling the flaming gas all over the floor and trapping us in the unventilated chart room. For a split second everyone took a step backward and hesitated. I yelled, "get out," and we all ran through the fire into the open air. I was aflame when I got outside and fell down to smother the fire. I wasn't burned at all. Fumes had gotten on my clothes and that was what burned. I know now how it feels to think you might die by burning to death. Thank God it happened after, not during, the enemy attack.

I sat on the ground for several minutes with other Marines after the danger passed, inhaling the fresh air. Within seconds, we all began to laugh, relieved to be alive, lesson learned. Afterwards, we always refilled the Coleman lanterns outside the bunker. The incident was a reminder of how unforeseen, preventable accidents could threaten a life as quickly as an enemy AK-47 round or a booby trap.

Unrest Back Home

I knew my father was a staunch Republican and supporter of the war effort and I understood my parents' puzzlement over the cultural changes underway around them. They had a son fighting there. By spring 1968, they felt the mood of America gradually turning against support for the conflict. Shortly after a younger sister had been confirmed in a local church, my family stopped attending services after the pastor spoke out from the pulpit against the war. I too had begun to lose touch with my own political culture, struggling to understand the dynamics of life back home.

I tried to block out reports of political and social upheaval and the growing anti-war movement back home, particularly when it grew in intensity after the Tet Offensive. Mission and keeping Marines safe remained my primary concerns. The *Stars and Stripes* newspaper did not flinch at reporting bad news, along with the good, about the war. Armed Forces Radio Vietnam seemed to play anti-war music without hesitation, anything popular back home. After all, music was music.

My negative view of the war had hardened. What goals were we now fighting for in Nam with our country so divided by the war? In-country, we mostly steered clear of any comment that might sound political around other Marines, not knowing who might be offended or take exception. We could ill afford disputes or arguments that might complicate the mission. We were not in Nam to debate whether the conflict was morally just or not, regardless of our personal views. Neither did we discuss whether our president and his advisors were conducting the war with a clear objective. But expressions hating the war surfaced in private comments, in particular from Marines who saw friends around them become casualties. They resented the puzzling strictures placed on us in the field, the Rules of Engagement—directives on what to do and not do—that seemed to benefit the enemy while hamstringing U.S. armed forces. We could not pursue the enemy beyond the borders of the RVN, for example. Operating within national borders meant nothing to the enemy.

Assassination

When Armed Forces Radio announced the assassination of Martin Luther King, Jr., on 4 April, I realized right away it spelled impending racial unrest and violence back home. A week later, I observed,

What a sad thing to happen to Martin Luther King. The far-reaching consequences are unknown.

I did not expect any disturbance from the handful of African Americans in Echo Battery, but I worried what might happen back home. I thought at the time that the King assassination would benefit Richard Nixon's presidential candidacy. While King had not endorsed Robert Kennedy, he had been moving in that direction. King's assassination, I thought, might suppress the Black vote for Kennedy without King there to encourage African American turnout at the polls. Looking back at that period, I am sure my parents supported Nixon. It didn't matter:

I like the Democratic [primary] race. Johnson's bombshell [announcing he would not seek re-election] has made this time a most unusual and exciting year in political history. I'm very hopeful for the possibility of peace. LBJ did a courageous thing, even though I don't like him as president. He seems to really be going after a peace settlement. We all hope so here. Cross your fingers.

Another Assassination

I had begun to track the Kennedy presidential primary run since March. I thought he had built momentum in April and May and silently applauded his primary win in California. On 6 June, the D-Day anniversary, I had the early morning watch in the FDC. The graveyard shift always seemed to drag by, the tactical radios crackling but quiet. Typically, it was a time for letter writing, ribald conversations, and relaxed laughter. That night I heard Bobby Goldsboro sing his saccharine "Honey" on the radio. Like other songs that remain fixed in memory and tied to a specific event, I listened closely, trying to understand the appeal of this sad, melodramatic tune. How in the world, I thought, could this song have reached the top of the pop charts and stayed there for weeks?

Then the news came in. Robert Kennedy shot in Los Angeles, in a coma, near death. My hope for a possible eventual ending to the war by a potential Kennedy administration disintegrated in an instant. Prolonged silence followed for what seemed like an hour, maybe more. Heads down, no one said a word. I sensed the deep shock, confusion, and sadness in the battery over his passing for days afterwards. His death, like that of MLK, did not result in notable conversation—but I felt the vibes. The day Robert Kennedy died I wrote home. I knew my parents didn't like him, he was a Kennedy, but it didn't matter.

> *I can't choose the right words to express what I feel at RFK's death. I didn't come right out and say it [earlier], but I was pulling for him in November if he was the Democratic nominee.*
>
> *What has this country come to? It has gotten to the point where if radicals disagree with a political public figure, an assassination is carried out. I strongly feel Kennedy was the best man—a courageous man—to enter the race before Johnson decided to drop out. What a horrible tragedy. I am sick.*

As usual, I received no response from home. Ten days later the RFK assassination still disturbed me; I was a chief mourner. I wrote,

> *The news of the Kennedy death has made a great many people here depressed.*

Increasing Enemy Attacks

Stationary firing batteries were always vulnerable to ground, mortar, or rocket assaults. Phase II of the Tet Offensive began in late April. Much of the enemy activity focused on renewed attacks in urban areas held by ARVN troops. But our battery became a prime target of NVA attempts to pressure, weaken, and pin down Marine artillery units in I Corps, according to the 2/11 Command Chronology. Our battery remained on the west side of the ridge overlooking Highway 1.

On 9 April we took 16 or 18 enemy 82mm mortar rounds, not the first attack that month by the enemy, but one that clearly appeared to be an escalation. I was not too alarmed. Luckily, we took no casualties. The battery responded with 105mm howitzer direct fire. Huey gunships raked the surrounding hills overlooking our position with rockets and machine gun fire. The enemy strike was likely a registration mission, shooting in targets they could later fire on without delay and with more deadly effect.

Just before dawn on 2 May, we absorbed approximately forty 81mm, twenty 60mm mortar rounds, and numerous B-40 rockets. Remarkably, the attack wounded only two Marines. We grew more concerned that the assaults might foreshadow an imminent enemy ground attack on the battery. Some of the distant hills already had been defoliated by possible Agent Orange spraying, thereby limiting the cover enemy ground units could use to hide. Hills closer to the battery still lush with triple-canopy foliage, however, could conceal enemy activity.

To neutralize the threat, on 5 May and 10 May we burned off dry undergrowth from areas that could serve as a possible launch point for a ground attack. We raised our cannons to maximum elevation and shot illumination rounds on the targeted areas. When the illum reached the ground, still burning, it ignited the dry brush and burned away much of the vegetation. We employed this effective defensive tactic several times in the coming months at different locations.

Shortly after midnight on 11 May, the enemy struck again, this time with mortars, recoilless rifles, and B-40 rockets. The attack was more accurate, more deadly. We returned fire with 270 high explosive rounds and five Beehive rounds—direct-fire, anti-personnel projectiles containing small metal darts—on likely areas from which the enemy could launch a possible ground assault. Not all casualties were medevacs, but we suddenly felt we were in the bullseye of enemy gunners. I wrote,

> We are on a [slight] hill so we were able to direct fire back. The [enemy] barrage lasted an hour. We took 19 wounded.

Friendly Fire

Friendly Fire. Marines in the field feared those dreaded words, for good reason. They knew arty could deliver them from the direst of circumstances, but were also inherently gun-shy of friendly artillery. They often had only a limited grasp of how to call in a fire mission, but few wanted to admit it. Arty seemed to them something of a mystery, awesome when used against the enemy, but always a potential danger. They downplayed their fears and most of the time, when possible, gladly left arty support to an experienced FO. To limit friendly fire incidents, artillery FOs in the field hammered home the importance of knowing where they were on the map at all times. Many grunts, by instinct and experience, were often expert map readers, but some friendly fire accidents were caused by units requesting a fire mission without knowing their precise location. As an FO with a grunt company, I viewed as vital teaching grunt squad leaders and NCOs on how to call in and direct a fire mission.

Harassment and Interdiction (H&I) fire, such as the errant one that likely killed Corporal Crigger in November 1967, were often requested on likely avenues of approach or possible assembly areas. I sometimes questioned the practice of firing random artillery missions. We had no evidence that H&Is had a negative impact on NVA morale, but shooting them made the battery personnel and Marines requesting them feel a bit safer. Strict procedural protocols were put in place to reduce the chance of possible deadly H&I rounds harming our Marines. Typically, the request for such artillery support was worked up by the two chart operators working independently and the resultant gun data triple-checked and verified by the officer on duty in the FDC, and again by the gun chief when the rounds were fired.

Recon teams were always steady customers; they often called for H&Is. Unfortunately, friendly fire incidents still occurred despite safeguards designed to minimize them. As dusk fell on 15 May, we received a whispered radio transmission from a recon team settling in for the night. They requested several H&I missions to be fired at random times during the evening on designated points on the map. The H&I plots were usually placed at safe distances from the unit requesting them. But requestors had to know their own location. I was duty officer in the FDC several hours after the recon team had requested the H&Is. Before daybreak, I fired rounds on one target. Shortly afterwards, we received a screamed, urgent "check fire, check fire" transmission from the recon team. They had, tragically, called in arty on their own position. I wrote later that day,

Fire Direction Center, An Hoa, showing the communication area and cartoon depictions of various Reconnaissance Team call signs, 1967 (courtesy Martin Dunbar).

> Recon called four H and Is in on top of themselves. We didn't have their actual positions, neither did the clearing agency. Echo Battery shot the rounds that killed one recon Marine and wounded two. I fired the rounds. It wasn't my fault, or the fault of any of the other FDC personnel. Since then, Recon has not had approval to shoot any H and Is. They can call in only observed missions instead.

Within hours of the incident, Major Cates, my first battery commander and now the artillery battalion operations officer, descended on the battery to conduct the mandatory investigation. Over the next few hours, Cates reviewed all the data—the initial call for fire plotted on the chart, the computed data relayed to the guns, and the data received by the guns that fired the artillery rounds. He found no errors and cleared the battery.

Tactical Displacement

Following escalating enemy attacks on the battery, we finally got the message: we had taken enough punishment in that location, why stay any longer than was necessary? Higher command understood we could not afford to remain there without risk of further debilitating casualties—perhaps from a massive enemy ground attack that might overrun the battery and impede our ability to function effectively.

On 20 May we moved a short distance to a new position—to the east, just off Highway 1, on the other side of the towering ridge line that overlooked our position. The new spot was a short drive from our battalion headquarters. Still, the same threatening ridgeline looked down on our position, uncomfortably close to the battery, a menacing mortar threat. The enemy could—and would—strike from the reverse slope. The battery's tactical relocation fit into the evolving strategy implemented after the Tet Offensive—to reinforce security on primary roads, according to the artillery battalion command chronology. It also provided a palatable rationale for our move: we were not retreating from the enemy. After our displacement, intelligence pointed to still another possible general enemy offensive in the works.

The battery's newly assigned position on a small hill a few hundred meters west of Highway 1 required establishing a secure perimeter, creating gun emplacements, and building a fire direction center and living quarters. We spent a week feverishly hardening the battery from possible attack. A rifle company from 2/5 moved in close to help provide security.

Concerned that vegetation on the hill overlooking the battery might provide concealment for the enemy, we again used howitzer illumination rounds to burn underbrush. Seabees came in and bulldozed the remaining vegetation from the immediate area around the battery. We dug deep underground bunkers with several layers of sandbags for overhead. Working twenty hours a day, we found adequate sleep impossible. Two weeks after arriving at our new location and hardening our bunkers from mortar attack as much as we could, we felt reasonably confident we could withstand an attack. Given the recent acceleration of NVA mortar strikes, we calculated it could come at any time.

Deadly Incoming

I always slept in my uniform with boots within reach, anticipating the worst—an enemy ground assault. My flak vest and loaded weapon lay under my cot.

The anticipated mortar assault began at 0245 hours on 27 May. Half-asleep in a bunker at the time, I heard two rounds in rapid succession leave the mortar with a distinctive, hollow "thunk, thunk." Shouts of "Incoming!" rang out along the gunline and battery defensive perimeter while the mortar rounds were still airborne. The cannoneers leaped into action and began to pump out counterbattery fire. The initial enemy rounds impacted somewhere near the Fire Direction Center, but exactly where, I could not determine. Grabbing my pistol, flak jacket, and helmet, I ran to the heavily sand-bagged FDC—about a 30-second dash. We numbered about ten Marines in the FDC, three officers, the first sergeant, and FDC personnel on watch.

The mortar fire paused for a minute as the enemy calculated what adjustments were required to hit the bunker. Little could be done in the FDC as the rounds began to rain in. We all fell on the dirt floor and curled up, helmets and flak jackets on, making ourselves as small a target as we possibly could. We had landline (wire) communication with the gun chiefs, but the crews knew what had to be done without being told. With a general idea of where the mortar tubes were emplaced, probably on the reverse slope of the high ridgeline overlooking the battery, our cannoneers began conducting immediate counterbattery fire without regard to their own safety or exposure to the incoming.

Despite our response from the gunline, the incoming mortar fire continued, round after round, amazingly accurate. At least ten 82mm rounds, one after the other, impacted on top of, or very near, the large FDC bunker. Each explosion shook the structure to its foundations with ear-splitting force. At least one round exploded near the low, sandbagged blast wall shielding the open entrance to the FDC. Each detonation elicited desperate epithets and moans from Marines inside the bunker. I thought perhaps the end might be imminent. I worried the barrage might be the prelude to a ground attack on the battery. If that occurred, we would have to rely on grunt security on the perimeter and the gun crews to defend the battery. If an NVA ground assault managed to reach the FDC all inside could be killed.

But then, as if by Divine Providence, the mortar rounds suddenly shifted, just when I thought one more direct hit on the roof of the FDC might penetrate it. The NVA began to walk the rounds down the gunline. They obviously had pre-plotted targets there as well. After about 40 rounds had landed inside the battery perimeter from at least one, maybe two enemy tubes, the incoming ceased. We rushed to the guns as the cannons were still pumping out counterbattery fire. Fourteen cannoneers had suffered various wounds; one of them later died. Trying to be useful, I helped carry his stretcher to a point he could be retrieved by corpsmen. As daylight broke, we spent the rest of the morning assessing the damage and evacuating our wounded. Our personnel strength had been diminished further. Replacements were not arriving quickly enough.

The courage and motivation of the gun crews had been remarkable since the NVA mortar attacks on the battery had begun the month before. Their morale sky-high, the cannoneers never complained. I felt some shame, along with pride, in what I had seen. I previously thought I would never witness the level of esprit de corps in the battery that I had experienced in the field with the grunts, but I had been wrong. I had sold my cannon cockers short. I now knew the battery was where I belonged. I realized Marines were Marines, no matter where they served, no matter which unit.

Continued Leadership Rotations

The number of senior NCOs in our battery had declined over the months. By early to mid–1968, many enlisted career Marines had already completed their tour in Nam. Most of them likely had no plans to return for a second time, if they could avoid it.

As noted earlier, the junior officer pipeline had already begun to diminish, unable to keep pace with the mounting casualties. From early 1968, enlisted FOs began to take over the deployed FO teams. Although I worried at first that the quality of our artillery support to rifle companies might be reduced, the trend had no discernible impact on the artillery support the battery provided.

Careerism and favoritism sometimes became a factor in officer assignments, as it always has in the professional military. It appeared to me that regular officers sought command time to advance their careers. Medals awarded for a command billet helped at promotion time. The endless churning of key, experienced leaders out of frontline units and their replacement by less experienced officers sometimes created a temporary void, I thought, but for the most part transfers did not interfere with the mission. When turnovers occurred, memories of prior operations and the lessons learned from them were limited to the enlisted Marines. But the officers were the decision makers. I had four commanding officers during my 13-month tour. As noted previously, by 1968 it seemed to me that most career-minded captains had been given a brief command in Nam, then often moved on to a staff position in a higher headquarters. Over time, senior lieutenants began to take over command of infantry companies and artillery batteries. At the end of May, our battery commander moved to a staff position at higher headquarters, leaving no captains in the battalion available to assume command. The senior lieutenant in the battery would have normally assumed command if a more senior officer from outside the battery were unavailable.

The battalion commander, however, had an officer in Echo Battery he wanted to install as the new CO. Two reserve, non-career first lieutenants were subsequently moved—one to command another battery in the battalion for three weeks before he rotated home. The other officer was transferred out to command the battalion headquarters company—not a firing battery. The battalion commander then installed his preferred candidate to become the Echo commanding officer.

The CO-designate, was weeks junior to me. I had no issue with the decision. I wanted to stay with Echo and do what I could to help run the battery. Despite the battalion commander's maneuvers, the new battery commander turned out to be a good choice. He had been assigned by the same battalion CO to command two 155mm howitzers, detached from the battery, during the Tet Offensive in February. He had proven success and command experience. He was smart to boot, easy to work with, a capable officer. He had no problem keeping me as the XO. I would focus on managing the guns, maintaining morale, and keeping our Marines focused on the mission. I knew it would work. Our Marines in Echo Battery were already motivated. The new battery CO kept the battalion commander happy and oversaw keeping the battery supplied with what it needed. I found the work challenging and my role fulfilling. The CO and I worked well together over the next three months. We supported each other as best we could and rotated out of Vietnam weeks apart. On later home leave, I visited him and we drove around town in his new 1968 Corvette, bought with savings from the war.

Body Counts

Following every artillery fire mission called in, the requestor—whether an infantry unit or an aerial observer—was provided a damage assessment. "Two confirmed KIA, three 'probables,' two secondary explosions," might have been a typical response. I had begun to focus on this bothersome issue after three months in-country while still an FO. The frequent reporting of inflated, estimated enemy body counts, accompanied by occasional underreporting of U.S. servicemen casualties, struck a nerve with me.

In November 1967 I enclosed in a letter an annotated article on the recently concluded Operation Essex published by *Sea Tiger*, an official weekly newspaper distributed throughout I Corps, the III Marine Amphibious Force area of northern South Vietnam. I had been processing and mulling over Operation Essex. I read accounts of Essex in the *Stars and Stripes* and *Sea Tiger* newspapers. In my view, *Sea Tiger* deserved its well-known reputation for biased reporting. Although the paper often used official reports from the field as a basis for news stories, I focused on its embellishment of some field accounts. While the goal might have been well-intentioned, perhaps to bolster morale, exaggerated stories created just the opposite effect. One article describing the recent Operation Essex struck me as misleading. I wrote that it was

> *a testament to the inaccuracies of enemy casualty reports I have become familiar with. Sea Tiger dwells on the sensational. Hotel Company never bushwhacked the NVA. In fact, as you know, they were bushwhacked and took heavy casualties. And it was Golf Company that checked out the village the following day and found eight dead, not 43!! This might have been written to save Hotel's reputation. Interesting.*

Sloppy or inaccurate casualty reporting was certainly not limited to *Sea Tiger*. The 2/11 Command Chronology for April 1968 took credit for a reported 56 enemy "confirmed" KIAs, and two enemy forced to surrender—six concrete emplacements destroyed, eight other structures destroyed, three structures damaged, six secondary explosions. On it went, month after month, the reports evolving into, for me, a feel-good paper exercise. Few, apart from high-ranking officers on secure bases, considered the reports reliable. Artillery damage assessments likewise seemed inflated to satisfy the firing batteries, which dutifully reported the numbers up the chain of command. The battalion's four batteries expended over 26,000 rounds that month. More than half of the rounds were shot at unobserved targets. The "confirmed" enemy casualties were more often estimated or exaggerated reports of enemy killed rather than actual "confirmed." I thought at the time that senior commanders had to be provided such data to keep them happy. The reports encouraged the pretense of progress in what had become an ugly, grinding war of attrition. Enemy casualty figures were almost always a guessing game. They were grotesque benchmarks meant to be positive indicators that we were winning the war.

Reported numbers of enemy dead, inflated or not, provided little to no comfort or cause for optimism. What mattered most to me and, arguably, to other Marines—and to their mothers and fathers, and friends—were the painful Marine casualties, such as those absorbed by 2/5 in the attack on the fortified village during Operation Essex on 6 November 1967: 23 killed, 56 wounded. Each Marine casualty left family members, friends, and Marine buddies, emotionally scarred. Over time this is what contributed to the fundamental weakening of American public support for the war in Vietnam. And for me, the sting of accumulating friendly casualties and the bodies of fallen comrades would not lessen. The steady numbers of Marines killed, week after week, would take a toll on me and those around me.

Echoes of Hue—Homesickness

I wrote in early June:

I got my orders. I'll be going to Parris Island for duty. I have three months to go and counting.

I had requested the assignment to be near friends in Charleston, South Carolina, but it seemed a lifetime away. I first had to survive until September. During quiet hours I sometimes caught myself thinking of the allure of life back home. Homesickness was an unavoidable malady. It often flared up when I least expected it. I tried to not let it interfere with my duties. I once thought of decorating my flak vest, but I didn't. I addressed my father, as I did whenever my morale seemed to sag or I felt sorry for myself:

It seems all of us have been through a period of stress the past several months. I've never been quite the same after Hue.

The Tet Offensive kept reverberating for me. The thinnest of hopes for a positive end to war in Vietnam had evaporated with the unexpected enemy attacks in Hue and elsewhere. At the time, my parents were dealing with trying to find my sister, who had run away from home. They, of course, read my letters, but only rarely reacted to them. They tried to shield me from the bad news on the home front, but found it difficult given my persistent requests for family information. I did not hesitate to "let it all hang out," popular slang of the time. I had to "tell it like it is"—another idiom from the late 60s. Not holding back from what I was experiencing or feeling had become a necessary emotional outlet.

> Of course, you all have lived through hell for a year and more. I worry about Dad—how stout and brave and unbending he is in the midst of all the confusion. I sure am proud of that man.
>
> I wish I could be home longer when September rolls around. We'll have to make the most of our time together. Eat like kings and enjoy our time, talk late into the night and wake up sort of late the following morning.

I fantasized about life back home. Despite the anguish and chaos my family was going through, for me the idealized home front always appeared more attractive from a distance than the hell cascading daily around me in Nam.

10

Dead Man Walking

Shared Experiences

The mortar attacks in April and May shook the battery. Morale remained high, but we began to feel the loss of experienced Marines. Mounting casualties, in my view, made Echo Battery look almost like a depleted rifle company. Replacements dribbled in.

The heavy enemy incoming we received the previous month prompted me to write in early June to friend Steve Joyner, whom I knew to be somewhere near the DMZ. I checked in with him for the first time since we left Okinawa in early April. I figured sending him a brief description of our mortar attacks offered a good excuse to write. I knew he could probably relate. Intense enemy activity near the DMZ and around Khe Sanh had continued unabated for over a year. I had received developed photographs taken in Okinawa in March, while we were both at embarkation school. I enclosed a couple of them in a letter—including one I took of him one rainy morning—and several shots of street scenes during our visit to Naha City. Steve responded several days later with a graphic description of the recent punishment his Lima Company had taken on Hill 689, near Khe Sanh. He wrote the following two letters on 8 June, probably his last ones. His company would leave Hill 689 on an operation two days later.

> Big Dan-
>
> Thanks for the great pictures and the info. You talk about incoming! Let me tell you what we received in the last 24 hrs. Within our company perimeter, over 126 82mm mortar rounds. The Arty battery at Khe Sanh, which I don't know off hand, really gives us support, e. g. H&Is at night and an 8" gun for close support!
>
> We are still at Hill 689, approx. 4,000 meters west of Khe Sanh. No word when we will leave. I hope soon. The weather is still very humid & hot ... today 107. Chow still C-rats. Our SPs [special food rations] sure help.

10. Dead Man Walking

I am commanding officer till our new skipper comes. Capt. McLaughlin rotated on 24 May. The Colonel has informed me his relief should be in-country around mid–June. At any rate, the experience is something else. Last night alone I had NDF [Night Defensive Fires] called into our area and the lines went 100% [alert]. All-in-all, I love it, you know that.

Well buddy, I might see you in Australia in July. That is where I am going. Let me know your dates ASAP. Thanks again for the pictures.

SJ

Unfortunately, we would not meet in July, or any other time on this earth. The same day Steve wrote me, he put the following letter in the mail run from Hill 689 to a cousin in California.

Received your warm letter today. Thanks for the info!

Mail here at Hill 689, Khe Sanh, sure brings me closer to home. I think often of the warm California hospitality, girls, girls, and more girls. I plan to go to Australia in July for my R&R. Do you know anyone there? If so, let me know.

The weather is the big factor here. 107 again today with humidity up to around 91%. The NVA hits our position daily with 82mm mortar rds. Only light casualties (6 WIAs).

Boy, without artillery and close air support, we would be in a fix. I believe it is a decisive factor when in close contact w/the NVA.

Lots of Love and hello to all.

PS: enclosed is a picture taken in Okinawa when I was TAD to Embarkation School. Thought you might like it.

The photo he enclosed in his letter to Donna was almost certainly the same one I had taken of him in Okinawa.

Lieutenant Steve Joyner, eating C-rations just before nightfall June 14, 1968, about 15 kilometers southwest of Khe Sanh, near the Laotian border. He is covered with ash from fighting brush fires ignited by napalm. Hours later, he would be killed in action leading a counter-assault against an overwhelming enemy force that had penetrated his company's perimeter (image courtesy Joyner's radioman, Bob Montgomery).

Another Brother Falls

Not all wounds are visible.

Mid-day, about 20 June, I took a short break from the stifling heat of the FDC. Walking to my bunker in the blinding sunlight, I carried a copy of a newly-arrived *Stars and Stripes* newspaper. I tuned in Armed Forces Vietnam Radio and sat on my cot to read. As Linda Ronstadt and the Stone Poneys sang "Different Drum," I turned to the page where the recent casualties were printed. It was something everyone in Vietnam did: casualty lists first. Which friends would not make it home? It was reflexive. I stopped breathing for a moment when I read the entry, "First Lieutenant Stephen D. Joyner, 15 June." I sat there in darkness for some time getting my head around it. First Stetson, now Joyner. Two Marines, both like brothers to me. We had shared stories, laughter, dreams, unspoken fears, and doubts. I must have been shaking as I sat there in silence, trying to grasp the reality on the page before me. Some minutes passed; I have no idea how long I remained immobilized before I closed the paper and returned to the FDC. How could I suppress the crushing weight of the news, I thought? I had to stifle inner howls of despair.

I sought out the CO, alone, at an opportune moment. I told him I had just learned of the death of my best friend and had to get away for a few days to deal with it, if it was okay with him. He agreed on the spot, no questions asked. He must have read my expression. "Go whenever you want," he said. I made it through the end of June before I left for Da Nang, struggling to conceal from everyone around me the enveloping gloom. I'm uncertain others in the battery knew what happened. Nothing was said to me to indicate anyone else was aware of it, but it didn't matter. We all dealt with our own demons and gave each other plenty of space.

In a letter home on 23 June, I tried to paint a positive picture of battery activity, but as I wrote, I could not conceal the creeping disillusionment and bitterness of recent events.

> *Summer is in full swing. Temperatures are in the 100s for most part of the day. Everyone hibernates from 1100-1300, out of the sun. Today we had a heat casualty from hiking up to an Observation Post near our position.*
>
> *I am still busy, but like it a great deal. As XO I can do almost exactly what I want with the battery. It's up to my judgment and imagination.*
>
> *Most Marines believe the VC are going to help us celebrate the 4th of July. I hope not.*
>
> *Personnel-wise we are stretched too thin. We have about 100 men in the battery. We rate 50-60 more than that. Units throughout I Corps are ridiculously undermanned. We can't afford to take any more casualties.*

10. Dead Man Walking

> *The tragic news has to deal with my old FO team. Five days ago, a new lieutenant who had gone to the field on 17 June was killed by 3 "Bouncing Bettys" [booby traps] about 10k meters south of our position. His radioman was killed also.*
>
> *The following day, two replacements from the battery were among a group of 20-30 Marines who landed in a minefield. One had his foot blown off, the other multiple shrapnel wounds, but isn't too serious. The poor FOs, I do feel sorry for them.*

Lieutenant Howard Howland, was the last new officer assigned to Echo Battery before I would rotate home in September. I have little memory of my dealings with him. He and his radioman, Lance Corporal Stephen Hadley, were with a company sweeping across a heavily mined peninsula on Howland's first morning in the field. Hadley tripped a mine, losing both legs and an arm. He died on a medevac chopper before reaching a field hospital. Howland died instantly from head wounds.

More bad news had closed in around me. When would I reach a saturation point of some kind, I asked myself? Would I break down? Had I played all my chips in this poker game? As I noted earlier, Shakespeare wrote, "All the world's a stage." Even in wartime. I sometimes felt like an actor playing a role: a happy warrior. Trying to mask my view of the war, while working with the Marines around me, required all the energy, resolve, and any acting talent I could muster. I had to maintain battery morale and effectiveness at all costs while hoping to cling to my own sanity and fighting the gloom. The upbeat, all-is-well facade I attempted to display to the Marines around me every day by no means reflected the reality of my mental state. I knew making it through my remaining time in-country would require a Herculean effort—like a runner who could see the finish line in the distance, but who felt consumed by exhaustion. Winded and near collapse, I kept moving forward just as I had done earlier in OCS and perceived setbacks earlier in my tour in Nam. I wanted to make it through to the end with dignity and purpose, contributing to the mission to the best of my ability and safeguarding my battery.

Go-Go Girls Galore

Days after I learned of Steve Joyner's fate along with our new FOs, I had a discussion on the value of war with an American civilian in Vietnam—a war profiteer. I wrote home:

> *Day before yesterday we had a show in the battery. A traveling show featuring four Vietnamese girls and a band of three. One of the girls*

> was a stripper and put on a good show. It will be another day or two before everyone settles down again.

After the band played several, almost unrecognizable, pop songs, I spoke with their cynical manager, a nondescript middle-aged civilian trying to make a buck off the war. I doubted he ever served in the military. Somehow, he must have received approval from senior officers up the chain of command to bring his troupe to the battery. I wasn't sure who was paying whom for the visit. Our battery doubtless was not the only field unit the group visited. I do not recall what I said or asked that prompted him to comment on the profitability of war. His sickening response startled me. It still shocks me. He had formulated a justification for war to suit his view of the world. I am unsure if I even offered a rebuttal. I later vented,

> The manager, an American, said he would always be in a place where there was war. Economically speaking, he said, all good comes out of war, peace is just a resting up period before men war again. All progress, he said, comes out of war.
> I don't agree. Economically there are just as many disadvantages to war as advantages. But think of all the suffering war brings. He doesn't care about this.

Repulsed, I walked away and said nothing more to him. Late that night, after the performance, at least two girls slipped into the command bunker. I'm sure the manager encouraged or directed them. Give the officers what they want, he likely thought, stay on their good side, earn a few bucks. We can visit the battery again. But for the enlisted Marines, the girls were not to be touched. One girl tried to climb onto my cot, but I was in no mood for sex. The recent losses of Joyner and the others days before and the revulsion over young women trafficked as objects by the war-loving manager for his own advantage and enrichment proved too strong. I have wondered what became of him, a pure, unadulterated pimp. Did he and his itinerant group survive the war? Did he continue to chase wars, wherever they were?

The following week I mentally prepared for a respite at China Beach. It would provide a much-needed opportunity to think without distraction and to unwind. Close to an emotional breaking point, my cluttered mind almost immobilized me.

China Beach

I arrived at the Naval Support Activity, China Beach, on 1 July for a four-day, tranquil in-country R&R. My small, clean, stand-alone plywood bungalow, contained a bed, desk, and an adjoining bathroom, nothing else.

It was a perfect setting for unwinding and sorting through recent experiences and disappointments. I ate in the club dining room, a five-minute walk away. China Beach offered much needed peace and quiet—no outgoing cannon fire, no incoming rocket or mortar fire. The war outside could have been a thousand miles away. The time spent there allowed me to regroup mentally and physically. I tried to put events into perspective, steel myself for the sprint ahead toward home, and grieve privately for Steve Joyner, Ken Stetson, and the others who hadn't made it. In the silence, I knew I wanted no more of war and death, but I still had over two months left in-country. I had to gut it out.

Other Marine officers staying at the complex also kept to themselves. A quiet, peaceful bubble is what we all sought. I had brief conversations with a few in the bar and dining room, but we all sat alone. We remained anonymous, first names only. We doubtless sought to block out, at least for a brief time, the reality of war raging outside. In a letter home, I noted the saved expense of not traveling abroad for R&R. But the actual reason? I could not justify it after spending a month in Okie. I knew it would not have been the right thing to do. Whatever credibility and respect I had managed to achieve since joining the battery in March would disappear in the resulting contempt.

Inching Toward the Exit

The time remaining on my tour—10 weeks—would not be easy, but I could see some daylight ahead. The road would be filled with frequent moves and at the end, a return to dreaded An Hoa, where I had begun my tour. I likened the homecoming there to a recurrent nightmare. I felt like someone who had taken a long and arduous trip, only to discover he had returned to the starting point with little changed. The saga seemed tailor-made for a Rod Sterling "Twilight Zone" segment. I tried to remain defiantly upbeat, but found it a struggle to disguise the fatigue:

> Being XO is a good job. It's time consuming and all that, but fun and never boring. It helps the time pass quickly. I like the job.
>
> A little more than a month longer and I will have been away a year. You know something? It seems a lot longer than that. It seems I've been here for three years. If I stay in the Corps, it's going to be like this from now on.

I had never contemplated a career in the Marine Corps, but now felt the need to put the thought on paper. It somehow made my plans irreversible. I assumed from the start of my enlistment that I would serve three years of active duty, followed by three years in the ready reserves, then out. Now I allowed myself to mentally inch toward the exit—ready to walk out of the darkness that was Vietnam, through the door, and into the sunshine outside.

I revealed at last the bad news of Joyner's loss—almost as an unintended afterthought—to my parents. As usual, they served as a silent sounding board. I expected no meaningful response, and I received none. I wrote to maintain my equilibrium and sanity. I never pictured them sitting at home, reading my letters, and commenting on them. Perhaps selfishly, I wrote for myself, sending a silent scream of rage and mourning.

> The quicker I get out of here the happier I will be. A close friend with whom I went to Embark School in Okie was killed last week near Khe Sanh. Steve Joyner is the Marine in a few of the pictures I sent to you from Okie. I sent copies to him and got a note from him where he thanked me for them. He was from La Habra.

That was all I wrote about Joyner. I reverted to the lure of a return to the world.

> A new month. About 60 more days now before time to leave for home. I left for Vietnam the 12th of August [1967]. I can't wait, you know that? I'm sure we'll have a lot to do. The money I have saved up will not be available, I discovered, until 60 days have gone by in the States. I might have to borrow until it comes through.

Sprint Toward Home

I returned to the battery from China Beach refreshed, my energies recharged. I thought I could now go forward and calm the turbulence inside my head. All I had to do was go balls to the wall for two months. I felt I could stand on my head for that length of time, if I had to. We kept the nearby hillside and undergrowth around the battery burned off with illumination rounds to discourage any ground attacks. With a nearby Marine infantry company as security, none came, but the NVA mortared us again with 45 rounds the night of 14 July. Amazingly, we took no casualties. They must have used a new mortar crew.

We received an alert in late July to stand ready to move by road from our position north of Da Nang. The approximately 40-mile drive back to An Hoa with our eight-gun battery took the entire day. Happily, we encountered no ambushes, breakdowns, or delays in route. It would be the first of four moves in the next four weeks as our artillery battalion strained to support now routine mobile operations by grunt units.

10. Dead Man Walking

> *30 July 1968*
>
> *It's been a while since I've last written. Reason is, we moved to An Hoa on 26th July. I've got just over one month to go now before I'm on my way home. Four weeks can't be too long, can it? The battery is located quite a distance from our old position, but we plan to move into it within a couple days. Right now, the old position is occupied by the ARVNs.*
>
> *No mail in a week, but it should catch up with us. There isn't much to say now. Maybe I'll have time in a couple days between building [battery positions] to write again.*

In fact, during my last few months in-country, I found letter writing almost impossible for various reasons, the intense press of duties paramount.

Another Flashback

One of the problems with serving in Nam? No formalized institutional memory of any kind that could coherently be passed down to others who recently arrived in-country, no lessons learned to pass down to reduce or prevent battlefield casualties. No one to tell you not to go near this village, not to walk down those trails. It could have saved lives and lightened the burden of those who occupied any base for the first time. Memories of places and events seemed not to be shared except, perhaps, with other Marines in your squad or platoon. Then again, casualty rates were so high, and the battlefield so fluid, there were few left who could explain those lessons learned to new arrivals. We must have all been too hell bent on getting out alive.

Bad memories of An Hoa enveloped me as I viewed the changes to the base. Any combat base in Vietnam took on a life of its own, changing over time with the personnel and the tempo of war. Each base held recollections of bad juju—moral, physical, and psychological—for me, and I am sure, for others who served there. During our battery's ten days on base, from late July to early August, I stared out again at the same hostile villages in the distance and reviewed the events from my initial five months in Vietnam. Those early shocks returned: memories still too fresh—the officer I replaced the year before after his bizarre death; the NVA ambush of a squad en route on foot from An Hoa to Phu Lac—all killed; the booby-trapped artillery rounds that ripped five Marines apart. Worst of all were the mounting numbers of fallen Marines I knew personally and had interacted with. Here today, gone tomorrow. So long, been good to know ya. I had one month to go.

Back to Antenna Valley

6 August 1968
>Sorry for the delay in writing. We have moved this time to a 300 meter hill which looks down on Antenna Valley. Remember Antenna Valley? Operation Essex.
>
>Each time I write I guess I have to mention my return in early September. Looking forward to it.

The battery had been airlifted to the top of a hill that afforded a breathtaking vista of the dangerous Antenna Valley, which appeared lush, green, and peaceful from the safety of the hill. If only I could close my eyes and imagine Nam without warfare. That's what I thought. When I came full circle and returned to visit Antenna Valley in 2008, from a distance it appeared unchanged. But the invisible ghosts still walked the paths of empty, fortified villages.

On Hill 300, we had as security a grunt company from 27th Marines. Our new fire base had been mostly cleared off before our arrival, but there remained plenty of work to be done to harden our perimeter and emplace the cannons. I had been near Hill 300 before—in November 1967. We had swept through the valley after the battle on the 6th when the battalion ran into the fortified NVA village that had likely contained elements of a regimental or division headquarters. A nightmare. The hill sat on the southern ridgeline of the valley and had an unobstructed view of almost everything that moved below. Over the next ten days, I would often scan the valley with binoculars hoping to spot movement, perhaps an NVA unit on the move, just as I had done from a different perch the previous November. Memories flickered. If we discovered enemy in the valley or surrounding hills, we would have to lower a cannon tube as far as possible to fire directly on the target. More plausibly, we would have to call in a fire mission to a battery that remained behind in An Hoa. Hopefully, we would not experience friendly fire.

Life on the hill wasn't bad at all. We were far away from the distractions and harassment from higher headquarters in An Hoa and thus escaped attempts to micromanage us. Threats of an enemy ground attack were remote due to the very steep gradations on all sides of us. The infantry company providing security further discouraged any serious enemy attempt to assault us. The two weeks spent on Hill 300 remained reasonably quiet. I focused on fine-tuning gun line efficiency and breaking in new gun chiefs I had chosen based on their leadership and motivation.

Only one medical issue arose. A rat bit one of our officers while he was asleep in a bunker. He underwent painful anti-rabies injections in his abdomen, requiring numerous airborne runs to the Battalion Aid Station in An Hoa and back. He was a laid-back Texan reassigned from another battery in the battalion for reasons never disclosed. He had a couple of months to go before he rotated. I learned later that he commanded the battery for a short time after I left. Perhaps he was the only available officer left in the battery. I found him easy to work with and had a good, relaxed relationship with him, but he had a serious attitude problem. He disliked authority of any kind. He did nothing to conceal his contempt for senior officers and the war. He expressed his opinions openly in front of the enlisted Marines around him. In my view, he was a potential walking morale problem, but he did not seem to bother the other Marines. Maybe they shared his views.

Two More Moves, Then Homeward Bound

Airlifting an artillery battery was always fraught with the possibility of accidents. Just when I thought I might cruise calmly and quietly to the end of my tour, we were ordered off Hill 300 on 20 August and spent the following week operating again from An Hoa. The CO and the Fire Direction Officer left the hill on the first chopper out to prepare for the battery's arrival in our old position, vacated by an ARVN battery. Our cannons, along with their crews, followed by helilift, one by one. I left on the last chopper. We settled into the old position, the FDC and Exec Pit still there, unchanged, standing just as they had more than a year before. Yet, so much had happened since then.

The move back to An Hoa reminded me of reports I heard months earlier of a similar battery move, miles away, in another artillery battalion. After arriving at a new position, near dusk, the cannons were laid in the wrong direction of fire. When the first fire mission came in later that evening, the rounds impacted in a "friendly village" and several Vietnamese were reported killed. The officers received letters of reprimand from the battalion CO. They were reservists with no plans to remain on active duty once their tour was over. That doubtless made it easier for the battalion commander to punish them. Accountability for junior officers could be severe.

On 28 August we moved again, on the dreaded Liberty Road, to a position on the north side of Liberty Bridge and the river, not far from Phu Lac. The dusty ride again brought back a flood of memories—we passed the area where a squad of Marines from Lieutenant Alton's platoon had been wiped out to the man by an NVA ambush one July morning 1967. We sped by areas where countless Marines were blown apart by booby traps. The tree line I took fire from on one of my first patrols in August 1967 passed as a blur. The memories flashed as we bounced along the road as fast as we could, red dust blanketing everything. We rolled into our designated battery position, about a kilometer north of Liberty Bridge, to support grunts trying to trap NVA troops east of An Hoa base, around Go Noi Island (Christmasville)—just as we had done in December 1967. I laid the battery in record time, energized, driven by awareness that my time in the field had now dwindled down to days. I wanted to leave, to return to what I hoped would be the welcome familiarity of home and America.

Last Days in Nam

The day arrived for me to depart the field, proceed to An Hoa overnight, then hop a chopper the next day for Da Nang and out-process. I contained my excitement and said low-key goodbyes in the battery before I left. I wanted to avoid celebrating or highlighting my departure. Others would be left behind to finish their own tours. They too were counting the days.

Late that afternoon, my jeep driver and I accompanied one of our trucks on the 15-minute run to An Hoa. I thought that if we ran into trouble, we would be effectively defenseless, though my driver and I were armed, as were the few Marines in the truck. With two hours remaining before nightfall, we took off at a rapid clip. We crossed Liberty Bridge, drove through Phu Lac, then made the dash along the dirt road toward An Hoa. The omnipresent red dust cloud followed our progress, alerting anyone on the way who might want to do us harm.

It was smooth sailing until we reached a spot about a thousand meters from the base. The driver and I leaned forward and strained to see ahead, scanning for possible signs of a hastily buried mine. Suddenly, without warning, the driver said nothing as he veered sharply to the left, leaving the road and rolling to stop in a dry rice paddy. The truck behind us braked to a halt. My life flashed before my eyes as I thought of the irony: I'm going to die on my last day in the field. "Why did you do that?" I asked the driver calmly, trying to control my anger and fear. "Lieutenant, I thought I saw something in the road that did not look right." What could I say but, "Okay?" I could not take exception with his decision—our lives were on the line. After a few seconds of catching our breath, the drivers of both vehicles skirted the suspicious area and continued. We arrived in An Hoa minutes later, grateful to still be alive. Now, all I had to do was get to Da Nang and I would almost be home free.

A year later, I stood with two officers on a parade deck at Parris Island recruit depot swapping war stories. We all had returned from Vietnam within the past year. Somehow, talk shifted to the circumstances of how we left Vietnam. I recounted my off-road experience, emphasizing the humor—not the terror—of the possible near miss. In the best Marine Corps tradition, the battalion XO one-upped me, countering with a dramatic saga of his own. I listened in quiet awe. On his last day in An Hoa, headed for home, he boarded a chopper late in the afternoon. He had turned in his service pistol. A few minutes after takeoff, about 6,000 meters from the base, the chopper began to lose power and had to land in the middle of nowhere. The crew and five passengers offloaded. The pilot, co-pilot, and door gunner were armed, but not all the passengers. The group formed a defensive perimeter around the aircraft, including those without a firearm. They were later extracted by another aircraft and safely flown to Da Nang.

His account beat my story hands down. It sounded like a bad anxiety dream, not all that different from one I sometimes have, of waiting at some combat base for an assault by an overwhelming enemy force, death assured. I would then force myself awake before being overrun.

11

Coming Home

Flight Out

I boarded a chopper in An Hoa for the last time and flew to Da Nang. I checked out with the arty battalion and regiment, and the following day hopped a truck to the transient BOQ at the Marine airbase. The plywood building with a tin roof, like all the others in various bases in Vietnam, offered the barest of necessities—a cot, an outhouse in close proximity, and a mess hall within walking distance. The arrangements didn't matter. I wasn't looking for comfort. I was returning to the world, my life no longer on hold. For the next two days, we were placed on rocket alert, often the case in Da Nang.

One evening I overheard a cluster of Marines talking outside the hooch, barely able to curb their excitement over leaving Nam. The group listened attentively to a Marine spinning a yarn he had heard. True scoop: right here, on a recent flight taking Marines back to the world, an enemy sniper shot and killed a passenger as the plane taxied down the runway. The guy made it all the way through his tour, only to be killed during his last minute in Vietnam—on a departing plane! A few of those present seemed to accept the tale as fact, shook their heads and uttered profound epithets. Stories such as that thrived, colorful indicators of just how much those who fought a war without meaning wanted to leave Vietnam and extinguish the memories they harbored. It would not be that easy for many.

The next morning, I boarded a chartered plane for Okinawa, where I would spend two days, collect my seabag with stateside uniforms and other personal effects in storage, and head home. As nearly every Marine on the Freedom Bird cheered wildly when it lifted off the runway, I sat back in the seat, closed my eyes in disbelief, and exhaled. One world filled with darkness and fear seemed to recede, another one of promise lay just ahead. What did the future hold? I took refuge in one thought: I had survived. Only problem was, those Marines closest to me had not made it.

Road Ahead

Those survivors on that Freedom Plane could not know the obstacles that lay ahead of them. We had all been changed, some almost beyond comprehension. Many would contend with an unsupportive home front, poor job prospects, shattered family lives and relationships, and difficulty adjusting to everyday life. Some would find cold comfort in alcohol or other addictions.

A sergeant rotated home a couple months after I did. I didn't know him, but his younger brother told me this story decades later. The first thing he said to his mother after he arrived at the airport and climbed in his parents' car was an urgent warning. He quietly told her he was not the same man she knew before he left for Vietnam. Within twelve hours, he would lose his life as a passenger in an automobile accident following a welcome home party in his honor. His father later said he wished his son had been killed in action instead. He would receive a posthumous Silver Star for fighting alongside Steve Joyner that fateful June morning south of Khe Sanh.

In Okinawa I had time to run to the well-stocked post exchange and bought a wristwatch while waiting for my seabag. I looked forward to retrieving the camera I bought the previous March. When the bag arrived hours later, I eagerly opened it and found it gone. The disappointment—a year spent in Nam and now victim of a theft of the one valuable item I possessed. That made it two cameras lost during my tour, both stolen. Yes, the loss disillusioned me, but more than that, a Marine at some level of complicity had to be involved in the crime. How many others serving in-country experienced a similar loss? Months later I submitted a claim for the theft and received $25 from the government for a camera that retailed for $500.

Touch Down

We landed at El Toro Marine Airbase in southern California with instructions to leave the base in civilian clothes. We arrived in a different country from the one we left a year before. Shaped, twisted by our experience in-country, neither were we the same people. The scene after deplaning was loud, exuberant, chaotic. Most of us deposited our uniforms and jungle boots in the trash bin and put on civvies that had been crumpled in sea bags for a year. It was an act heavy with symbolism. One life, one identity ostensibly discarded, the promise of another one shining ahead. I kept my jungle boots as a reminder of my tour. I still have them, still showing the scruff marks and traces of caked, red mud from months in Nam.

I called home, collect, on a pay phone. In the twinkling of an eye, it seemed, my family appeared to retrieve me—parents, two sisters, and my brother. We all packed into dad's dark-blue, four-door Mercury sedan as I surrendered to their collective, emotional embrace. "Yeah, I'm fine, great to see you," I said. I could only answer in brief sentences, avoiding my mother's searching eyes. At the time, the joy of setting foot in America and being surrounded by a loving family temporarily blocked out the memories that would begin to return as time wore on. Unlike the sergeant who warned his family he was a changed man as he climbed in the car at the airport, in the days, months, and years ahead, I chose not to discuss the negativity of my experience in Vietnam. I didn't talk about it at all during home leave and very little—except with my wife, Pat—for decades afterwards. I wanted to forget what lay behind and strained forward to what lay ahead—a mission impossible.

A Visit

Although I had several weeks of home leave coming, I was on an urgent, crucial mission. As soon as possible, I looked up the contact information for Steve Joyner's mother. I almost felt as though I knew her already, based on Steve's description. June Joyner arranged a time for me to visit days later at her small, neat apartment in Fullerton, California. I didn't know at the time that she had recently moved from the home where she raised her family. She did not have the financial resources to keep up the mortgage.

In attendance also the day of my visit were a cousin of Mrs. Joyner, the cousin's husband, and a younger daughter. I wasn't expecting a group welcome, but it was not a problem. The reception was polite and restrained. The family appeared attentive and wanted to hear what I had to say. During the hour-long somber gathering, I explained how I came to know Steve and how much he had been respected by all who knew and worked with him.

It had only been three months since June had been informed of Steve's death. She was still dealing with anger and grief. Why Stephen? I thought, momentarily, did she want to know why I made it back, not Stephen? Following a brief pause in our conversation, the cousin's husband leaned forward, wanting to speak. Straining to control his emotions, he explained how the family had refused to accept the initial news that Stephen had been Killed in Action. They demanded that a family member identify his body, despite the Marine Corps' guidance not to open the casket. After insisting, he was allowed to view the remains. When it was opened, he explained, Stephen's head and face were completely wrapped in bandages, making identification impossible—until he saw an identifiable childhood scar. He confirmed it was Stephen's body.

A visit that began in relative silence and tearful mourning ended on a more positive note. Mrs. Joyner asked me what I thought she should do with his uniforms. Stephen would be buried in his dress white uniform. I had no clear answer, other than to suggest she might consider donating them, which she angrily dismissed. Perhaps she could give them, on consignment, to the Camp Pendleton uniform shop. She recoiled with a flash of anger toward the Marine Corps, indicating that too was not an option for her.

At the time, I did not tell her of the promise I had made when I learned of Steve's death: that one day I would tell his story. It was far too early. That project took nearly 50 years to come to fruition. She managed a weak smile at the end of our meeting, thanked me for the visit, and weeks later sent a newspaper clipping of Steve's Bronze Star ceremony.

June Joyner would never recover from losing her only son—who could? But she ended up not blaming the Marine Corps for his loss. I hope she found a suitable home for his uniforms. In time, she took pride in his service and sacrifice. For the rest of her life, she kept a photograph on her dresser of Stephen in his dress blues, his right arm raised in an eternal salute. She later remarried and lived out her remaining years financially secure.

As I walked away from Mrs. Joyner's apartment, I felt a burden lifted, if only for a short while. The meeting was a mixed blessing. My life was still ahead of me. But Steve had given his for his brother Marines and his country. How I dealt with that became a long journey of trying to live up to the values he espoused and the example of the Good Life he had set through his sacrifice. There was something saintly about him, his life an outward and visible sign of an inward and invisible grace. I wanted his loss not to be in vain. Something positive had to come out of it. I am sure the millions of productive, patriotic Vietnamese Americans would have inspired him.

As I drove away from June's apartment and headed home, I teared up from relief and sadness as I listened on AM radio to Dion's "Abraham, Martin, and John" and loudly sang along with "Hey Jude." I, too, knew I was not the man I used to be.

Not all wounds are visible.

We Remember the Fallen

Not just on Memorial Day. The following anonymous poem attributed to Nam-Band-of-Brothers seems appropriate. We tell our fallen,

> Slip off that pack. Set it down by the crooked trail. Drop your steel pot alongside. Shed those magazine-ladened bandoliers away from your sweat-soaked shirt. Lay that silent weapon down and step out of the heat. Feel the soothing cool breeze right down to your soul ... and rest forever in the shade of our love, brother.

"Love one another," we have been instructed. We did in Nam, and we still do. Relationships forged with brothers in arms can, in some instances, be closer than those with actual family. Losing friends and those we love in combat is a long-lasting trauma that fades over time but never goes away. Is there ever "closure"? In Nam, we almost never grieved openly over those we lost. Perhaps it reminded us too acutely of our own fragile mortality. It was unprofessional. The fallen exited our immediate world without warning, and we found it too painful to talk about them with others. Too heartrending to think about them, no time or occasion to mourn them, except perhaps in memorial services led by a chaplain who did not know them. Where the fallen-in-battle have gone, we cannot follow in our lifetime. Vietnam vets have often used the plaintive phrase, "See you on the other side," when addressing in writing a deceased brother killed in action. Years later, we still remember them, mourn them, cry over them, see and talk to them in dreams, share stories about them, honor them, often incessantly. But we can never bring them back, which is what we really want to do.

That is why the Vietnam Veterans Memorial is so important to the Vietnam War generation. The engraved names symbolize our living memory, we can touch their names and, on one level, bring them back. It's better than visiting a gravesite. Yes, touching the engraved name on The Wall of a fallen comrade is the next best thing to seeing and talking with them again.

I have volunteered at The Wall since 2014. For the first few years while serving there, I could not hold back the tears with emotional visitors. Sometimes it happened when no visitors were there. I do that less frequently now. One day a couple years ago a Vietnam veteran who visited The Wall for the first time asked me to locate a friend. I found the name in the directory. We walked to the panel. I found the etched name and pointed to it. Aware the visitor was about to lose it, both of us racked with emotion, I began to tear up. He said the name aloud repeatedly as he rubbed his finger across the engraved letters several times as if he were communicating with his friend, then fell to his knees. He began to

(Left to Right) Vern Arndt, Tracy Alton, and the author, at Joe's Burgers, McLean, Virginia, 2012.

weep uncontrollably. Two Vietnam vets with him stepped up and placed their hands on his shoulders as I have seen priests do in church in somber moments. Other visitors at The Wall stopped and turned towards him. A few gathered around him for support. After about a minute of loud mourning, he stopped crying, stood up with friends holding each of his arms. He looked at me and said he felt better, he had accomplished what he came for. As he walked away, I marveled at his apparent self-control and capacity to put it all behind him in a near-instant. But had he really done so?

I have also met other vets at The Wall who tell me it is their first actual encounter with it, although they have tried to walk through the memorial many times before to find a name. Typically, they would make the trip to DC to visit, but could not bring themselves to come face-to-face with The Wall. Once they have taken that step, however, they explain, they feel liberated, elated, as if an unbearable weight has been lifted. There's something spiritual about it.

Basic School Classmates

Every so often, Steve Joyner visits me in a dream. Sometimes we talk, but the exchanges are brief. While the scenarios of the dreams differ, there is one constant. Steve is unaware that he has died or will be killed in action, but I know. Of course, I don't mention it to him. I then force myself awake. Yes, fallen friends keep reappearing in memory and sometimes in dreams. In OCS we wore our stenciled last names on utility shirts. I knew more names than the actual candidates who wore them. Some of those names reappeared almost as old acquaintances when I read them in 2012 outside the National Marine Corps Museum on the bronze memorial to our fallen OCS and TBS brothers.

I must admit, I have imagined, in recent years, returning to Basic School in 1967 and—knowing what I do now—imploring the 47 lieutenants in my class who would not return from the war, to avoid going to Nam. It's a futile thought. I know that if time travel were possible, my effort would be fruitless. Thinking it through, I have concluded that even if I could somehow accomplish such a supernatural feat of revisiting those times of my youth, my pleading would almost certainly fall on deaf ears and meet resistance. "We want to go, to serve our country, defeat communism, prove ourselves to friends and family," they would doubtless tell me. "Don't try to stop me, I'll be okay." They will remain forever young and heroes in my book. They answered the call.

The author at TBS 3-67 and OCC 41 Memorial, National Museum of the Marine Corps, Memorial Walk, Quantico, Virginia, October 2016.

On the TBS 3-67 Memorial to our fallen the inscription reads:

These are the names of our friends, our brother Marines, who fell in battle. They did not choose to die nor we to live, but we promise them, as they would promise us, that they will not pass on, but will live on in our in our minds and hearts as long as we shall live.

Semper Fidelis,
The Lieutenants of The Basic School 3-67 and 41st OCC

We are honor bound to keep their memories alive.

Epilogue: Aftermath and Return

Best of the Best

Upon return from Vietnam, I spent more than two years supervising recruit training at Parris Island Marine Corps Recruit Depot. The base and the people there provided the space that allowed me to make a soft-landing, a re-entry into a community that honored military service and whose values I shared. I experienced none of the public hostility and isolation of many returning Vietnam vets. I enjoyed the work. Looking through a photo album recently, I came across an image of Series 368, I Company, Third Recruit Training Battalion, Recruit Training Regiment, the date—29 August 1970, taken at a rehearsal for the series graduation parade. The series of four platoons won every possible colored "streamer," each one attained through a 90 percent success rate in about ten graded training segments. Although the war had been winding down for the Marine Corps, some of the recruit graduates received orders for Vietnam. Most, if not all, of the drill instructors pictured had already served there, some bearing fresh combat wounds.

For me, first as a series, and then as a company, commander, Parris Island offered an unforgettable, positive experience, especially the honor of working with the drill instructors and having the great privilege to know them as ordinary human beings. I learned that behind the public bluster they mastered when dealing with their recruits, they too had self-doubts and concerns about their careers and reputations. They were undeniably tough with their charges, but they also cared deeply for them. On the whole, their integrity and their humanity came across loud and clear every day. With rare exceptions they were several cuts above the average NCO or staff NCO. Carefully chosen in a competitive selection process for the roles they played so admirably, they worked superhuman hours. The skills and values they instilled in their recruits would last a lifetime and impact the Marine Corps. Little did recruits understand the depth of respect their drill instructors had for them. Yes, DIs were hard taskmasters, but they took great pride in their recruits. I am reminded of that even today. I've read several tributes left at The Wall by former DIs honoring their recruits who did not return from Vietnam. They came to the memorial to pay homage to them.

A final comment about the amazing series commander in the photo, Lieutenant Fred Scherer. Fred was a tank officer in Vietnam. His stood a little over five feet tall. Despite his small stature, Fred had the heart of a lion. He was, in fact, a giant in the eyes of many, such was the professionalism he exhibited and the respect he commanded from those who worked with him. Fred was a true free spirit of the times. After his return from Nam in 1969, he reported to duty at Parris Island driving a vintage 1958 model tan Cadillac hearse bearing tailfins that looked taller than he was. He shared a run-down trailer near the base with another series commander. Off-duty, he liked to ride his motorcycle. When discharged from active duty, he played drums in a rock band for a while in Peoria. We met in Chicago for lunch the summer of 1976. After decades of searching, I established contact with Fred in late 2023.

To all Series 368 drill instructors—and to every drill instructor and series officer I served with—Hand Salute! Thanks for your service. Wherever you are, I hope you've had a good life! Semper Fi!

War—What Is It Good For?

Some months before I left active duty, I boarded a bus headed to Advanced Infantry Training at Camp Lejeune, North Carolina. I accompanied several hundred newly-graduated Marines, along with their drill instructors. After turning over the Marines to their new trainers, I walked to the club for a beer and dinner. The war in Vietnam had begun to die down for the Marine Corps, but racial tensions flared almost out of control on Marine Corps bases stateside. As I sat alone at a table, someone put a quarter in the jukebox to play Edwin Starr's anti-war protest song, "War." The song was a powerful statement then and it remains so today. It brought back waves of inner turmoil I had wanted to leave behind in Vietnam. I listened to Starr shout out the question, "What is it good for?" then answer it emphatically with the chorus: "Absolutely nuthin'." I felt the same way, as did, I am sure, the Marine who decided to play the song.

In 1970, emotional and psychological constraints related to the war would not allow me to express that sentiment publicly. I had shut it out as I immersed myself in the Parris Island training regimen. As an officer at Parris Island, I could not acknowledge or admit to others what I thought of

The author at Parris Island Marine Recruit Depot rifle range, 1970.

the conflict in Vietnam. I walled it off as much as possible. At Parris Island I only wanted to do the job expected of me to the best of my ability. I had the responsibility to ensure my recruits had the best training possible and were ready for deployment to Vietnam. Still, it was tough knowing I was sending some of them to Vietnam.

Following release from active duty I spent the next few decades in and out of the Marine Corps Reserves. Stateside duty as a reservist, a weekend warrior, could never measure up to the urgency and sense of purpose I experienced as an active-duty lieutenant in Vietnam. The bad memories sometimes surfaced, but the pride of serving at that time, in that place, with those Marines, never dimmed. Although I sometimes felt I was "playing a Marine" when attending drills, I did not want to sever my connection to the Marine Corps and the exceptional men and women who served.

Interlude in Academia

After release from active duty in 1971, I spent nearly ten years getting my master's and doctoral degrees in history, while managing to stay active in the reserves. Immersed simultaneously in those two cultures made for interesting experiences. I straddled both worlds, accepted by both, but fully at home in neither. It probably took all that time in academia to gain my equilibrium after Nam. Graduate school offered a safe haven from the memories of Vietnam, which continued to lurk in my subconscious. I collected books on the war, but, with rare exceptions, did not have the emotional energy to pick them up and read them. I recoiled from movies and TV drama that glorified gratuitous violence of any kind.

In the mid-1970s, I tried to write about the war, to no avail. I started a memoir, but soon abandoned it. My anger and frustration made it impossible. Emotional healing and reconciliation could only come years later. Not once during my graduate school years did I have a negative experience regarding my service in the Marines or in Vietnam. I later heard many stories, however, of other veterans who struggled, trying to restart their lives.

After my retirement in 2013, I finally embarked on fulfilling the promise I made in 1968 to write Steve Joyner's story. I brought all my academic training to bear. Researching and writing *Promise Lost: Stephen Joyner, the Marine Corps, and the Vietnam War* took on a life of its own and still reverberates. I discovered along the way that Steve had many other friends who recognized his singular approach to life and admired his adherence to unwavering principles, even in the face of insurmountable adversity in Vietnam. One person who knew Joyner in college has written:

> Steve Joyner was Everyman. With all his flaws he was a tragic hero. His introspective letters, the focus on the numbing fatigue of the highs and lows of the battlefield, and the accounts of his fellow Marines, family, coaches, and college classmates flesh out the man who faced the long odds of a generation of young men.

Family

I met my wife, Pat, in graduate school. She has been a consistent supporter without whose love and dedication I could not have navigated all these years. She understood the anxiety, anger, and situational depression I dealt with after the war, and stood by me resolutely as I found my footing.

Following field research in 1978, and completing all but one chapter and conclusion of my dissertation, I accepted a job offer from the Central Intelligence Agency in 1980. Our first child, Bennett, was on the way, to be joined by his brother, Gibbs, two years later. I completed the dissertation in 1983, inspired by their presence.

Return to Nam

Four decades after my tour, I began to emerge from my Vietnam hiatus. Pat and I joined a small group of vets, led by my former Golf Company commander, Chuck Meadows, to celebrate the 40th anniversary of the battle of Hue. The steady, bone-chilling drizzle and breeze from the north eerily duplicated the weather of Tet 1968. We were a group of 12 paid participants, including three vet guides, and a government-approved Vietnamese tour guide. Each man had specific battlefields he wanted to revisit, for the first and probably the last time. Each of us understood what the others were going through and respected and supported them emotionally. After spending a couple of days in Hanoi, we flew to Hue International Airport, the former sprawling Phu Bai air base, and from there drove north to what once had been the area of operations for the Third Marine Division.

Hue, 2008

Now in the old imperial capital, our tour group stood with Chuck Meadows in a cold, light drizzle at Ambush Corner. That was where Golf Company took withering fire from a fortified entrance of the Citadel, leaving Meadows with a critical decision. Should he follow orders to enter the grounds and attempt to rescue the ARVN general from NVA troops assaulting the general's headquarters, or withdraw from the area to save his Marines? The local populace streamed around us on bicycles and scooters as they went about their daily business. We received few inquisitive or hostile stares. Over the years, Hue inhabitants had seen, with some regularity, similar small bands of aging men walking the streets where a devastating battle once raged. Unlike many of us American war veterans, however, it seems to me that the Vietnamese in general have put the war behind them, choosing the promise of the future over revisiting the past with sorrow or regret.

Our tour group paused, listening to Meadows describe the events of 31 January 1968. He told us with surprising candor that some Marine officers had criticized and second-guessed his decision to return Golf Company to MACV after the fight for Hue. Surviving Marines from Golf Company have agreed all along with his decision that day. He saved his company from what would have been a catastrophic attempt to push into the Citadel. It's possible the entire company might have been wiped out had the Marines managed to fight their way inside. More out of sorrow than bitterness, he said he believed the views of some of his contemporaries had

Epilogue: Aftermath and Return

damaged his professional reputation. But Meadows insisted he thought he had done the right thing. He did not have to convince us. None of us gathered there could even begin to disagree.

As we passed Ambush Corner and walked toward the stone gate that once spit machine gun fire at Golf Company, I thought the area probably looked very much as it did in 1968, small shops on one side, a long wall on the other side of the street that led to the Citadel gate. Passing through the portal, I saw what appeared to be battle damage from Tet 1968, pockmarked stone from small arms fire and scars from larger caliber hits.

Three Silver Stars for valor were awarded to Golf Company Marines for action on 31 January 1968. Many more acts of courage over the next few weeks went unrecognized. Although Bill Tant's view of the action was restricted that day, he contends that corpsman Donald Kirkham's gallantry and sacrifice was the most courageous act he witnessed in Vietnam. Squad leader Barney Barnes also believes Kirkham deserved the Medal of Honor.

We later walked the axis of attack that Golf Company took during the battle south of the Perfume River. We revisited the Hue University Faculty Housing complex that had contained the 2/5 headquarters for part of the battle. I stood outside the compound walls and took a photo of the courtyard where Stetson and I talked for the last time. I somehow managed to retain my composure. We walked toward the Hue Railway Station, a short distance away, once the scene of unspeakable NVA atrocities against the Hue populace. A former corpsman with us carried a blood-stained towel he had used when he had been wounded there 40 years earlier. We took his photo, towel draped around his neck, at the very spot he was wounded in February 1968.

Traveling north to Quang Tri Province, near the old DMZ, we stopped at various former Marine bases along east-west Highway 9, the scene of intense battles in 1967–68. Former Marine Tom Jacobs had brought something given to him by a nurse after he was wounded in 1968. At the site of the C-2 combat base near the DMZ—with his son, who was in his early 20s—he walked in dense fog to what was the northern perimeter, where he had been wounded. He and son Ben buried the object along with his dog tags. It was a symbolic act—a traumatic chapter in his life partially completed, but not fully closed. Fifty years later, he eloquently commented on his long journey coming to grips with the war. Jacobs spoke for all of us.

> As I look back, I realize there are truths and selective memory. Somewhere between reality and wishful narrative are lies and omissions that we all tell ourselves to make sense of it all. Until we tell our story about Vietnam and own it, we glide through life half empty, sometimes numb. Something seems to be missing. Perhaps it is shared truth. Holding back stories of our traumas

and fears, our sorrow and tears, keeps us from fully living. We go through the motions of life with painful secrets and wounds that have deep scars. As combat Marine veterans, we are souls who yearn to be forgiven and to be understood.

Leaving Hue, we proceeded south to Da Nang, then continued to Antenna Valley, where I stood on a distant hill taking in the unchanged

Tom (right) and son Ben Jacobs, at former C-2 combat base, Quang Tri Province near the old DMZ, February 2008.

beauty, recalling the events that took place there many years before. I saw no evidence of human activity from my vantage point. The valley still appeared uninhabited and uncultivated. Was it perhaps due to the unexploded ordnance there, or perhaps the ghosts that still walked the trails? I wanted to descend to the valley floor, maybe in hopes of seeing The Village and confronting the memories there, but the government guide informed us the area was off limits, travel there prohibited by the Vietnamese military.

Do You Know Carl?

Later that day, our minibus pulled up to a small, run-down, hut-like restaurant mainly open to the elements on the South China Sea, north of Hoi An. It was cool, the wind blowing. We needed jackets. The windswept beach looked deserted. There were about six Vietnamese in the shack when we entered, all appearing to be in their 50s or 60s, sipping tea or coffee at several long, wooden tables with benches. They paused to look at our group as we entered. We were told by our guide that the woman who owned the business had once been a hostess in an officers' club in Da Nang during the war. She remained a poised, proud, imposing figure and spoke good English, as did several of the Vietnamese customers there. It soon became clear that the little restaurant was a usual stop for the American company that sponsored the tour.

As we sat, one of the Vietnamese men approached our table and held out an old, faded and bent photograph, taken of him as a child of about eight years old, with a young Marine by his side. His gesture did not appear canned or rehearsed. "Do you know Carl, from Texas?" he asked. He explained that Carl befriended him as a boy at one of the U.S. bases. He had been trying to locate Carl for many years. We asked if he had a last name for Carl. No, he said, looking down in disappointment. We would not be able to help him. Surely, he had posed the same question to any number of the tour groups before and received the same answer. After a few moments of terrible silence, we gently raised the subject of the war with him. He and the other Vietnamese present, he confirmed, were all in some way associated with the South Vietnamese government and the U.S. military presence. They were considered outsiders in their own country because of it.

The conversation carried me back several days before, to our visit to Hue. Thanks to the generosity of Chuck Meadows, who doubtless paid for it, we had been invited to a dinner with a Vietnamese family. The father had been an officer in the Army of the Republic of Vietnam. He spent an untold number of years in a re-education camp after the takeover by the Communist North. Because of his service in the RVN armed forces, he and his family had been pushed to the fringes of society and the economy. His children were not admitted to the best schools and were shut out of government jobs. Only because of support from his sisters who immigrated abroad was the family able to have close to a middle-class existence, including a home with an indoor kitchen and plumbing.

Before we left the beach, I managed to speak with Carl's friend for a few moments alone. I told him I was sorry he had been unable to find Carl and apologized for what the war had done to Vietnam. He looked at me and with sad acceptance, replied: "In every war, there are winners and losers. I just happened to be on the losing side." Although I wanted to weep, I did not. We were all losers in the Vietnam War. This encounter brought home how the consequences and reverberations of a long-ago, faraway war remain with us. Our group boarded the bus and left, but the talk with Carl's friend haunts me still.

Last Visit to An Hoa

We continued on to An Hoa. Few traces remained of that critical base. The most prominent feature was the former 1000-meter-long runway,

Former 2/5 Command Bunker, An Hoa, February 2008.

now little more than a short dirt road to nowhere. What looked like pasture grass was pocked with shallow holes dug by locals to recover spent metal they could sell. What I thought might have been the former battalion combat operations center, once a large bunker, now appeared to be just another shallow hole. One of the guys in our group scrounged about, then held up in triumph a broken vinyl 33 LP record. Was it the Stones, The Beatles? A fragment of our former presence had survived.

The local villagers began to gather at a distance, watching us with curiosity. They had not built over or cultivated what had been the base for some reason. I wondered, did they consider the area haunted, perhaps? Too dangerous from possible ordnance? But if that were the case, why had they established a settlement at the former combat outpost of Phu Lac?

The return to An Hoa was cathartic. Gone was the fear and anxiety from living there during the war. I was unafraid of stepping on booby traps, assured no one was going to shoot at me. The local villagers around An Hoa that afternoon appeared passive, curious, and non-threatening. Yet, I could not help but wonder if the older ones, perhaps the parents or grandparents of younger Vietnamese, had caused the deaths of Marines long ago.

It was getting late in the day when we left An Hoa, but not before our minibus got stuck in mud for several minutes. The experienced driver rocked the vehicle back and forth until it lurched free from near axle deep mud, sending us on our way. We would not have to circle the bus in a defensive posture, draw weapons and watch for any nighttime attack.

Curious local villagers gather to observe our visit to former An Hoa Combat Base, February 2008.

Our last two days in Nam were spent at a China Beach resort. I remembered my in-country R&R spent there, perhaps near the very spot Pat and I waded into the water, washing the sand—and bad memories—away.

Another Look at Chuck Meadows

Chuck Meadows lived a post-active-duty life of public service. In 1995 Meadows became chief executive officer of a U.S.-based nonprofit that removed U.S. bomb ordnance from remote areas of and replaced the

Dan and Pat on China Beach, February 2008.

product of war with trees. After that, he privately supported entrepreneurial development among underprivileged groups in Vietnam. In a sense, he went native, in a good way.

Chuck also promoted American veterans' reconciliation with the Vietnamese people. He provided unconditional emotional support for Vietnam vets, especially those who fought alongside him in Nam. Leading groups of vets on tours to revisit the battlefields of their youth, he understood and shared their anguish and pain. Chuck made 44 trips back to Vietnam leading tours for vets, helping them heal. Each tour group he led included a mandatory 15-minute pause for prayer and reflection at the Hue Cathedral in remembrance of the Vietnamese and Golf Company Marines killed during the month-long battle.

During our trip to Vietnam to commemorate the 40th anniversary of the battle of Hue, I still retained some resentment over the circumstances of Stetson's death. I also carried some guilt about feeling resentful. Months later, Chuck sent me the Eric Hammel book on the battle of Hue, *Fire in the Streets*. Inside the cover he wrote an inscription:

> This portrait is a vivid reminder of our service together and our walking the streets of Hue in Vietnam. I am proud we had the good chance to share some of history in the crucible called Hue City this book describes. We won't forget ... and won't regret ... and we will always remember our

Chuck Meadows (left) and the author, An Hoa Combat Base, February 2008.

brothers who fell ... and those who came home. You are my brother. Thank you for your service to your country. God Bless and Semper Fi.

I stood alone with an emotional Meadows after a memorial service for the Hue fallen at a 2009 USS *Hue City* reunion, a year after our pilgrimage to Vietnam. I had begun to emerge from a decades-long, self-imposed ban on unwelcome talk of Vietnam. I asked Meadows what he thought of the prevalence of PTSD among Vietnam War veterans. Did he think the media exaggerated it? How common was it? He looked straight at me, without flinching, in the same manner he did in February 1968 in Hue, after Stetson had died. Everyone who served there, he replied with fierce conviction, has experienced it to some degree. When he said that, it sounded right. Perhaps I wanted him to say it, just as I welcomed his response in 1968 that he no longer needed an FO in Hue. His passionate views lightened in an instant much of my own burden and doubts. I began to release the anger and allow myself to recall those times with less guilt.

Chuck Meadows made postwar resolution easier for Golf Company and other vets, and with the Vietnamese. He helped them come to terms with what they saw and suffered. Emotional vulnerability over the war was something Chuck accepted and embraced. In a comment to a reporter weeks before he died in 2018, Meadows said he thought about Vietnam every day and felt the need to undo some of the damage of the war. In retirement, he led his men toward catharsis and reconciliation. He acknowledged, "It's still a Marine thing to cry with your buddies."

Visit to The Wall

I did not see the Vietnam Veterans Memorial until four years after its dedication in 1982. One summer evening at twilight I carried to The Wall a copy of Steve Joyner's only letter to me in a protective covering. Concerned I might be overcome with emotion, I checked the directory of "The Names on the Wall" for the locations of Steve's name and that of Ken Stetson. I stopped by Ken's name on the East Wall, then walked to Steve's on the West Wall. I stood, looking at his name for a long time. When I thought I was alone, with nightfall approaching, I placed the letter down and walked away. I hoped it would be preserved, along with Steve's memory, with other artifacts left at The Wall by others who had paid homage to the etched names. At the time, I thought my encounter with the memorial, and the war, might be over. As it turned out, it was only beginning.

Glossary

Adjutant: The administrative officer of a Marine battalion or regiment.

AK-47: Standard field assault rifle carried by Communist forces.

Arty: Artillery.

ARVN: Army of the Republic of Vietnam; a South Vietnamese soldier or unit.

B-40: Shoulder-fired rocket used by NVA and Vietcong.

Boonies: The Bush, areas outside the base where contact with the enemy is possible.

Boot: A new arrival in Vietnam.

Bouncing Betty: A grenade booby-trap.

Bush: The "Field," areas outside base areas.

Buy Lunch: Slang for Killed in Action.

C-130: Large cargo plane capable of carrying personnel.

C-Rations: The original Combat Ration, developed in the late 1930s, was replaced in 1958 by the Meal Combat Individual. MCIs were commonly called "C-Rats" by Marines in Vietnam.

Cannon Cockers: Marines in the artillery battery.

CAP: Combined Action Platoon, joint Marine/South Vietnamese platoons set up to protect villages, usually one squad of Marines and three squads of Popular Forces.

Chain of Command: The rank structure.

Chow: Food of any kind.

Clearance: Approval to fire artillery and air ordnance.

CO: Commanding Officer.

COC: Combined Operations Center.

Decks: Floors.

Deflection: A numerical reading for an artillery piece that moves the tube to the left or right.

DMZ: Demilitarized Zone, dividing North from South Vietnam.

Doc: Common nickname for a Navy Corpsman.

DOR: Drop on Request, a self-initiated action resulting in departure from Marine Corps Officer Candidates School.

Exec Pit: The area used by the Executive Officer to fire the battery.

FAOBC: Field Artillery Officer Basic Course, Fort Sill, Oklahoma.

FDC: Fire Direction Center. Where the artillery calculations are made, verified, and sent to the battery.

Fire for Effect: The final correction used to bring fire on a target.

Flak Vest: More commonly called Flak Jacket, sleeveless armored vest. Often left unbuttoned due to the heat and inconvenience.

FNG: Fucking New Guy, a new arrival in-country.

FO: Forward Observer, directs artillery fire, usually assigned to the infantry unit supported by the battery.

Free Fire Zone: An area, thought to be populated by the enemy, open to fire on without restrictions.

Gear: Personal items and uniforms and equipment.

Grunts: Nickname for Marine combat infantryman.

Gunline: The emplacement of artillery cannons.

Gunny: Gunnery Sergeant. The senior enlisted Marine of a company when in the field.

H&I: Harassment and Interdiction Fires, artillery targeted usually on trails and other terrain features on a map. Normally fired at night at random times.

Hamlet: Used interchangeably with village.

Hat Out: To leave.

The Head: The toilet, in Vietnam the outhouse.

Keep on Truckin': Continue to march, carry on.

Kit Carsons: Also called Tiger Scouts or Scouts, former Communist military who defected and volunteered to fight with the Marines and served as intelligence advisors and translators.

Landline: Wire, phone communications.

Liaison Officer: Officers from the supporting arms assigned to a Combat Operations Center.

LP: Listening Post.

LZ: Landing Zone for helicopters.

M16: Standard issue rifle by 1967.

MACV: Military Assistance Command Vietnam, a joint command with overall responsibility for conduct of the Vietnam War, headquartered Tan Son Nhut Airport, near Saigon.

Medevac: Medical evacuation, usually by helicopter.

MOS: Military Occupational Specialty, as in 08 (artillery), 03 (infantry).

New Life Village: A pro–South Vietnam government village used a counterinsurgency tool by allied forces.

Newbie: A "boot," a new arrival in-country.

NVA: North Vietnamese Army; a North Vietnamese soldier(s).

Passageways: Hallways.

Perimeter: The defensive portion of a base, usually with bunkers and razor wire.

Piasters: Military scrip in-country.

Popular Forces: PFs, local South Vietnamese paramilitary militia often used to guard villages.

Quadrant: The numerical calculation that moved the artillery piece up or down in order to hit a target.

R&R: Rest and Recuperation, a weeklong respite, often to Hong Kong, Hawaii, Singapore, Taipei, Tokyo, and Australia. Each serviceman rated one for each tour.

Racks: Bunks.

Reveille: Wake-up call.

Rubber Lady: An inflatable rubber mattress.

RVN: Republic of Vietnam, South Vietnam.

S-2: The intelligence section or officer on a battalion or regimental staff.

S-3: The operations section or officer on a battalion or regimental staff.

Salty: Experienced, confident, sometimes impervious to rank.

Scout Observer: An enlisted artillery FO who received formal arty training at Fort Sill.

782 Gear: Field equipment, usually cartridge belt, helmet, flak vest, ammunition pouches, canteens, pack.

Short: as in, "I'm Short," having little time left in-country.

Skipper: A Marine captain or commanding officer of a Marine company.

Squad Bay: Houses a platoon.

Stingers: Marine ambushes.

III MAF: Third Marine Amphibious Force, headquartered in Da Nang.

VC: Viet Cong, Communist insurgents from South Vietnam.

XO: Executive officer, second-in-command of a company or battery.

Recommended Reading

Archer, Michael. *The Gunpowder Prince: How Marine Corps Captain Mirza Munir Baig Saved Khe Sanh*. Self-published, 2018.
_____. *The Long Goodbye: Khe Sanh Revisited*. Ashland, OR: Hellgate Press, 2016
_____. *A Patch of Ground: Khe Sanh Remembered*. Ashland, OR: Hellgate Press, 2005.
Bowden, Mark. *Hue 1968: A Turning Point of the American War in Vietnam*. New York: Atlantic Monthly Press, 2017.
Braestrup, Peter. *Big Story: How the American Press and Television Reported and Interpreted the Crises of Tet 1968 in Vietnam and Washington*. Garden City, N.Y.: Anchor, 1978.
Broyles, William. *Brothers in Arms: A Journey from War to Peace*. New York: Alfred A. Knopf, 1986.
Bryan, C.D.B. *Friendly Fire*. New York: G.P. Putnam's Sons, 1976.
Ca, Nha. *Mourning Headband for Hue: An Account of the Battle for Hue, Vietnam 1968*. Bloomington: Indiana University Press, 2014.
Caputo, Philip. *A Rumor of War*. New York: Holt, Rinehart and Winston, 1977.
Childers, Thomas. *Soldier from the War Returning: The Greatest Generation's Troubled Homecoming from World War II*. Boston: Houghton Mifflin Harcourt, 2009.
Claiborne, Al. *A Time Past, or What Might Have Been ... The Odyssey of Norman Lane*. Self-Published, 2023.
Coan, James P. *Con Thien: The Hill of Angels*. Tuscaloosa: University of Alabama Press, 2004.
Cox, Franklin. *Lullabies for Lieutenants: Memoir of a Marine Forward Observer in Vietnam, 1965-1966*. Jefferson, N.C.: McFarland, 2010.
Doubek, Robert W. *Creating the Vietnam Veterans Memorial: The Inside Story*. Jefferson, N.C.: McFarland, 2015.
Edelman, Bernard. *Dear America: Letters Home from Vietnam*. New York: W.W. Norton, 1985.
Fall, Bernard B. *Hell in a Very Small Place: The Siege of Dien Bien Phu*. New York: Da Capo Press, 1985.
_____. *Street Without Joy*. New York: Stackpole, 1961.
Faust, Drew Gilpin. *The Republic of Suffering: Death and the American Civil War*. New York: Alfred A. Knopf, 2008
Finlayson, Andrew R. *Killer Kane: A Marine Long-Range Recon Team Leader in Vietnam, 1967-1968*. Jefferson, N.C.: McFarland, 2013.
Fitzgerald, Frances. *Fire in the Lake: The Vietnamese and the Americans in Vietnam*. New York: Vintage, 1972.
Fuller, Lewis. *Fortunate Son*. New York: Grove Press, 1992.
Fussell, Paul. *The Great War and Modern Memory*. New York: Oxford University Press, 1975.
Glasser, Ronald J. *365 Days*. New York: George Brazillier, 1971.
Graves, Robert. *Goodbye to All That*. New York: Doubleday, 1957.
Greene, Graham. *The Quiet American*. New York: Bantam, 1955.
Hammel, Eric. *Fire in the Streets: The Battle for Hue, Tet 1968*. Pacifica. CA: Pacifica Military Press, 1991.

Herr, Michael. *Dispatches.* New York: Alfred A. Knopf, 1977.
Herring, George. *America's Longest War: The United States and Vietnam, 1950–1975.* 4th ed. New York: McGraw-Hill, 2003.
Jacobs, Tom. "A Dance with Death." Presented by Robert L. Fisher, *Echoes of Our War: Vietnam Veterans Reflect 50 Years Later.* Parker, CO: BookCrafters, 2020.
Junger, Sebastian. *Tribe: On Homecoming and Belonging.* New York: Twelve, 2016.
Karnow, Stanley. *Vietnam: A History.* New York: Viking, 1983.
Kovacs, Ronald. *Born on the Fourth of July.* New York: McGraw-Hill, 1976
Kovic, Ron. *Born of the Fourth of July.* New York: McGraw-Hill, 1976.
Laurence, John. *The Cat from Hue.* New York: Public Affairs Press, 2002.
Lehrack, Otto J. *Road of 10,000 Pains: The Destruction of the 2nd NVA Division by the U.S. Marines, 1967.* Minneapolis: Zenith Press, 2010.
Longley, Kyle. *The Morenci Marines: A Tale of Small Town America and the Vietnam War.* Lawrence: University of Kansas Press, 2013.
Manchester, William. *Goodbye, Darkness: A Memoir of the Pacific War.* New York: Dell, 1980.
Mason, Bobbie Ann. *In Country.* New York: Harper Perennial, 1985
Millam, Ron. *Not a Gentleman's War: An Inside View of Junior Officers in the Vietnam War.* Chapel Hill: University of North Carolina Press, 2009.
Moore, Dan. *Promise Lost: Stephen Joyner, the Marine Corps, and the Vietnam War.* Abingdon, VA: Hidden Shelf Publishing House, 2016.
Moore, Harold G., and Joseph L. Galloway. *We Were Soldiers Once ... and Young: The Battle That Changed the War in Vietnam.* New York: Random House, 1992.
Nolan, Keith William. *Battle for Hue: Tet 1968.* Novato, CA: Presidio Press, 1983.
Oberdorfer, Don. *Tet!* New York: Avon Books, 1971.
Pham, Andrew X. *The Eaves of Heaven.* New York: Harmony Books, 2008.
Puller, Lewis B. *Fortunate Son.* New York: Grove Weidenfeld, 1991.
Shay, Jonathan. *Achilles in Vietnam: Combat Trauma and the Undoing of Character.* New York: Scribner's, 1994.
———. *Odysseus in America: Combat Trauma and the Trials of Homecoming.* New York: Scribner's, 2002.
Shulimson, Jack. *U.S. Marines in Vietnam: The Defining Year 1968.* Washington, D.C.: History & Museums Division, Headquarters U.S. Marine Corps, 1997.
Sledge, E.B. *With the Old Breed at Peliliu and Okinawa.* New York: Ballantine, 2007.
Van Devanter, Lynda. *Home Before Morning.* Amherst: University of Massachusetts Press, 1983.
Weiss, Daniel H. *In that Time: Michael O'Donnell and the Tragic Era of Vietnam.* New York: PublicAffairs, 2019.
Wells, Jack. *Class of '67: The Story of the 6th Marine Officer Basic Class of 1967.* Self-published, 2010.
Wilbanks, James H. *The Tet Offensive: A Concise History.* New York: Columbia University Press, 2006.

Index

Numbers in **bold italics** indicate pages with illustrations

"Abraham, Martin, and John" 225
acceptance 9–10, 16, 53, 60, 109, 238
accountability 104, 130, 219
Adams, Sgt. Bill 106–107, 143, 181–183
Advanced Infantry Training, Camp Lejeune 231
adversity 127, 233
advisors: Chinese and Russian 99, 122, 163; U.S. 11
African Americans 19–20, 34, 96, 199; *see also* Black Marines; Taylor, Sgt. Booker T.; Weekfall, Cpl. Eddie Lee; Williams, Lt. Theodore (Ted)
Agent Orange 194, 200
"All You Need is Love" 70–71; *see also* The Beatles
Alligator Lake 111
Alton, Lt. Tracy 5, ***56***, 93–96, 98, 113, ***227***
AM Radio 26, 35, 225
Ambush Corner (Hue) 153–156, 234–235; *see also* Hue; Meadows, Capt. Chuck
ambushes: by enemy 52, 55, 57, 60, 64, 91, 93, 108, 120–126, 172–173, 217; by Marines 162–163
American Forces Vietnam Radio 70, 81, 132, 140, 158, 198, 212
An Hoa Base ***48***, 238–***239***, 241
"Angel in the Morning" 197
The Animals *see* "We Gotta Get Out of This Place"
Antenna Valley: fighting in ***73***, 90, ***98***, 87–109, 112–113, 126; history and NVA safe haven 76–79, 82–84, ***85***–86, 87; return to 218, 236; *see also* Operation Essex
anxiety 17, 22, 73, 90, 107, 175, 189, 233, 239; *see also* fear
Ap Ba ***90***–91
Archer, Michael 46, 141

Arkansas 74, 79, 82, 107, 117, 122, 135; family 7–8, ***9***, 14
Army of the Republic of Vietnam (ARVN) 45, 47, 76, 82, 120, 122, 148, 150, 152–154, 162, 178, 200, 219, 234
Arndt, Lt. Vern ***55***, 84, ***227***
artillery liaison officer 127, 142, 158
ass-chewing 15, 67–68, 117, 129
assassinations 198–200
The Association *see* "Never My Love"
atrocities 163–165, 235
attacks: during Tet Offensive 56, 146, 149–150, 157, 159, 178–179, 208; on Echo Battery 146, 200–201, 205, 210, 216
Australia 108, 184, 192, 211

Baez, Joan 12
Banana Wars 61
banquet 86–87
The Basic School (TBS) 28–34; classmates 171, 196, 227–229
Barabbas 145
barbed wire 42, 91
barbers 109
Barnes, Cpl. Barney ***58***, 90, 112; on Tet, 150–156, 160–162, ***164***–165, 186, 235
Barnum, Capt. Harvey (Barney) 35
baseball 10, ***142***; *see also* World Series
baseplates: artillery illumination 123–124
The Basic School (TBS) 28–34; classmates 171, 196, 227–229
battalion aid station 84, 99, 127, 194, 198, 201, 207–208, 253; jump 180–181, 207
The Beatles *see* "All You Need Is Love"; "Hey Jude"
Black Marines 96, 113; *see also* African Americans
blue funk 127

250 Index

body counts 61, 112, 131, 207–208
Bolt, Robert *see A Man for All Seasons*
booby traps 47, 57, 64, 71, 112–114, 128, 131–132, 137, 207, 213, 219, 239
books 81, 88, 111, 233; *also see* mini-library
"boots" 49
BOQs: Camp Hansen 187; Da Nang 44, 222; Fort Sill 36; TBS (O'Bannon Hall) 30, 32–33
boredom 62, 65, 71
The Box Tops *see* "The Letter"
brandy 84, 111; cognac 101, 187
Brave New World 81
Bremerton Naval Shipyard 7–8
brotherhood 25, 33–34, 182
brothers in arms 106–107, 114, 226
Brown, Lt. Stewart 182–183
Bunker, Amb. Ellsworth 150
bunkers: enemy 89, 94, 99; Marine 42, 59, 67, 80–81, 83, 204
Butler, Jerry *see* "Only the Strong Survive"

c-rations 59, 77, 101
Ca, Nha *see Mourning Headband for Hue*
Cai Do Peninsula 147
Callaghan, Adm. Daniel J. 8
camaraderie 53, 134
cameras 70, 106, 152, 165, 187; loss 166–167, 223
Camp Hansen, Okinawa 187, 191
Camp Lejeune 174, 231; *see also* Lejeune, Maj. Gen. John A.
Camp Pendleton 40, 225
Camus, Albert *see The Fall*
cannoneers 195, 204–205
career officers 92, 110, 185, 193
casualties 26, 35–36, 39, 51, 61, 65, 79, 114, 122, 127, 130–131, 208, 217; on the DMZ 211–212; in Echo Battery 189, 200–201, 203, 205, 210, 212; in Hue 138–139, 156–157, 167, 170, 180–181, 185–186, 189, 198; Operation Essex 87, 89, 93, 106, 108, 207–208
casualty officers 121
Cates, Capt. George 48, 65, 67–69, 81, 110, 203; *see also* ass chewing
catharsis 201, 239
Catholic Church 139, 239
cause 69, 92, 130–131
Central Intelligence Agency 233
chaplains 65, 106, 114, 136–137; *see also* Demers, Richard
Charleston, S.C. 14–15, 34, 36, 208; *see also* College of Charleston
chart operators 132

Cheatham, Lt. Col. Ernest 127, 130, 161, 176, 178, 185
checkpoints 90, 176
Child, Julia 34
children 62, 64, 82, 118–119, 130–131, 139, 152, 238
China Beach 214–215, 234, **240**
Christmas 84, 111, 114, 118–120; *see also* Peace Christmas Tree
The Citadel (Hue) 148, 150–151, 153–154, 156, 159, 166, 168–169, 234–235
Clifford, Clark 57
close air support 93, 211
cluster munitions 100
cognac 101, 187
The Cold War 11–13, 18
Coleman Lanterns 132, 197
collateral damage 130
College of Charleston 12, 36, 117
Collins, Judy 12
combat loss 108, 114
combat operations center (COC) 127–130, 145–146
combat photographer 77
combined action platoons (CAPs) 61, 88
command chronology 76, 87, 99, 101, 108, 172, 175, 185, 193, 200, 203, 207
communications 122, 149
Con Thien 39
corpsmen (docs) 61, 72, 93–95, 98–99, 104, 107, 109, 113, 115, 124–125, 169, 173, 180, 205; *see also* Meridith, Navy HN (Doc) Gary Lee; Potter, Navy HN (Doc) Roy
Coryell, Coach Don 188
counterculture 12, 71
counterinsurgency 61–63, 88
courage 38, 40, 88, 94, 96, 183, 205
Crigger, Cpl. Henry 104–105, 201

danger close 93, 168, 177
Darin, Bobby *see* "If I Were a Carpenter"
death 38, 40, 82, 97, 106, 116, 121, 215; *see also* suicide
Death in Venice 81
decisions 81, 92, 130, 135, 189
Demers, Christopher 137
Demers, Chaplain Richard 136, **137**–140
Demilitarized Zone (DMZ) 38–39, 57, 110, 115, 134, **141**, 149, 159, **236**
"Different Drum" 212
dignity 30, 121, 128, 213
Dion *see* "Abraham, Martin, and John"
Dispatches 27
displacements 203
divine providence 169, 205
Domino Theory 13

Index

Donovan 12
doubts 20, 23, 32, 69–70, 118, 128, 131, 134–135, 212, 242
downtime 26, 40, 81
the draft 12, 74, 154
dreams 226–228
drill instructors 230–231
drop on request (DOR) 20, 26
drug use 12, 196–197
Dunbar, Lt. Martin 68, 133, *142*, 193, 202
Dyer, Capt. Edgar (Buck) 59–60, 69, 79–84, 92, 93–95, 102, 110
Dylan, Bob 12

ear plugs 36, 196
Echo Battery Eleventh Marines (Echo Battery): assignment to 47–*49*; description 51–*52*, 104, 110, 129, 133, 199; inside view 194, 199, 203, 206; move to Phu Bai 134, 192–193; under fire 210
Echo Company, OCS 18
Echo Company Second Battalion, Fifth Marines 158–159, 162
Echo Company, Second Battalion, Third Marines (2/3) 120–121; *see also* Operation Auburn
Edwards, Lt. Ted 39, 171
82nd Airborne Division 179
El Toro Marine Air Base 40, 223
embarkation school 98, 184–185, 192, 210–211
esprit de corps 205
Exec Pit 67–*68*, 108, 110, 133, 194–195, 219
eyeglasses 93–94, 99–100

Fagan, Capt. Brian 30–*31*, 33
The Fall 81
family 7–10, 16, 23, 37, 40, 69, 198, 209, 224, 233
farewell feast 34
fate 106, 141–142, 188, 213, 223
fatigue 61, 109, 123, 146, 215, 233
favoritism 23, 205
fear: in battle 90, 183; of death 53, 73; of enemy 44, 45, 65, 175, 220; of failure 22; of Marines 64; of the unknown 66, 95–96, 114, 153, 175, 239
Ferguson, Gibbs 74–75, 116–117
Ferguson, Joe Pat *9*
field gear 19, 70
fire direction center (FDC) 36–37, 50, 67, 110, 132–*133*, 134, 177, 194, 197, ***202***
Fire in the Streets 148, 241
fire missions 36, 37, 64–65, 68, 71, 81–83, 102–103, 115, 129–130, 132–*133*, 146, 168, 177–178, ***195***–196, 201, 207, 218–219

fire support coordinator 159
firing tables *133*
1st ARVN Division 148, 153
1st Battalion, First Marine Regiment (1/1) 152
1st Battalion Ninth Marine Regiment (1/9, "The Walking Dead") 188
1st Marine Division 42, 57, 148, 160
flare ships 95–96
flashbacks 217–218
flooding 78
food 89, 111, 118, 124, 139, 152, 187, 210; *see also* c-rations
foot problems 86, 100, 109, 112
forced marches 19–20; *see also* OCS
Fort Sill 35–40, 52, 141, 171
fortified villages 91, 95–99, 101, 208, 218; *see also* Operation Essex
forward observers (FOs) 167–168, 171, 184, 201, 207; enlisted 167, 185, 205, 242; FO teams 51–53, 167–168, 205, 213; pipeline 110–167; *see also* Fort Sill
fragging 196–197
Franklin, Aretha *see* "Respect"
Freedom Bird 222
Freeman, PFC Ardenia 94; *see also* Operation Essex
friendly fire 53, 69, 96, 103–104, 201–202, 218
friendships 25; *see also* brotherhood
Frost, Robert *see* "The Road Not Taken"
Fuller, Cpl. 129

Gallup Poll 179, 186–187
German Red Cross 47–48, 130
GI Bill 14
Gibbs, Coach Joe 188
go-go girls 213–214
Go Noi Island (Christmasville) 120, 220
Goldsboro, Bobby *see* "Honey"
Golf Company (2/5) 53–60
grief 105, 114, 169, 174, 190, 192, 224
Groover, George 34; *see also* Henry's
Gruber, Marguerite 34; *see also* Henry's
grunts 33, 49, 52–54, 59–61, 63, 66, 71, 84, 88, 91, 102–103, 111–112, 115, 121, 123–124, 126, 128, 131, 134, 146, 163, 168, 170–174, 178, 184–185, 193, 195, 201, 205, 220
Guadalcanal, battle of 8, 13
The Guess Who *see* "No Time"
guilt 128, 170, 184, 187, 194, 214

H&I fires 80, 201
Hadley, LCpl. Stephen 213
halazone (tablets) 77, 79
hamlet 66, 100, 122, 194
Hamlet 116; *see also* Shakespeare, William

252　Index

Hamm, Lt. Harley 132–134
Hammel, Eric see *Fire in the Streets*
Hancock, Lt. Steve 153
Harden, Tim 35
Harris Poll 179, 187
Harvey, Lt. Bill **54**–56, 183
Hawaii 7, 10, 127
Hawkins, Lt. William D. 28
hearts and minds 61, 129–130
Hemingway, Ernest see *The Old Man and the Sea*
Henry's 34
Herr, Michael see *Dispatches*
"Hey Jude" 225
high explosive (HE) rounds 124, 168, 178, 201
Highway 9 235
Highway 1 45, **142**–143, 145–147, 152, 158–159, 162–164, 193–194, 200, 203
Hill 42 182
Hill 103 176–177
Hill 689 201–211
Hill 63 (LZ Baldy) 45
Hill 300 218–219
Hill Trail, Quantico 23
Hill 230 147, 152
hippies 12
H&I fires 80, 104, 136, 195, 201–202, 210
Ho Chi Minh 149; sandals 62, 160; trail 76
hobo stew 81
home leave 37, 40, 206, 224
homesickness 50, 208–209
homeward bound 219
"Honey" 199
hooches 44, 46–47, **54**, 78, 106, 109, 112, **137**, 140, 194, 222; burning 64
Hotel Company (2/5): in Hue 159, 167, 180, 182–183; Operation Essex 90–92, 95–97, 99, 101, 207
housekeeping 19, 109
Howland, Lt. Howard 213
Hue hospital 160–161; railway station 164–165, 172, 235; university faculty housing 165–**170**, 235
Hue Citadel 148, 150, 153–154, 156, 159, 166, 168–169, 234–235
USS *Hue City* 242
Hunter's Point Naval Shipyard 38
Huxley, Aldous see *Brave New World*

I Corps 44–45, **46**–47, 57, 64, 111, 121, **141**, 145, 150, 200, 207, 212
"If I Were a Carpenter" 35
illumination (artillery) 47, 51–52, 67, 69, 95, 118, 123–124, 147, 168, 200, 203, 216
Imperial Japan 7–8, 10, 41

incoming (hostile fire) 37, 39, 95–97, 99, 104, 123, 147, 177, 194, 204–205, 210, 215
USS *Indianapolis* 7
integrity 25, 32–33
intelligence: battlefield 57, 62, 66–67, 110, 174–175, 203; Hue 129, 141–146, 148–150, 157, 162; Operation Auburn 120–122; Operation Essex 76–77, 86, 89, 96, 101
intercepts (radio communications) 99
investigations 33, 104, 130, 203

Jacobs, Ben **236**
Jacobs, Tom 235–**236**
Johnson, Gen. Harold K. 66
Johnson, Pres. Lyndon B. 56–57, 119, 149, 157, 159, 178–179, 187, 192, 200
journal 126, 128
Joyner, June 224–225
Joyner, Lt. Stephen 188–190, 210, **211**, 212–213, 216, 218–221, 243, 245, 247
judgment 84, 110, 144, 212
Julius Caesar (play) 81
jungle utilities 47, 70, 109
junior officers 26, 49, 92, 107, 134–135, 167, 182

Kaukola, Allison 43, 58, 90, 151
Kelly, Commandant P.X. 197
Kelly, Sam 80
Kennedy, Robert 190, 199–200
Khe Sanh Combat Base 134, **141**, 144–150, 160, 186, 210–211, 216, 223
King, Martin Luther, Jr. 198–199
Kinny, PFC Gerald 156
Kirkham, Navy HN (Doc) Donald 154, 235
Kit Carson Scouts 62
Korean War 14, 25, 70
Krulak, Lt. Gen. Victor H. 61

USS *Laffey* 8
Lagerkvist, Par see *Barabbas*
Lamoureux, Lt. Wes 27–28
leadership 28, 44, 68, 96, 101, 117, 134, 139, 161, 166, 182, 191, 194, 205, 218
Lee, Lt. Ken **56**, 62
leeches 79
Lejeune, Maj. Gen. John A. 17; see also Camp Lejeune
lessons learned 19, 114, 197, 206, 217
"The Letter" 158
letter writing 37, 59, 69–70, 74, 94, **144**, 199, 208, 216–217
Lewis, LCpl. John 172–173
Liberty Bridge **58**, 59, 115, 219–220
Liberty Road 55, 57–**58**, 63, 219
lieutenants: artillery at Ft. Sill 36, 38, 40;

at TBS 27–35; in Vietnam 57, 64, 83, 92, 113, 136, 140–141, 191, 206; Tet (Hue) 153
Life magazine 12
Lima Company, Third Battalion Fourth Marines 192, 210
listening posts 59, 95, 124–125
logistics 70, 107, 145, 175
Lonborg, Jim 79
USS *Los Angeles* 10
Lucas, Cpl. Glenn 154–155
Lulu *see* "To Sir with Love"

M16 50, 70–71, 77, 83, 90, 97, 111, 162, 172
MACV compound (Hue) 148, *151*–153, 156, 234
Madden, Coach John 188
malaria 83
A Man for all Seasons (play) 81
Mann, Thomas *see Death in Venice*
map reading 66, 84, 107, 201
Marine Corps Birthday 84, 101–102
Mary Washington College 25
USS *Maryland* 7–8
Mauriac, Francois *see Vipers' Tangle*
mayhem 93, 95–97, 106, 175
McCormick, Ensign John 38
McCullers, Carson *see Member of the Wedding*
McGuiness, Cpl. 129
McKenzie, Scott 35
McNiel, Lt. Michael 154–*155*, 172
Meadows, Chuck: in An Hoa 110, 115, 117–118, 120; in Hue 150, 152–153, 155–156, 162, 170–174, 186; post-Vietnam 234–235, 237, 240, *241*–242
Member of the Wedding 81
memorial services 106, 175, 226
memories 30, 69, 85, 90, 108, 128, 158, 163, 206, 217–220, 222, 224, 232–233, 237, 240
mental stress 109, 116
mentors 10, 117, 142
Meridith, Navy HN (Doc) Gary Lee 105–106, *125*–126
Meyer, Tony 14; *see also* College of Charleston
midrats 129
Mike Company, Third Battalion, Fifth Marines 101
mines 47, 57, 64, 131–132
mini-library 42, 88, 101; *see also* books
Mr. Rogers 23; *see also* Owens, Capt. Harold
monsoon 47, 76–77, 90, 111, 131
Montgomery, Bob 211
Moore, Bennett 233
Moore, Gibbs 233
Moore, J.D. (father) 7–*11*, 13–16, 21, *27*–28, 40, 47, 50, 70, 81, 140, 151, 198, 208, 228, 241
Moore, Nancy *11*
Moore, Patricia (wife) 233–234, *240*
Moore, Paula *11*
Moore, Polly (mother) 7–9, *11*, 17, 40, 70
moral and ethical issues 63, 71–72, 120, 163, 198, 217
morale 25, 48–49, 59, 61, 71, 83, 85, 111, 117–118, 132, 135, 158, 194–195, 197, 205–208, 210, 213, 219
mortars: enemy 39, 147, 172, 201, 204–205, 210–211, 216; U.S. 50, 52, 63, 84, 161, 171
mourning 114, 170, 216, 225, 227
Mourning Headband for Hue 163
Muir, Bob 10
Mundy, Capt. Carl E. 14
Murray, Staff Sgt. 18–19, 21, 28; *see also* OCS
Myllymaki, Lt. Carl (Bud) 32

Naha City 187–188, 210
National Marine Corps Museum 228
NCOs 49, 96, 117, 129, 135, 145, 197, 201, 205, 230
"Never My Love" 81
New Life Village 61–63
New Year's Truce 122
"newbies" 60, 82, 100
Nicholson, Cpl. 128
night defensive fires (NDF) 65, 78, 80–81, 211
night movements 65–67, 174–176, 200
Nimtz, Adm. Chester 185
1910 Fruitgum Company 158
"96 Tears" 26
"No Time" 33
Nong Son Coal Mine *55*, 76, 79–*80*, 81–84, 87–*90*
Norman, Lt. Henry (Hank) 39, 171
Nyuyen Hoang Bridge, Hue *151*, 153

Oakes, Sgt. Mark 106–107, 143, 145–146, 190
Oelsner, Lt. Jay 141
Officer Candidates School (OCS) 13–14, 16–17, 19, 22–29, 30, 32–33, 74–75, 116, 118, 140, 173, 213, 220
The Old Man and the Sea 166
"Only the Strong Survive" 24
Operation Auburn 120–122
Operation Essex 73, 87–*90*, 91–106, 108–111, 207–208, 218
Owens, Capt. Harold 19–23, 28, 30

Parris Island Marine Recruit Depot 128, 137–138, 208, 220, 230–231, *232*

Peace Christmas Tree 118–119
Peace Corps 24
Pearl Harbor 7–8
peer evaluations 32
Perfume River (Hue) 148, 150–*151*, 153, 166, 168, 173, 235
Peterson, Lt. Dennie D. 39–40, 171
Phu Cam Canal *151*, 165, 176
Phu Lac (6) *46*, 50, 55, 57–*58*, 59–67, 71–72, 83, 114–115, 116–120, 124, 217, 219–220, 239
Phu Loc *141*, 145–149, 159, 193
platoon commanders 30, 36, 54–55, 84, 86, 95, 99, 109, 112–113, 118, 143, 182
popular culture 71
Popular Forces (PFs) 61, 129, 163
post-traumatic stress disorder (PTSD) 145–146, 190, 242
Potter, Navy HN (Doc) Roy 93–94, 126
Powerline Trail, Quantico 21
precision destruction mission, Hue 168–169
prep fires (artillery) 97, 124; see also reconnaissance by fire
Procol Harum see "Whiter Shade of Pale"
Promise Lost 189, 192, 233
propaganda (enemy) 118–120; see also Peace Christmas Tree
psychiatrist 100
public opinion 123; see also Gallup Poll; Harris Poll
Puff (gunship) 96
PX (post exchange) 132, 140, 145, 152

Quang Nam province 47
Quantico Marine Base 22, 24, 26–*27*, 28–29, 33, 35, 71, 74, 116, **228**
Que Son Mountains 102
Question Mark and the Mysterians see "96 Tears"

R&R 70, 108, 127, 134, 142, 174, 184, 187, 192, 211; in-country 214–215, 240
rats 50–51, 218
Raub, PFC *73*–74, 78, 84, 91–93, 95, 172–173, 184
recoilless rifles 72, 161, 201
recon by fire (artillery) 64
recon teams 115, 195, **202**
reconciliation (postwar) 233, 241–242
reconnaissance by fire 124
recruit training 230–232
regional forces (RF) 88
replacements (personnel) 45, 60, 100, 110, 165, 176, 185–186, 205; see also "newbies"
reserve officers 29–30, 92; see also junior officers

"Respect" 35
return to Nam 234–242
reunions 33–34, 182
rifle battalions 70, 193
"The Road Not Taken" 14
Robertson, Maj. Gen. Donn J. 44
Rodgers, Cpl. 128, 145, 147
Rogers, Lt. Bill 95, 106–107, 143–***144***, 181–182
Rolling Stone magazine 158
Ronstadt, Linda see "Different Drum"; The Stone Poneys
A Room of One's Own 81
Roosevelt, Pres. Franklin 123
rotations (leadership) 205–206
Rowden, John Wayne 152
rules of engagement 67, 198
Rush, Merrilee see "Angel in the Morning"
Rusk, Sec. of State Dean 57
Russell, Bill 10
Ryberg, Lt. Charles 39, 171

"San Francisco (Be Sure to Wear Flowers in Your Hair)" see McKenzie, Scott
The Sands of Iwo Jima 25
Scherer, Lt. Fred 230–231
Sea Tiger 207
seabees 59, 204
search and destroy (operations) 61, 63, 79, 87, 89–91, 112, 120–122, 131, 175, 184
Second Battalion, Eleventh Marines (2/11) 45, 193
section chiefs (artillery) 195
self-doubt 16, 32, 192, 230
senior officers 76, 79, 91, 129–130, 135, 168, 214, 219
shades (sunglasses) 99–100
Shakespeare, William see *Hamlet*
Sheridan, Gen. Philip 35
short-timer calendar 128
Sill, BG Joshua 35
"Simon Says" see 1910 Fruitgum Company
sleep deprivation 25–26, 45, 61, 103, 105, 108–109, 123, 136, 156, 204
soccer 86–87
Song Thu Bon River *58*–59
sorrow 105, 192, 234, 236
South China Sea 45–*46*, 237
Spalding, Phinizy 117
spider holes 94, 121–122
squad leaders 65, 69, 71, 100, 109, 143, 201
Starr, Edwin see "War"
Stars and Stripes (newspaper) 198, 207, 212
Steele, Maj. Orlo (O.K.) 173–174
Sterling, Rod see "Twilight Zone"

Index

Stetson, Jan 152, 169, 191
Stetson, Ken: in An Hoa 52, 74, 78, 83, 87, *115*, 127–128, 137; Hue 142–143, 146–147, 158, 167–68, 184; legacy 235, 242; post 186, 212, 215
stingers 124–125; see also ambushes
The Stone Poneys *see* "Different Drum"; Ronstadt, Linda
stress, mental 9, 22, 98, 109, 116, 208
suicides 111–112, 118, 155

Tant, PFC Bill 19, 21–22, 28
Tarawa 28; *see also* Hawkins, Lt. William D.
Task Force X-ray 150, 168
Taylor, Sgt. Booker T. 21, 23, 28
Taylor, Gen. Maxwell 57
TBS 3-67: memorial *228*–229; survey 158
teargas 99
Tet Offensive (foreshadowing) 107, 136, 142, 144, 147, 149–152
Thieu, President 86
Third Battalion Fifth Marines (3/5) 120
Third Battalion Fourth Marines (3/4) 192
III MAF 57, 61, 207
3rd Marine Division 38, 44, 57, 110, 120, 148, 188
Threet, PFC Tony 152
Thuong Tu Gate *151,* 154
"Tiger Piss" 86
"To Sir with Love" 93
trauma 65, 84, 98, 109, 145–146, 190, 226
Tuchman, Barbara *see The Zimmerman Telegram*
Tully, Lester 112, 152, 154, 156
tunnels 76, 97, 109, 122, 161–162
27th Marine Regimental Landing Team 179, 218
"Twilight Zone" 215
typhoon 77–79

U.S. Navy 7–8, 10, 12–15, 27, 37–40

valor 38–40, 94, 124–126, 174, 184–185, s235
The Ventures *see* "Walk Don't Run"

Viet Cong (VC) 44–45, 57, 59, 61–62, 64, 67, 77–79, 87, 109, 122, 129, 146, 148–150, 157, 172, 175, 179, 212
Vietnam, beauty of 62, 84, 176, 237
Vietnam Tactical Zones *43*
Vietnam Veterans Memorial (The Wall) 226, 242
Vietnam Veterans Memorial Fund (VVMF) 104
Vietnam War veterans 99, 120, 135, 140, 196, 226–227, 230, 234, 242
Vietnamese interpreters 62, 118, 120
Vietnamization 179
Vipers' Tangle 93

"Walk Don't Run" 20
Walt, Lewis W. 61
"War" 231
Warner, Cpl. David 172–173
The Washboard 36; *see also* Ft. Sill
water buffaloes 72, 82, 102–103
Wayne, John *see The Sands of Iwo Jima*
"We Gotta Get Out of This Place" *see* The Animals
Weekfall, Cpl. Eddie Lee 97, 113
Wennes, PFC Robert 112; *see also* suicides
Westmoreland, Gen. William I. 61, 149–150, 178–179, 186–187
white phosphorous round (WP) 80, 124, 177
"Whiter Shade of Pale" 35
Who's Afraid of Virginia Woolf? (movie) 143–144
Wilk, Lt. William 51–52, 124
Williams, Lt. Theodore (Ted) 20; *see also* African Americans
Wiseman, Lt. Richard 27
Woolf, Virginia *see A Room of One's Own*
"the world" 189, 216, 222
World Series 79
World War II 18, 36, 38–39, 70, 135, 149, 156

Yoshida, Cpl. Cliff 10

The Zimmerman Telegram 81